Cultivating Compassion

Cultivating Compassion

A Psychodynamic Understanding of
Attention Deficit Hyperactivity Disorder

Francine Conway

ROWMAN & LITTLEFIELD
Lanham • Boulder • New York • London

6/15/17
$40.00 LB

Published by Rowman & Littlefield
A wholly owned subsidary of The Rowman & Littlefield Publishing Group, Inc.
4501 Forbes Boulevard, Suite 200, Lanham, Maryland 20706
www.rowman.com

Unit A, Whitacre Mews, 26-34 Stannary Street, London SE11 4AB

British Library Cataloguing in Publication Information Available

Library of Congress Cataloging-in-Publication Data

Names: Conway, Francine, author.
Title: Cultivating compassion : a psychodynamic understanding of attention deficit hyperactivity disorder / Francine Conway.
Description: Lanham : Rowman & Littlefield, [2017] | Includes bibliographical references and index.
Identifiers: LCCN 2016057699 (print) | LCCN 2017000118 (ebook) | ISBN 9781442269644 (cloth : alk. paper) | ISBN 9781442273009 (pbk. : alk. paper) | ISBN 9781442269651 (electronic)
Subjects: LCSH: Attention-deficit-disordered children—Treatment. | Attention-deficit hyperactivity disorder.
Classification: LCC RJ506.H9 C665 2017 (print) | LCC RJ506.H9 (ebook) | DDC 618.92/8589—dc23
LC record available at https://lccn.loc.gov/2016057699

∞ ™ The paper used in this publication meets the minimum requirements of American National Standard for Information Sciences Permanence of Paper for Printed Library Materials, ANSI/NISO Z39.48-1992.

Printed in the United States of America

Contents

Preface

Attention Deficit Hyperactivity Disorder (ADHD) has been a part of the lexicon of psychotherapists since its inclusion in the *Diagnostic and Statistical Manual of Mental Disorders* (DSM-III) in 1980. Some of the predominant symptoms commonly found in children with ADHD include distractibility, difficulty paying attention, hyperactivity, impulsive behaviors, disorganization, poor judgment, poor ability to plan for the future, and impoverished social skills. These symptoms have far-reaching implications for the children and their families. Specifically, ADHD symptoms often result in increased frustration and stress among caregivers, family members, and teachers that may lead those adults to form negative views of the child. For example, teachers may describe the ADHD child as oppositional and willful. Parents may experience a sense of helplessness and frustration in their efforts to change the child's behavior. Other adults may give up on any expectation that the child will be able to accomplish typical life milestones. The adverse impact of ADHD thus weighs on the child, their parents, and teachers alike as all parties engage in a somewhat coordinated attempt to bolster the child's functioning.

Throughout the course of this coordinated intervention, the behavior of the same ADHD children those efforts are intended to assist may at times elicit negative emotional responses from their caregivers, other adults, and their peers. For this group of children, many of whom typically struggle with self-image, these negative interpersonal interactions may lead to an exacerbation of their already intolerable feelings of frustration and anxiety. For example, ADHD children's experiences of failed relationships may lead to a lack of confidence in themselves. The resulting insecurities further complicate and interfere with their ability to function effectively. As failed efforts mount, they lose hope. The spiral of negative emotions quickly leads to the disintegration of the child's sense of self and may result in inconsistencies in their performance. These sequences of experiences described above explain why ADHD children may be at risk for lower self-esteem compared to children without ADHD (Slomkowski, Klein, and Mannuzza, 1995; Weiss and Hechtman, 1993).

In clinical and research situations, the term "ADHD" is used to refer to a broad spectrum of etiologies. For example, ADHD has been used to refer to children who have difficulty with attention, whether it stems from trauma-related hypervigilance or some neurological insult. This lack of severity in the diagnostic nomenclature has led to a diversity of views about ADHD. Some view ADHD as a gift affording the child above-average creative abilities (Honos-Webb, 2005). While for others, there is a fear that ADHD reflects poor parental practices (Harborne, Wolpert, and Clare, 2004) . Because there are multiple pathways to ADHD symptoms, the individualized approach of psychodynamic psychotherapy is ideal because it is flexible enough to treat children with this clinical presentation regardless of its etiology.

However, despite its suitability for this treatment population, psychodynamic psychotherapy has been largely excluded from ADHD psychotherapy research. The most recent multisite study by the National Institute of Mental Health, for example, considered only cognitive therapy, medication, and parent training (MTA Cooperative Group, 1999). To date there are very few studies that look at psychodynamic psychotherapy interventions, but those that exist have found promising results. Work done by researchers such as Fonagy and Target (1996; 2002) and by Leuzinger-Bohleber and colleagues (2011) begins to show evidence of psychodynamic intervention with ADHD children. As more psychodynamic-oriented researchers search for ways of measuring their interventions, this work will continue to grow. In the meantime, this book focuses on the therapists who work psychodynamically with children presenting with ADHD symptoms stemming from a range of etiological factors. Their positive results provide compelling evidence that psychodynamic psychotherapy treatment is effective with ADHD children.

The exclusion of psychodynamic psychotherapy's contributions has resulted in a dialogue about ADHD that is mostly descriptive. Conspicuously missing from the discourse is an understanding of how the child's intrapsychic processes contribute to their symptomatology. A psychodynamic understanding of ADHD allows those who have charge of the child to broaden their attention beyond the child's behavioral compliance to include the cultivation of compassion for the child. More importantly, psychodynamic psychotherapy provides a path for the ADHD child to develop an appreciation for their own challenges and develop compassion for themselves.

In the process of completing the research for this book, I interviewed psychoanalysts, psychodynamic therapists, and psychoanalytic researchers concerned with the psychological well-being of children with ADHD. Very early on in the interview process it was apparent to me how the narrative of the psychodynamic therapist departs from a focus on the child's behaviors. For instance, I began my interview by asking therapists "What is ADHD and how do you treat it?" This question was a difficult one for therapists to answer. I soon realized that for many psychodynamic-oriented therapists, the question I posed was the wrong one. One analyst explained *"It's like asking 'Have you stopped beating your wife yet?'"* [DON]. This analyst experienced the question as inappropriate. He explained, *"How does one respond? Yes? No?"* Inherent in the way the question is phrased is an emphasis on the ADHD child's behavior and a preferred outcome. The question assumes the child's behaviors are wrong from the onset and, therefore, the only acceptable outcome is to stop the behavior. (He later added, *"By the way—it is wrong to beat your wife."*)

I also relied heavily on my own clinical and research experiences with ADHD children. One of the things that stands out after more than a decade of clinical practice in child psychotherapy are questions parents and teachers often ask, such as "When will she behave better?" and "When will he be able to focus better, sit still, and follow instructions?" These questions are the domain of therapists who are more focused on behavioral outcomes than on the more holistic outcomes related to overall emotional well-being that concern psychodynamic-oriented psychotherapists. For example, behavioral therapists may have little conflict when responding to these kinds of questions because they subscribe to a view that behaviors can be modified by contingencies, such as rewards. The same questions, however, elicit conflict in psychodynamic therapists because those practitioners generally hold a view that behaviors or symptoms are symbolic of the child's struggle to communicate their difficulties. Therefore, a dynamic therapist is not so much focused on *stopping* the behavior as much as they are on *understanding* the behavior.

This book brings to life what psychodynamic analysts and therapists do in a way that beginning therapists, nondynamic-oriented practitioners, and other mental health professionals can understand so that they may integrate psychodynamic thinking into their work. The information from the interviews integrated throughout the book are presented using the analysts' own words so that the reader is privy to the therapists' thoughts and can gain insight into their work with children.

In contrast to a behavioral focus, the psychodynamic approach is characterized by an individualist approach that embraces the notion that although children's symptoms may be similar, the origins and the communications of their actions vary. Consequently, it is the therapist's position that the therapy provides the child a space or an opportunity to express himself and be known. In therapy, the child is understood and responded to in a way that differs from the usual response he receives from others (frustration, anger, annoyance, etc.). It is only through this process that the child can resolve some of his struggles. For some children, having the opportunity to be understood leads them to accept their reality or find other ways of coping with what ails them. This opportunity for exploration and self-expression sets the stage for other therapeutic work, such as reconstructing mental structures of the mind (ego development, resolution of superego conflicts, etc.). Evolving out of this therapeutic space are new or strengthened abilities for self-regulation, reality testing, impulse control, motivation, improved sense of self and self-esteem, and so on. This focus on the internal life of the child and interventions targeting the child's inner experiences do lead to lasting changes in behaviors and relationships with others (see Leuzinger-Bohleber and colleagues, 2011). This therapeutic approach is not a quick fix; in fact, it is recommended that therapy occur at least twice weekly. Treatment duration ranges from one to two years.

The intent of this book is to equip therapists with a psychodynamic perspective of psychotherapy that is especially useful for addressing the ADHD child's difficulties. A psychodynamic approach offers a window into the inner lives of ADHD children, arguably a more compassionate view than one that is focused primarily on extinguishing undesirable behaviors. When the views of the psychodynamic therapist are embraced by others in the child's life, relationships between ADHD children and others improve. Those who read this book will have an opportunity to develop a psychodynamic conceptualization of ADHD and formulate psychodynamic treatment interventions for this population. In doing so, therapists can continue to explore, understand, and facilitate the development and resolution of inner psychic matters that are pertinent to the ADHD child's functioning and help the child respond to the demands of the external world.

ACKNOWLEDGMENTS

I wish to thank my colleagues who encouraged me to add my voice to the discourse on ADHD. To my publisher who helped to make this book a reality: I appreciate your guidance and support. To the many scholars, clinicians, psychoanalysts, and researchers who agreed to be interviewed: thank you for the generous manner in which you shared your time and clinical expertise.

I am grateful to my graduate students, Catherine Holder, Masha Borovikova, Marie Barnett, and Sarah Joffen-Miller, who contributed to this work through coordination of the research efforts along with transcription and coding of interviews, and who provided listening ears for my ideas and enthusiastic support for this project. Special acknowledgments to a talented illustrator of the book's cover, Francesco Adriatico and to his instructor Dale Flasner, director of Adelphi University's Graphic Design Program, for this captivating representation of my ideas.

Finally, I thank my "*village*" for their unwavering support: my parents, whose belief in me has inspired me to do this work; my sister, Fiona, who sat with me weekly in our writing sessions, I am grateful for your companionship; and my dear "sister and friend," Kim, whose belief in my efforts persists beyond my doubts, I am grounded by your love and faith in me. I especially wish to thank my children who inspired me to write this book. It is through the journey of being your mother that I am reminded each day of the transformative power of compassion. Thank you to my husband, Dr. Samuel Jones, for his continuous listening and his willingness to be a receptacle for the vetting of my ideas.

Introduction

A Historical Context of ADHD:
From Moral Indictment to Compassion

The search for descent is not the erecting of foundations: on the contrary, it disturbs what was previously thought unified; it shows the heterogeneity of what was imagined consistent with itself.
—Michel Foucault, 1991 (p. 147)

Attention Deficit Hyperactivity Disorder (ADHD) is one of the most frequently diagnosed psychological disorders in children in the United States (Kessler et al., 2005), with prevalence rates from 3 to 5 percent (Barkley and Biederman, 1997; Mash and Barkley, 2003). Common symptoms include developmentally inappropriate levels of attention, impulse control, and activity level (American Psychiatric Association, 2000; Barkley, 2006a). ADHD symptoms have an adverse effect on children, interrupting their learning and contributing to negative social relations with peers and family members. Although ADHD is not a new diagnosis, its use has increased exponentially over recent years. National surveys conducted by the Centers for Disease Control and Prevention, such as the National Survey of Children's Health (NSCH) and the National Health Interview Survey (NHIS), have documented increased prevalence rates of ADHD over the past decade (Pastor, Reuben, Duran, and Hawkins, 2015). National surveys of ADHD diagnoses in states across the United States report increases in ADHD incidences ranging from of 3.7 to 12.8 percent in 2007 to 4.2 to 13.3 percent in 2011. Similarly, parent reports of ADHD across the United States have also increased, ranging from 5 to 11.1 percent in 2003 to 5.6 to 17 percent in 2011 (Visser, Danielson, Bitsko, Holbrook, Kogan et al., 2014).

Due to ADHD's high prevalence rate and the negative impact of its symptoms on those who suffer from it, the disorder has gained the attention of clinicians and researchers nationwide. How did we arrive to this point in child psychopathology?

As we consider the history of ADHD, we must keep in mind the confluence of factors that shape historical accounts—that is, documentation of the historical events; the perspective of the recorder; the prevailing cultural and societal values; and the narrator's view. This chapter will demonstrate how the combination of these factors resulted in the emergence of a dominant perspective of ADHD—a medical one. Given that physicians chronicled the most documented cases of ADHD, it is not surprising that their view of ADHD persists. Neither is it difficult to imagine that there is another view of ADHD's history—a psychological one—that parallels the medical perspective. Here I attempt to present a comprehensive view of the historical context through which our understanding of ADHD has emerged: one that takes into account both medical and psychological perspectives. This chapter thus discusses the shared historical origins of the two models and the points that they have diverged, intersected, and merged.

Usually, what sets us on the path of historical review is our quest to find answers. In this case, parents, treatment professionals, teachers, and researchers are curious about the etiology of ADHD and the effectiveness of current treatments. And in reviewing the development and progression of our understanding of the disorder, it becomes apparent that the current treatment approaches are informed mostly by a medical model and, to a lesser extent, by psychoanalytic theories and treatment. It is the very process of examining the history of ADHD that revealed the gaps in our current understanding and has led to the search for other points of view. A guiding principle in this search is the realization that knowledge is co-constructed. Much of what we know is derived from a variety of societal and personal factors that shape our perceptions and understanding of our experiences. In as much as our view of history is a social construction of our own unique patterns of observations and perspectives, our current psychological practices also adhere to these views. An acknowledgment of this co-constructive process allows us to be aware that the course we pursue is only one of many possible avenues; this awareness, in turn, allows us to open ourselves to other perspectives. Cognitive flexibility is thus the basis for what constitutes advancement, growth, and learning.

Although an "ideal" treatment path for ADHD children remains unclear, we know two things for certain: The prevalence of the disorder has increased, and ADHD has an adverse impact on individuals, families, and societies. Therefore, remaining open to fresh perspectives that may shed light on how to help those who may be afflicted and affected is necessary. By no means am I advancing the psychoanalytic version of ADHD's history as a singular truth. Rather, I argue that a psychoanalytic perspective contributes to the existing fund of knowledge, and its integration into current treatment practices can stem the sense of despair that most individuals with ADHD, and families with an ADHD child, experience.

ADHD has evolved along two main pathways: the *medical* and the *psychological*. The medical model views ADHD as associated with disease or structural anomalies in the brain. In this model, medication is one of the primary treatment interventions. In contrast, in the psychological model, identification of errant mental processes and engagement in the process of psychotherapy is primarily used to bring about behavior change. During the evolution of ADHD's history, some aspects of the disorder and treatment approaches have been obfuscated by the marginalization of disciplinary approaches while other elements have gained prominence. For example, within the last decade, psychoanalysis has received less attention than other approaches despite the fact that, historically, world-renowned psychoanalysts such as Sigmund Freud and Melanie Klein have made notable contributions to the understanding of ADHD.

Before Freud, the physician who developed psychoanalysis, became interested in what has come to be known as ADHD, the symptoms associated with the disorder were chronicled exclusively within the literature and treatment records of medical doctors. Although the term ADHD did not appear in the DSM until its third edition, published in 1980, the earliest record of documented ADHD symptoms dates back to 1798. The published work of Sir Alexander Crichton (1763–1856), a Scottish physician, describes a child's inability to constantly attend to an object. He described a child who is inattentive and easily distracted due to a "sensibility of the nerves" (Crichton, 1798, reprint p. 203). According to Crichton, the child's sensitivity to everyday sounds (such as people walking, dogs barking, doors opening or closing, and movement of furniture) results in distraction ranging from an agitated response to anger. Crichton characterizes this inattentive state as restlessness that he refers to as "the fidgets" (Crichton, 1798, reprint p. 203). Crichton refers to patients who respond to extraneous stimuli as having a "disease of attention." These symptoms are believed to be consistent with the "inattention" criteria for ADHD as it is currently described and diagnosed (Lange, Reichl, Lange, Tucha, and Tucha, 2010; Palmer and Finger, 2001).

Another period in the pre-psychoanalytic evolution of ADHD was shepherded by German physician Heinrich Hoffmann, in the mid-nineteenth century (Hoffmann 1846, 1948 in Lange et al., 2010). Hoffmann wrote and illustrated a children's storybook of characters referred to as "Fidgety Phil" and "Johnny Look-in-the-air." Some consider the characters' inattention and hyperactive behaviors descriptions of ADHD (Burd and Kerbeshian, 1988; Thome and Jacobs, 2004). In his book about Fidgety Phil, for example, Hoffmann tells a story about a little boy who could not sit still at the dinner table. Due to Fidgety Phil's difficulties, the tablecloth, dinner, and his chair often ended up on the floor. The boy's father asks at the start of dinner, "Let me see if Philip can be a little gentleman; Let me see if he is able to sit still for once at the table" (Hoffmann 1846, English edition in Lange et al., 2010, p. 243). This story reflects not only the child's difficulty but also the cultural and societal moral expectation associated with being able to "sit still." Whereas Fidgety Phil's behavior may now be interpreted as hyperactivity, another symptom of ADHD (Burd and Kerbeshian, 1988), some may attribute Fidgety Phil's behavior to a lack of discipline and an attempt to challenge his father's authority. In other words, the stories can be viewed as a warning to "naughty" children who defy their parents (Lange et al., 2010). This story thus evokes a persistent question regarding ADHD children: To what extent do the symptoms expressed by ADHD children represent willful disobedience and lack of discipline, or is the behavior a function of the "disorder" and therefore beyond the child's control?

The following description ushers in the next era in the treatment of ADHD-like symptoms in children:

> (1) passionateness; (2) spitefulness – cruelty; (3) jealousy; (4) lawlessness; (5) dishonesty; (6) wanton mischievousness – destructiveness; (7) shamelessness –immodesty; (8) sexual immorality; and (9) viciousness. (Still, 1902, p. 1009)

A perception of children as oriented toward self-gratification and with a lack of regard for others, was the entree into what is considered a more "scientific" accounting of ADHD. In 1902, the Goulstonian Lectures of Sir George Frederic Still (1868–1941) documented the above observations of children's behaviors. According to Still, children's actions stemmed from a "defect of moral control" and was "a morbid manifestation" that could not be explained by a general impairment of intellect or physical disease (Still, 1902, p. 1079, as cited in Lange et al., p. 245).

Contemporary researchers like Barkley (2006b) have reinterpreted some of Still's characterizations to mean "impulsivity." According to Barkley (2006b) and Connors (2000), Still's description of passion speaks to current ADHD children's difficulty in delaying gratification and impulsive behavior. Unfortunately, Still's stories of the children he worked with were not merely behavioral descriptions; they also implied that these children were morally and socially at odds with a desirable value system. The stories suggested the very disposition of these children pushed against the fabric of society. This discourse continues today; researchers cite the percentages of ADHD adults in the penal justice system and who have accompanying symptoms of antisocial personality disorder (Barkley, 2008; Eme, 2009; Young, 2007). Among children, comorbid diagnoses of conduct disorder and oppositional disorder are common (Loeber, Keenan, Lahey, Green, and Thomas, 1993; Young,

Sedgwick, Fridman, Gudjonsson, Hodgkins et al., 2015). In my private practice and in interviews with therapists, reports of parents, teachers, family members, and other adults' descriptions of their experience with the child echo those of Still's: "lazy," "unmotivated," "lying," "cheating," "willful," "manipulative," "lack of remorse," and so on. What escape us in these characterizations are the experiences of the children themselves as they negotiate their lives.

Case studies were the predominant approach in developing these theories about children with inattention and hyperactivity symptoms. However, what was compelling about Still's work was the extent to which there was variability in the children's symptoms. Among the twenty children he studied, some of his discussion included cases about children who exhibited *aggressive* behavior toward another child: "He would suddenly seize two of them [children] and bang their heads together, making them cry with pain" (Still, 1902, p. 1165). In another description, a child exhibited obsessive compulsions to say "good night." In other cases, Still discussed instances of predominant inattention—a child whose difficulty in paying attention during class resulted in academic failure, despite his intellectual abilities—and hyperactivity—a fidgety girl. Some argued that Still included a broad range of disorders under the diagnosed "defect of moral character."

Although Still's notion of *moral defect* is a concern among those who view ADHD as a disease, he is credited with having made a contribution to the study of mental disorders in childhood. Still's contributions changed the understanding of children. He introduced the idea that there are other causes (nonmoral) for defective or immoral behaviors—intellectual retardation, physical diseases, and brain damage (Barkley, 2006b; Conners, 2000; Rafalovich, 2001). Still's work also speaks loudly to the individualization of symptoms associated with ADHD. His work offers substantial support for the idea that there are many pathways to ADHD, and that, because of this, the individual experience of the ADHD child and her circumstances are relevant when thinking about treatment. Children do not necessarily fit neatly into diagnostic categories. Often, there is an overlap of contributing factors, and it's hard to make precise distinctions.

Still's work, considered "scientific," may have led to the medicalization of deviant behavior in children after the encephalitic period. *Encephalitis lethargica*, a viral form of encephalitis with a debilitating impact on the basal ganglia and midbrain structures of the brain, caused an epidemic that resulted in the death of 20 million people between 1916 and 1927 (Conners, 2000; Kiley and Esiri, 2001; Rafalovich, 2001; Rail, Scholtz, and Swash, 1981; von Economo, 1931). Symptoms of the disorder included sleep disturbance, lethargy, and stereotypic extrapyramidal movements. A range of neuropsychiatric disorders, including obsessive-compulsive behavior and catatonia, were observed among survivors. In child survivors, actions akin to those exhibited by ADHD children became associated with the disease—among them were hyperactivity, difficulty in focusing and attending, destruction of property, and disruptive behavior in the classroom. Although these behavior changes were not sufficient to meet the current diagnostic criteria for ADHD, it was enough to warrant a diagnosis of *post-encephalitic behavior disorder* and ignited an interest in children's hyperactive behavior. Because treatment professionals of the time established a physiological connection between the brain and children's deviant behavior, that relationship set the stage for the medical pathway to ADHD diagnosis (Lange et al., 2010; Rafalovich, 2001).

Physicians were the primary treatment providers for the psychosis that resulted from the encephalitis lethargica epidemic. The founder of the disease, von Economo, struggled to identify a cause of the illness, generating many theories but no clear conclusions. Some physicians adopted a medical treatment approach that was informed by a belief that infectious diseases were the cure for psychoses: a similar approach had been used in 1917 when a Viennese physician, Julius Wagner von Jauregg, successfully treated psychotic soldiers with malaria injections. Physicians experimented with patients suffering from post-encephalitic behavior disorder by injecting them with typhus. Some of the symptoms associated with ADHD were successfully treated with this approach, thereby opening the door for medical treatments of behavioral problems. Von Jauregg won the Nobel Prize in 1927.

Although von Jauregg's treatment was considered successful, the idea of injecting ADHD children with thyphus is probably not one that would be well received today. Fortunately, during the late nineteenth century, Freud shifted the focus of mental health treatment from a medical one that sought answers in the brain to a psychological one that looked for solutions associated with the mind. This shift was largely a result of Freud's discovery that *hysteria* was not a disease of the brain, but rather a neurosis that stemmed from disordered thoughts (Mitchell and Black, 1995). He began to turn the tide from medical interventions to successful psychological treatments based on his development of the scientific psychotherapy method, noting that "the neuroses of our unpsychological modern days take on a hypochondriacal aspect and appear disguised as organic illnesses" (Freud quoted in Carlson, 1999, p. 74). Freud's interpretation of the societal reaction to neuroses was not far-fetched given that this was a time in medical history where medical treatment was ineffective in curing a subset of patients whose neurological symptoms were debilitating, yet had no identifiable medical etiology.

Although treating the psychosis resulting from encephalitis lethargica was not his focus, it is likely that, given the historical context in which he was writing, he had the condition in mind when he criticized the medicalization of neuroses. Thus, Freud's development of the psychoanalytic treatment technique can be seen as offering the first nonmedical conceptualization of the post-encephalitic epidemic. Indeed, some believe Freud's work on hysteria overshadowed the work of von Economo, who was less successful in developing a treatment for post-encephalitic behavior disorder—also a disease of unidentifiable etiology.

Currently, there are some studies attempting to establish a scientific connection between brain physiology and ADHD. As our understanding of ADHD evolves, the belief that a neurological cause is central to the symptoms of inattention and hyperactivity grows. Studies of the brain made possible through advances in brain imaging techniques have begun to map out how the brain's structure and function relates to behavior. This topic is explored in chapter 2.

The findings of two German physicians, Franz Kramer (1878–1967) and Hans Pollnow (1902–1943), mark the next era in the history of ADHD. These physicians observed the presence of a motoric drive and restlessness in children that they termed *hyperkinetic disease* (Kramer and Pollnow, 1932, in Lange et al., 2010). In their observations of children with hyperkinetic disease, Kramer and Pollnow witnessed children who climbed furniture, ran around the room, and experienced difficulty sitting still. The children's movements conveyed a sense of urgency, as though they were being driven, but their interactions with objects seemed to be without a clear purpose. The children moved from one activity to another indiscriminately, touching things and interacting with objects in their environment in ways that ignored the objects' functions. Children also presented with mood instability and often encountered difficulties in their academic and social functioning (Kramer and Pollnow, 1932, in Lange et al., 2010). Lange and colleagues (2010) draw many parallels between current ADHD symptoms (hyperactivity and distractibility) to hyperkinetic disease. The term *hyperkinetic disorder* is still being used in many European countries and is often used interchangeably with ADHD. It is important to note, however, that the age range of hyperkinetic disorder, once circumscribed to early childhood—ages three to seven years—now extends into adulthood (Barkley, 2006a, Okie, 2006; DSM-5).

The period of Kramer and Pallnow's (1932, in Lange et al., 2010) identification of hyperkinetic disease overlaps the emergence of a "medical" explanation for hyperactive or hyperkinetic behaviors: *minimal brain damage*. The conclusion that minimal brain damage causes hyperactivity derived from various reports of brain-injured patients being observed demonstrating the hyperactive behaviors. Hyperactive behaviors have been associated with gross lesions in the brain (Ross and Ross, 1976, p. 15); acute diseases such as encephalitis (1917 to 1928); history of head trauma (Kessler, 1980); birth trauma (Kessler, 1980); infections, lead toxicity, and epilepsy (Barkley, 2006a); brain-injured soldiers (Goldstein, 1942, cited by Kessler 1980, p. 22); and asphyxia illness in infancy (Rosenfeld and Bradley, 1948). These medical etiologies are associated with a range of behaviors common to

ADHD including mood changes, hyperactive behaviors, impulsivity and in-attention—a sequelae of ADHD (see Lange et al., 2010 for a review). Based on these findings, some practitioners refer to ADHD behaviors as caused by brain damage despite the dearth of evidence to the contrary (Barkley, 2006a; Ross and Ross, 1976; Strauss and Kephart, 1955; Strauss and Lehtinen, 1947). This extension of behavioral problems commonly found in an ADHD presentation to the medical domain of minimal brain damage exemplifies a sociological phenomenon referred to as *domain expansion* (Conrad and Potter, 2000). Conrad (1976) zeroes in on this domain expansion when he argues that the extension of behavior problems to the medical field is a prime example of what he refers to as the *medicalization of deviance*.

During the mid-twentieth century, doubts about the generalized use of the minimal brain damage diagnosis increased and led to further explorations (Birch, 1964; Herbert, 1964; Rapin, 1964, in Lange et al., 2010). Laufer, Denhoff, and Solomons (1957) compared children demonstrating hyperkinetic behaviors with those who did not exhibit any hyperkinetic behaviors. They found that differential responses to the threshold levels of children administered Metrazol disappeared when the hyperkinetic children received amphetamines. Their findings suggest that hyperkinetic children who did not experience biological insults to their brains were as responsive to Metrazol as those whose behaviors stemmed from organically based injuries. Hence all hyperkinetic children responded similarly to the medication compared to non-hyperkinetic children. Based on these findings, Laufer, Denhoff, and Solomons concluded that a dysfunction of the diencephalon region of the brain was also common among hyperkinetic children regardless of their history of brain damage.

In 1963, the diagnosis of minimal brain damage was changed to *minimal brain dysfunction*. The change was due in large part to the efforts of two groups—the Oxford International Study Group on Child Neurology and the National Institute of Neurological Diseases and Blindness (Bax and MacKeith, 1963, in Lange et al., 2010). The predominant symptoms of minimal brain dysfunction no longer included "below-normal" intellectual functioning but were instead characterized by inattention, impulsivity, and hyperactivity (Lange et al., 2010). Arguments about the lack of specificity of the minimal brain dysfunction diagnosis (cited by Conners, 2000, in Lange et al., 2010) and the absence of hyperkinetic behaviors in children with brain dysfunction (Birch, 1964, in Lange et al., 2010) provided a basis for the DSM II (1968) inclusion of hyperkinetic reactions of childhood as a disorder. This change in 1968, from a diagnosis of minimal brain dysfunction to one of *hyperkinetic reaction of childhood* was characterized as beginning in early childhood and lasting through adolescence. Hyperkinetic Reaction of Childhood included symptoms of hyperactivity, restlessness, distractibility, and inattention (American Psychiatric Association, 1968).

Excluded from the diagnosis of both minimal brain dysfunction and hyperkinetic reaction of childhood were considerations for the role that environmental factors, including family and society, played in the child's behavioral symptoms (Barkley, 2006a; Clements and Peters, 1962). The contributions of psychoanalysis has been even more sidelined. Psychoanalytic approaches are marked by a more phenomenological understanding of an individual's psyche and less so by nosology or diagnostic classifications. The introduction of diagnostic manuals became the predominant approach to mental health and simultaneously, the psychoanalytic approach lost a foothold in psychiatry. For those who value psychodynamic and psychoanalytic approaches, their sentiments have been expressed in review articles such as Andreasen's (2007), *DSM and the Death of Phenomenology in America: An Example of Unintended Consequences* regarding the shift toward reliance on the DSM:

> DSM has had a dehumanizing impact on the practice of psychiatry. History taking—the central evaluation tool in psychiatry—has frequently been reduced to the use of DSM checklists. DSM discourages clinicians from getting to know the patient as an individual person because of its dryly empirical approach. (p. 111)

Prior to the development and use of diagnostic classification systems, an understanding of children that reflected psychoanalytic thought considered understanding the child's psyche and internal conflicts as a goal of treatment. Psychoanalytic conceptualizations of ADHD that offers a comprehensive view of the child and the interplay of social and environmental factors are a missing component of the discourse on ADHD.

Psychoanalysis is concerned not only with the etiology of ADHD but also with the impact of ADHD on the individual's life. Although there is an acknowledgment that the origins of ADHD may have some basis in brain abnormalities and neurological pathways, psychoanalysts are equally aware that children's inattention may also stem from past and current environmental occurrences. Given the heterotypic reasons for ADHD symptomatology, analysts have adopted an approach to ADHD that is tuned into the individual. Diagnostic impressions of the child's behavior consider how the child's relationship to himself and others supports the persistence of hyperactive and inattentive symptoms. Depending on the particular school of psychoanalytic thought being used, theories about how symptoms impact the child's psyche vary. But a central focus of the psychoanalytic approach is the importance given to the child's experience of himself and his world in the context of his ADHD symptoms.

The evolution of the psychodynamic understanding of ADHD has not been a linear process. Psychodynamic treatment of ADHD involved taking into account how several dimensions of the child's personality structure, the defensive stance adopted in the face of anxiety, and other dispositional considerations contributed to a complex matrix of factors the analysts then wove into their treatment approach. Although this formulation was often useful, reliability among its users varied, and as the call for more scientific and measurable treatment methods increased there was a shift away from internal (intrapsychic and underlying) to more external (behaviors) views of ADHD. This shift, in turn, led to a parallel shift in the treatment of ADHD, which became less focused on the internal experiences of the child and more concerned with external behavioral change. This split has created a bifurcation in the field of psychotherapy leading to the abandonment of psychoanalytic approaches in treating ADHD for more behavioral and neuropsychological ones.

Across the period during which the DSM-III through DSM-5 were published, psychoanalytic views on children's behaviors were increasingly abandoned and replaced with more medical categorizations of ADHD. Before the ADHD diagnosis was adopted a diagnosis of "hyperkinetic disorder" was used. However, beginning with the DSM-III in 1980 (American Psychiatric Association, 1980), hyperkinetic disorder underwent a name change to *attention deficit disorder (ADD) with or without hyperactivity*, reflecting a change in emphasis on attention rather than hyperactivity (Douglas, 1972). The responsiveness of these symptoms—inattention and impulsivity—to stimulant medication treatments coupled with Douglas's work—identification of impulse control and inattention aspects of hyperkinetic disorder—led to the name change (Barkley, 2006a; Rothenberger and Neumärker, 2005). The change did not last; in the 1987 revision of the DSM-III, the name was again changed—this time to *attention deficit hyperactivity disorder (ADHD)* (Barkley 2006a). Those presenting without hyperactivity symptoms were diagnosed with ADHD and placed in the "not otherwise specified" category.

The introduction of the DSM-IV in 1994 again reflected changes to the organization of the ADHD diagnosis. The American Psychiatric Association identified three clearly defined groups: predominantly inattentive type, predominantly hyperactive-impulsive type, and combined type with both hyperactive impulsivity and inattention (American Psychiatric Association, 1994). Lahey and colleagues' (1994) study on ADHD led to this reorganization. In the late 1990s, the review of the DSM-IV that led in the publication of the DSM IV-TR in 2000 did not result in any name change. However, there were concerns raised about the paucity of evidence supporting a diagnosis of ADHD in adults. Since most of the research thus far has been limited to children, more empirical support for an adult onset of the disorder is needed.

With the introduction of the DSM-5 (2013), very little about the criteria for ADHD has changed. ADHD's predominant symptoms of inattention and hyperactivity remain the same. However, the age of onset was raised from seven years old to twelve years old. This new diagnostic manual also presents examples of how ADHD is presented developmentally—throughout childhood, adolescence, and adulthood. These changes expand the developmental trajectory of the diagnosis, which can now be documented in undiagnosed adults. Among young adults, particularly college-aged individuals, ADHD is often overlooked and less studied (Konold and Glutting, 2008; Reilley, 2005). College aged students with ADHD may experience difficulty adjusting to the social and academic aspects of college life resulting in disruptions in their academic pursuits (Norvilitis, Sun, and Zhang, 2010). Some college students with ADHD disclosed in a focus group their need for one-on-one coaching, academic assistance, assistance developing schedules to complete academic tasks on time, and social support groups (Conway, McLaughlin, Tyler-Best, and Minutella, 2015). ADHD symptoms of hyperactivity and impulsivity may be even more difficult to detect among adults who are no longer in academic settings, but evidence from a longitudinal study following children over a ten to twenty-five-year period supports the persistence of ADHD symptoms through their adolescent and adult years (Weiss and Hechtman, 1993). Documentation of ADHD symptoms in adults emerged during the late 1960s (Okie, 2006) with reports of aggression (Doyle, 2004) and destructiveness (Quitkin and Klein, 1969) alongside symptoms of hyperactivity and impulsivity. More recently, in a longitudinal study, which followed six- to twelve-year-old children for ten to twenty-five years, 75 percent of the participants experienced the symptoms of ADHD into their adolescent and adulthood years (Weiss and Hechtman, 1993).

This trend may reflect the possibility that society is more knowledgeable about ADHD symptoms than they were previously, or, as Conrad (1979) argues, it may reflect an increasing tendency toward the medicalization of deviance.

Psychoanalysis promises to play a pivotal role in the current treatment of ADHD despite the expansion of neurological contributions. It is quite possible that science has not yet caught up with the ADHD diagnosis and that we will learn much more in the years to come. However, in the meantime we find ourselves once more at a crossroads. For example, during the period of the encephalitis epidemic, the emergence of psychoanalysis paralleled the medical explorations of treatment. Freud developed a technique to treat those with seeming neurological impairments that led to the creation of psychoanalysis and the establishment of psychotherapy as a viable treatment alternative. Similarly, current developments in neuropsychology have made bold claims that ADHD is a neurobehavioral disorder (National Institute of Neurological Disorders and Stroke; Sroubek, Kelly, and Li, 2013).

Neurological findings fall short of providing answers regarding nonmedical ADHD treatment and raise a myriad of other questions. Most of these neuropsychological claims are based on correlational findings that compare the brains of ADHD and non-ADHD individuals (Barkley, 1990; Goldstein and Goldstein, 1998; Ross and Ross, 1982). The problem with this approach is that because there are many reasons for differences in brain structure, the mere existence of differences in brain structure is insufficient evidence to establish ADHD as a cause for any observed differences in behavior (Galves and Walker, 2002). Galves and Walker (2002) argue that noticeable changes in brain functioning can be affected by the environment (Rozensweig, Bennett, and Diamond, 1972); drug and cognitive psychotherapy (Schwartz et al., 1996); placebo treatments (Leuchter et al., 2002); and other therapeutic activities (Pennebaker, 2000). Moreover, a review of neuroimaging studies on ADHD shows no clear evidence for the predicted relations between ADHD and structural or functional brain abnormalities (Baumeister and Hawkins, 2001). At the heart of Galves and Walker's (2002) argument is the notion that current ADHD treatment pathways pay very little attention to the children's experience of themselves and how they negotiate their difficulties. They argue that this is problematic because how children think and feel and the environment they live in is of great importance and may impact their brain functioning.

In addition to the neurological findings on ADHD, some researchers have advanced an argument that ADHD is a genetic disorder. High rates of ADHD disorder occur among monozygotic twins relative to dizygotic twins (Biederman et al., 1992; Edelbrock, Rende, Plomin, and Thompson, 1995; Gillis et al., 1992; Goodman and Stevenson, 1989; Pauls, 1991; Sherman, Iacono, and McGue, 1997). According to Galves and Walker (2002), assumptions that these differences are due to genetic factors are based on erroneous assumptions that monozygotic and dizygotic twins grow in similar environments. Instead, they argue, the research shows the circumstances differ markedly for these two twin populations, with identical twins having more similar styles of dressing, more friends in common, and closer sibling relations compared to fraternal twins (Joseph, 2003). A higher standard of rigor is required to make genetic conclusions, including segregation and linkage studies (Ross and Ross, 1982). Furthermore, even though neural anatomy determines a range of possible experience or potentiality of the brain, experience plays a significant role in the realization of these possibilities (Lewis, Amini, and Lannon, 2000). The parent–child environment is important in shaping the emotions of the child and her self-development. It would be unethical and irresponsible to focus only on neurological aspects of ADHD without full consideration of the contributions of the environment to the symptom development.

History thus far has been one-sided in its view of ADHD, leading to a skewed focus of treatment—behavioral symptom amelioration and the use of pharmaceutical interventions. Conspicuously missing from the discourse on ADHD's history is an examination of nonmedical contributions to the ADHD symptomatology. Environmental factors, such as parent–child relationships, have not been considered in previous recordings of ADHD's evolution. Starting in the early 1970s researchers began looking at contributions to ADHD behaviors that are external to the child and more focused on the environment. In terms of the caregiving environment, research has shown the following parental factors associated with ADHD behaviors:

1. Parental attitudes toward the child's achievement and learning that are pessimistic and tied to severe disciplinary practices (Lambert and Harsough, 1984; Ross and Ross, 1982);
2. Parent–child interpersonal conflicts leading to feelings of inadequacies in the parent (Lambert, 1982);
3. Critical, negative, and commanding parental interactions (Barkley, 1990; Goodman and Stevenson, 1989; Ross and Ross, 1982; Thomas and Chess, 1977);
4. Impoverished maternal psychological well-being, including anxiety, depression, aggressive behavior, parental stress, low self-esteem, and other emotional disturbances (Barkley, 1990; Cameron, 1977; Goldstein and Goldstein, 1998; Patterson, 1982; Sameroff and Chandler, 1975; Thomas and Chess, 1977); and
5. Hostile and conflictual family environments due to marital discord, anger, and/or mother–child disharmony (Battle and Lacy, 1972; Cameron, 1977; Lambert and Harsough, 1984; Robin, Kraus, Koepke, and Robin, 1987).

These environmental considerations would require interventions beyond the reach of neuropsychological interventions. Rather, they lend themselves to psychotherapy interventions like psychoanalysis, which is designed to explore these parent–child relational issues that are central to the development of a core self and to the emotional life of the child.

Several key psychoanalytic/psychodynamic institutions, researchers, and clinicians took the initiative to form a task force leading to the development of the psychodynamic diagnostic classification system (PDM Task Force, 2006). Unlike the DSM, the *Psychodynamic Diagnostic Manual (PDM)* includes a comprehensive view of the individual ranging from personality structure to an integration of individuals' behavioral, cognitive, emotional, and social functioning. The manual combines the rich history of psychoanalysis with current research on child development, personality assessment, and neuroscience to provide a system for understanding the ADHD child's symptoms in the context of his development and intrapsychic positioning. Psychoanalytic/psychodynamic therapy is concerned with the child's emerging personality functioning, mental functioning, and subjective experiences. In terms of the child's mental functioning, the practitioner is less oriented toward her behavior and more toward how she deals with her experiences of relationships, emotions, and anxiety. Regarding the child's presenting symptoms, his subjective experience of those symptoms—rather than their eradication—is of primary interest. Thus, the dynamic-oriented therapist examines how these symptoms emerge in the dynamic context of the child's development and seeks to understand the child's unique experience of the symptoms—of specific interest are the child's healthy responses to situations, her response to developmental and situational crises, and her disordered affective responses. For the ADHD child, a psychoanalytic view would reference the child's interactive problems—disruptive behaviors, regulatory sensory problems—and symptoms of inattention.

Over the years, the medical view of ADHD existed alongside a moral indictment of children. It is only since the early twentieth century that researchers began to look at how the child's environment—especially how the *parental* environment—contributed to the child's behavioral symptoms. From a psychoanalytic perspective, discord in the parental environment most often impacts the development of the child's attachment relationship with the parent. Attachment provides a foundation for the child's ability to regulate his emotions and behaviors, as well as his capacity to pay attention. We are at a point in our history where we are willing to be self-reflective and consider the role we play in influencing the outcomes in our lives. This openness toward self-exploration has created an opportunity in the field of child mental health to look at parental and other practices that shape our children's spiritual life. We have begun to move away from a point of view that solely seeks to locate the cause of a disorder in the symptom carrier. Rather, a psychodynamic viewpoint is concerned with how the child's behaviors provide the therapist with insight into the child's perspective. For example, the child attempts to communicate, cope, self-regulate, and function psychologically by reacting behaviorally and emotionally to their experiences of the parental and other environments they find themselves in. There is a need to understand and bear witness to the experiences of these children and their families, to help them develop a healthy sense of themselves in the world, and to provide opportunities for them to thrive psychologically. These efforts, when achieved in a psychodynamic-oriented psychotherapy, repudiate moral indictment and bring a sense of compassion for the plight of the ADHD child.

Psychoanalytic contributions to the understanding of ADHD not only are essential to the history of the disorder but also set the stage for developing compassion for ADHD children. The analysts interviewed for this book spoke compassionately about the children they worked with. After speaking with them and analyzing their responses, the therapists' capacity to empathize with both ADHD children and their parents was most compelling. Given the historic and continued maligning of children with ADHD, the psychodynamic approach to working with ADHD is one that is respectful of individual differences—one that provides a compassionate response to children who often encounter harsh rebuttals for their ADHD-related difficulties. Chapter 1 synthesizes and describes a *psychodynamic understanding* of the ADHD child's difficulties that is inclusive of neurological, environmental (disruptions in early parent-child relationships, trauma and complex trauma), and intrapsychic determinants (self-concept and emotions). Chapter 2 offers a description of a *psychodynamic approach* to working with ADHD children. The psychodynamic approach is based on two main models—ego developmental and relational—used by dynamic therapists in approaching this work. These models were identified based on the responses of those interviewed and on a review of psychodynamic literature. Chapter 3 begins the second part of the book with a discussion of psychodynamic *psychotherapy interventions* useful in working with ADHD children's ego and relational issues. In chapter 4, I present guidelines for a *treatment model for psychodynamic psychotherapy* with ADHD children that applies the ego and relational approaches to treatment in clearly laid out phases. The psychodynamic therapists interviewed for this book also discussed their thoughts about behavioral approaches. To provide a context for their perspective, I provide an *overview of behavioral and cognitive behavioral therapies* in chapter 5. This final chapter also discusses a psychodynamic approach used by the dynamic therapists for *working with parents and schools*. The book concludes with an epilogue that provides a discussion of some unanswered questions about ADHD with larger societal and cultural considerations.

CHAPTER HIGHLIGHTS

For a graph on the evolution of ADHD, see figure 0.1 on the following page.

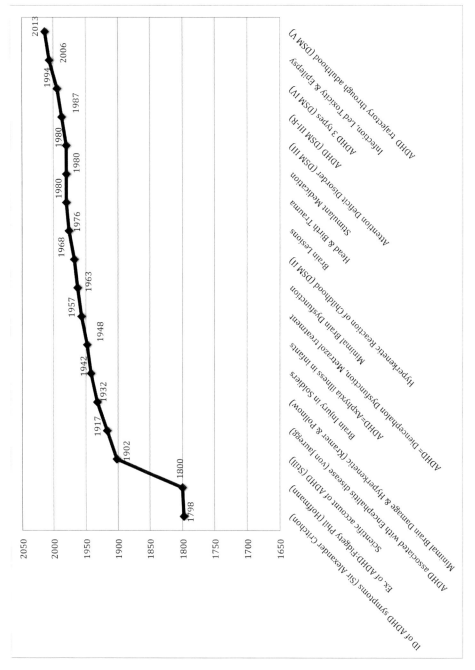

Figure 0.1.   Evolution of ADHD

Chapter One

A Psychodynamic Understanding of ADHD Symptoms

Engendering Compassion

We know what we are, but know not what we may be.
—William Shakespeare, *Hamlet* (4.5.43–44)

Therapists hold a range of beliefs about the behavioral manifestations of inattention, hyperactivity, and related symptoms in children that are commonly referred to as Attention Deficit Hyperactivity Disorder (ADHD). While interviewing psychoanalysts and psychotherapists who treat children, I found that some were very reluctant to use the diagnostic classification of ADHD. After encountering this resistance in interview after interview, I realized there is still considerable controversy surrounding the ADHD diagnosis. Given the conflicting views on ADHD among treatment professionals, it is therefore important to begin this discussion of psychodynamic perspectives of the disorder by first addressing the question: *What is ADHD?*

In this chapter, I discuss therapists' views on the etiology of ADHD. The psychodynamic therapists and analysts I interviewed believed the etiology of ADHD is twofold—that it is both biological and psychological. This chapter represents their views on neurological contributors to ADHD, as well as their views on the psychological determinants of ADHD. When available, I present research and relevant literature to support their clinical experience.

For psychodynamic therapists who do not primarily focus on their client's symptoms, the question *What is ADHD?* is a nuanced and complex one. Psychodynamic therapists acknowledge the ADHD classification; however, they do not find it useful. The ADHD classification is limited in that it fails to consider the behaviors of others in the child's environment. For example, others interacting with a child exhibiting symptoms of ADHD may exhibit responses to the child that range from mild irritation to extreme frustration. Some therapists view these interpersonal interactions as creating dynamics that either provoke or perpetuate these symptoms in the child. In either case, most can agree that the responses of important others in the child's life are a crucial consideration in determining the course of ADHD treatment and the occurrence of comorbid symptoms such as anxiety and depression.

For the psychoanalytically oriented therapist, the first issue in treating ADHD children is confronting how they are labeled and categorized. Children presenting with this cluster of symptoms are often brought to a therapist with requests to *fix* them—to improve their attention and reduce their hyperactivity. Often out of desperation, parents turn to medication as an option to reduce "problematic" symptoms. In fact, when a child begins therapy, her parent often informs her therapist that she "has ADHD," and in many cases, she has already begun taking some form of stimulant medication.

The problem with that approach is that ADHD symptoms have multiple determinants that include interpersonal, neurobiological, and environmental factors. Instead of focusing on symptom elimination, then, the psychodynamic therapist is concerned with what produces these ADHD responses in the first place. Rather than asking *How can we fix this child?* the psychodynamic therapist is more likely to investigate questions such as *What function do the child's symptoms serve?* and *What is the child attempting to communicate?* If there is a biological basis for these symptoms, *What role does biology play in the manifestation of the child's symptoms?* and *How does the child negotiate these limitations?* Finally, *What role does the parental environment play in this disorder?* Explorations of these *questions of etiology* from a psychodynamic perspective provide insight into the depth of the ADHD child's struggles. In this way, psychodynamic therapists avoid categorizing the child's behavior and instead adopt a sense of curiosity and inquiry about all aspects of the child's life.

Appreciation for the varied etiology of ADHD symptoms is a prerequisite for understanding that ADHD symptoms extend beyond inattention and hyperactivity. Depending on the child's unique experiences—both interpersonal and environmental—a complex matrix of symptoms emerges, all of which interact with each other to affect the child's psychological functioning. The child's view of himself, his views of others, and the intersection of these views with reality determines the core psychological issues with which he must grapple as he negotiates his interpersonal world. Matters related to the child's self (self-concept, self-esteem); how he mediates internal experiences of conflict; the extent to which he can regulate his emotions; and his experiences of emotions associated with shame and aggression are all important considerations for psychodynamic therapists.

Psychodynamic psychotherapists derive their understanding of ADHD from their consideration of the impact of neurological, environmental, and psychological factors on the child's psychological well-being. It is often difficult to disentangle the influence of these factors on a given child. Neurological factors may change behaviors, which in turn influence interpersonal interactions and, ultimately, children's sense of themselves. At the same time, psychological dispositions and the dynamics of the child's mental processes lead to a set of behaviors that evoke responses in the environment. For the purpose of clarity, these factors will be discussed separately.

First, this chapter reviews current neuropsychological perspectives on ADHD, highlighting some of the prevailing models of ADHD etiology such as executive dysfunction; impairments in motivation/processing reward; dual and multiple pathway models (specifically, the cognitive-energetic model and the integrated affective and cognitive model); and developmental models. Since neurological research on ADHD is a relatively new area of research, this research has been more concerned with the direct relation between the brain and behavior and less concerned with the dynamics of human relationships. These dynamics, interpersonal and intrapersonal, may be attributed to either the origin or the result of ADHD. Therefore, this chapter will then turn to a consideration of factors relevant to psychodynamic psychotherapists and analysts when working with children diagnosed with ADHD. Thus, intrapsychic and environmental determinants of symptoms associated with ADHD are important considerations for therapists as they seek to understand the child's conscious functioning (academic development; peer, parent, and teacher relationships) and unconscious functioning (intrapsychic issues related to self-esteem, self-concept, interpersonal relationships, and emotion regulation). A focus of this chapter attends to the mental life of the child by examining relational impingements, intrapsychic issues, and the relationship between the two that leads to ADHD-symptom manifestation.

NEUROLOGICAL PERSPECTIVES ON ADHD

Pete's a very interesting kid who has a NOS diagnosis . . . he's what they used to call in the olden days "FLK—Funny Looking Kid." He's atypical for sure, very bright, exceedingly anxious. . . . He has a father who's exceedingly anxious as well, and a mother who's exceedingly anxious in different ways. This boy has a lot of anxiety. But I'm pretty sure from his developmental history that he was born with this atypical pattern of behaviors. And so, he's afraid of thunderstorms. This summer was a bad summer. We had three or four thunderstorms. When he came to my office, his mom would drive right up to the driveway within two feet of my office door so he could run in without getting . . . "killed." So he does well, he's in an integrated inclusion class where some of the children are typical, and some of them have atypicalities like him, and he does well in general. He has some oddities to him. . . . They're not all attentional. I'm not sure if it's even ADHD, but that's his diagnosis, and he does take medication. [MOL]

The research efforts to identify neurological determinants of ADHD are relatively new. Leading neuroscience researchers, such as Dr. F. Xavier Castellanos, a pediatrician and child psychiatrist who heads up ADHD research at the National Institute of Mental Health, believe the answers research provides to be sparse and note that very little is known about the ADHD diagnosis. In an interview with *Frontline* (October 10, 2000), Dr. Castellanos admitted "We don't have an objective way of definitively saying 'This person has ADHD or does not,' in part because we don't really understand what it is." ADHD is a heterogeneous disorder affecting varied areas of the brain, and support for the diverse etiology of ADHD has been provided by numerous neuroimaging and neurocognitive research studies (Faraone, 2000; Sprich-Buckminster, Biederman, Milberger, Faraone, and Lehman, 1993). This diversity means that not all children presenting with ADHD symptoms have the same neurological abnormalities, so an individual approach to understanding and treating ADHD is necessary. That is not to say that this neurological information is not useful in understanding ADHD. On the contrary, it is important to recognize and appreciate that biologically based deficits can lead to inattention and hyperactivity. For example, in the quote that begins this section, Pete presents with attention issues, but it is clear that he has a biological disposition that adds to the complexity of his presenting problems.

Neurological Determinants

Neuroimaging

Advances in techniques available to study and understand the brain's functioning have been and continue to be employed to improve our understanding of ADHD. Here I discuss three methods used thus far in studying the brains of ADHD children—Magnetic Resonance Imaging (MRI), Diffusion Tensor Imaging (DTI), and Functional Magnetic Resonance Imaging (fMRI).

Magnetic Resonance Imaging Over the past two decades, researchers have been conducting Magnetic Resonance Imaging scans of children's brains looking for differences in brain structure between ADHD and non-ADHD children. These neuroimaging techniques entail the use of *Structural Magnetic Resonance Imaging (MRI)* technology to capture either static or active (fMRI to be discussed in a separate section) images of the brain. Research using static neuroimaging techniques shows that many areas of the brain in ADHD children are notably smaller than those of their non-ADHD peers; as a result, their overall brain size is also comparatively smaller. The affected areas of the brain include the posterior inferior vermis, caudate nucleus, prefrontal cortex, globus pallidus, corpus callosum, cerebellum, and posterior cortical region.

Neuroimaging studies have established irrefutably that the size of the overall brain and specific brain structures are smaller in ADHD children (Castellanos, Lee, Sharp, Jeffries, Greenstein et al., 2002). Using MRI techniques, Castellanos and his colleagues scanned the brains of 152 children with ADHD and compared them to the scans of 139 children without ADHD. The researchers were able to examine the children an average of four times over a ten-year period and found smaller cerebral and cerebellar volumes, 3.2 percent and 3.5 percent respectively, in ADHD patients. These differences, which persisted throughout adolescence, were observed in children as young as five years old.

With regard to specific regions of the brain, according to Dr. Castellanos, two decades worth of research has led to conclusions that a part of the cerebellum, the *posterior inferior vermis*, is 12 percent smaller in ADHD children. The cerebellum is generally thought of as being responsible for the coordination of movement and therefore may explain the motor inhibitory difficulties common to hyperactive children (Berquin et al., 1998; Castellanos, 2001; Castellanos et al., 1996; Castellanos et al., 2002; Durston et al., 2004; Mostofsky et al., 1998; Posner and Petersen, 1990). However, a more critical function is its ability to coordinate the functioning of other processes in the brain. In his *Frontline* interview, Dr. Castellanos refers to the function of this part of the cerebellum as a "co-processor" that bolsters the efficiency of other brain processes. In his imaging research, Dr. Castellanos also found that the *caudate nucleus* is approximately 6 percent smaller in the brains of ADHD children, but these differences may disappear during the mid- to late-teenage years. The caudate nucleus is responsible for a range of cognitive functions such as memory, affect, and inhibition (Castellanos et al., 1996; Castellanos et al., 2002; Filipek et al., 1997; Hynd et al., 1993). These findings suggest that as the child gets older, his ability to control his impulsive behaviors improves. Again, the implications of these findings are unclear, and researchers like Dr. Castellanos and his team are working to gain a clearer understanding of these results.

Taken together, the body of neuroimaging studies suggests that children with ADHD have smaller brain structures in regions of the brain that are associated with many well-known ADHD symptoms. Gopin and Healey (2011) summarize these findings in their article on *The Neural and Neurocognitive Determinants of ADHD*. In addition to the areas previously discussed, the areas of the brain showing reduced sizes include:

1. the *prefrontal cortex*, responsible for planning and decision making (Castellanos et al., 1996; Castellanos et al., 2002; Durston et al., 2004; Filipek et al., 1997; Hynd et al., 1990; Kates et al., 2002; Mostofsky et al., 2002; Sowell et al., 2003);
2. the *globus pallidus*, regulating voluntary movement (Aylward et al., 1996; Castellanos et al., 1996);
3. the *corpus callosum*, which facilitates the transfer of information between the right and left hemispheres of the brain (Baumgardner et al., 1996; Giedd et al., 1994; Hill et al., 2003; Hynd et al., 1991; Lyoo et al., 1996; Semrud-Clikeman et al., 1994); and
4. the *posterior cortical region*, responsible for visuospatial processing (Durston et al., 2004; Filipek et al., 1997; Sowell et al., 2003).

In addition to these identified areas, researchers found that in the brains of ADHD children, *cortical thickness*, a measure of general cognitive abilities, lags in development by two to three years (Shaw et al., 2006; Shaw et al., 2007a; Shaw et al., 2007b).

There is a wealth of studies supporting immature brain development in ADHD children. However, these studies are unable to offer any clear explanation regarding the reason these differences exist. Castellanos and colleagues have established that there is a biological difference in the brains of ADHD children and have speculated that these natural processes were possibly present as the child was developing in the prenatal stage. They have ventured as far as to say that these differences may be due to *genetic factors* or some *impingement on the developmental process*, but they cannot yet say what factors may cause these impingements on brain development during the prenatal period and early childhood years.

Diffusion Tensor Imaging Aside from MRI technology, neuroscientists studying the brain structure of ADHD children have made use of *Diffusion Tensor Imaging (DTI)* techniques. DTI, also referred to as *Diffusion MRI*, is an MRI-based neuroimaging technique that provides a visual representation of the location, orientation, and structure of the brain's white matter tracts, thus highlighting *pathophysiology*—that is, whether the tissue is normal or in a diseased state. Using the DTI technique, Dr. Manzar Ashtari, an associate professor of radiology and psychiatry at North Shore–Long Island Jewish Health System in New York, along with his colleagues, studied the structural aspects of the brain in ADHD children looking specifically at the brain's neural circuitry (Ashtari et al., 2005). Dr. Ashtari and his team used DTI to make comparisons between the brains of eighteen ADHD children and fifteen non-ADHD children. They found that the brain fibers' pathways used to transmit and receive information to the frontal cortex, basal ganglia, brain stem, and cerebellum were abnormal in ADHD children. These areas of the brain correspond to brain areas that influence the child's ability to self-regulate, which is significant given that attention, impulsive behavior, difficulty controlling motor activity, and decreased inhibition are common areas of difficulty for ADHD children.

In this way, DTI studies have been able to extend the understanding of the ADHD child's brain. We now know not only that several subregions of the brain tend to be smaller among ADHD children but also that ADHD is associated with a pathophysiology in the communication system between the frontal lobe and cerebellum—one that specifically involves the right hemisphere motor circuitry (i.e., the right supplementary motor area, right anterior limb of the internal capsule) (Gopin and Healey, 2011). Studies using DTI to document the degree of abnormality in the brain's circuitry have also identified both increased and reduced nerve sheath myelination in the white matter fiber wiring specific to attention and executive functioning (Casey et al., 2007; Hamilton et al., 2008; Li et al., 2010; Makris et al., 2007; Pavuluri et al., 2009). These studies have also identified abnormalities in tracts specific to movement such as the cerebellum and the striatum (Silk et al., 2009).

Functional Magnetic Resonance Imaging Unlike the studies previously discussed, this next set of findings reports on the brain's functioning when activated. These studies, which use fMRI techniques to capture images of the brain when the participant is engaged in a task, are designed to assess whether the levels of activation in the brain areas associated with the work are adequate—allowing researchers to focus on the functional aspects of the brain. The findings suggest that several functional aspects of the brain deviate from expected or normal patterns. According to Gopin and Healey (2011), the range of aberrant functions associated with ADHD include "inhibitory control (Casey et al., 1997; Durston et al., 2003; Schulz et al., 2004; Schulz et al., 2005; Tamm et al., 2004; Vaidya et al., 1998), conflict resolution (Bush et al., 1999; Tamm et al., 2004), motor control (Rubia et al., 1999), timing (Durston et al., 2007), attention (Cao et al., 2008; Sonuga-Barke and Castellanos, 2007; Uddin et al., 2008), and working memory (Valera et al., 2005)" (p. 15).

In a more recent examination of ADHD studies using fMRI techniques, Cortese and colleagues (2012) conducted a review of fifty-five studies with the goal of identifying the average level of activation in the brain when the child engages in a task. The results of the analysis confirmed that *hypoactivation* were observed in the relevant brain regions when ADHD children were required to participate in activities supported by networks responsible for:

1. goal-directed executive processes, decision-making, and integration of external with internally represented information—the *canonical frontoparietal network* (Corbetta, Patel, and Shulman, 2008);

2. the child's ability to reorient themselves to attend to relevant stimuli in the environment—the *ventral attention network* (Helenius, Laasonen, Hokkanen, Paetau, and Niemivirta, 2011); and

3. motor inhibition—the *right somatomotor system* (Gilbert, Isaacs, Augusta, Macneil, and Mostofsky, 2011).

While these networks are being discussed in a linear manner, it is important to note that they do interact, and changes in one may impact functioning in another. Cortese and colleagues (2012) confirmed this dynamic in their finding that children with impaired function in executive processes showed higher levels of activation in brain areas associated with visual, spatial, or motoric processing (Fassbender and Schweitzer, 2006). While it serves the child to have higher levels of activation in their attention and regulation brain networks, it is beneficial for the child to have lower activation levels in their neural networks that control processes that may prove distracting to the child who is trying to focus, pay attention, and inhibit their impulses. Cortese and colleagues (2012) found evidence to support the *hyperactivation* of this "default-mode" network, suggesting that other tasks intrude on cognitive functions and thus contribute to an increase in distractibility (Sonuga-Barke and Castellanos, 2007). One effective intervention that aids in the amelioration of the default network was the medication *methylphenidate*.

In sum, neuroimaging findings to date suggest that children with ADHD have difficulty with their networks responsible for attention, reward/feedback-based processing systems, and the "default mode" that modulates responses in support of other, more dominant processes.

The Neurocognitive Approach

Unlike structural and functional studies on the brain, which rely on brain imaging, neurocognitive research relies on neuropsychological assessments. These assessments have allowed researchers and clinicians working with ADHD children to identify cognitive deficits associated with abnormalities in certain areas of the brain. While the neurocognitive approach to the question *What is ADHD?* gives us another perspective, the diversity of its findings serves as a reminder that the domains in which ADHD children experience difficulties are diverse and reflect a range of cognitive deficits and general intellectual abilities.

In assessments of overall intellectual functioning, children diagnosed with ADHD perform significantly lower on measures of *general cognitive ability* (Full Scale IQ) compared to their non-ADHD peers (for review, see Frazier, Demaree, and Youngstrom, 2004; Barkley, DuPaul, and McMurray, 1990). These deficits range from mild global cognitive dysfunction to cognitive impairments in multiple areas (Frazier, Demaree, and Youngstrom, 2004).

The most commonly recognized symptom of ADHD is a deficit in *attention*, which is commonly understood as referring to the child's difficulty in sustaining attention over a prolonged period. However, understanding the ADHD child's attention deficit requires a nuanced understanding of attention as being multidimensional. It is true that ADHD children struggle with sustaining attention over time, but that's only one way of measuring attention—most ADHD children also present with additional deficit(s) in at least one of the three attention *types*: *selective attention*, the ability to focus on relevant information while ignoring distractions; *executive attention*, characterized by the ability to inhibit responses to stimuli that are not the focus of attention; and *orienting of attention*, the ability to direct one's attention to a particular location and reorient one's attention to a new location as necessary (Tsal, Shalev, and Mevorach, 2005, in Gopin and Healey, 2011). Attention deficits may also adversely impact the child's comprehension and language to the extent that the child experiences difficulty in inhibitory control associated with executive attention (Loge, Staton, and Beatty, 1990). ADHD children also have slower reaction times, referred to as *processing speed*, compared to their non-ADHD peers. Slower response times are attributed to deficits in sustained attention and difficulties with inhibitory control (see Gopin and Healey, 2011 for these references).

Another hallmark of ADHD is characterized by deficits in *executive functioning*—a set of cognitive skills, such as motivation and problem-solving, that allows individuals to organize their experiences and to plan and execute a set of behaviors oriented toward achieving their goals. Deficits in executive functioning associated with the prefrontal cortex impact set-shifting (executive functioning ability that allows one to shift attention from one activity to the other), working memory, and planning (see Gopin and Healey, 2011). Secondary problems resulting from executive function deficits are negative impacts on the child's capacity for verbal learning and memory. Regarding memory, ADHD children are particularly challenged in recalling unstructured information. Some attribute their recall difficulty to the ADHD child's lack of organizational skills needed to arrange information in a manner that is useful (Felton, Wood, Brown, Campbell, and Harter, 1987).

The *hyperactivity* in ADHD is associated with motor dysfunction in the brain and is most apparent when the child is required to integrate sensory and motor abilities (Werry et al., 1972). For some children, gross motoric activity can be either slow or excessive. The ADHD literature has the most support for observing these deficits in children's handwriting (Barkley, 1990; McMahon and Greenburg, 1977; Shaywitz and Shaywitz, 1984; Szatmari, Oxford, and Boyle, 1989; Whitmont and Clark, 1996). Some researchers link motor activity to the child's capacity to pay attention. For example, children with inattention perform poorly on manual tasks and tests of fine motor skills (Piek, Pitcher, and Hay, 1999; Whitmont and Clark, 1996). Motor activity is also associated with some visiospatial abilities located in the right hemisphere (Heilman, Voeller, and Nadeau, 1991; Resta and Eliot, 1994; Stefanatos and Wasserstein, 2001). It is debatable whether these deficits are more attributable to the motor or attention deficits (Garcia-Sanchez, Estevez-Gonzalez, Suarez-Romero, and Junque, 1997).

Neurological and Neurocognitive Models of ADHD Etiology

Given the heterogeneity in brain structure and function as well as in the neurocognitive impairments associated with ADHD, some researchers have developed a framework for approaching the question of ADHD's etiology. Some of the prevailing models of ADHD etiology include a view of ADHD as stemming from deficits in executive functioning, impairments in motivation/reward processing, as having dual or multiple pathways (such as in the cognitive-energetic model and integrated affective and cognitive model), and as resulting from some ontogenetic occurrences. These models will be briefly summarized here. (For more detailed discussions of these models, see Gopin and Healey, 2011.)

Barkley advances a view of ADHD as a result of *deficits in executive functioning* stemming primarily from the individual's inability to inhibit or delay behavior responses (1997). *Behavior inhibition* or *self-control* plays a central role in the facilitation of other executive functions including:

- *working memory*, a system responsible for holding and processing new and stored information that can be retrieved and used to predict future behaviors;
- *affect and self-regulation*, the ability to respond to emotional experiences with a range of responses while remaining flexible in expressing or delaying the expression of behaviors in socially appropriate ways;
- *internalization of speech*, the ability to rely on and generate internal speech to determine behavior; and
- *reconstitution*, the ability to create a goal in one's mind and to use that image to direct actions toward achieving the goal.

ADHD individuals experience difficulties in self-regulation and impulsivity that interferes with their goal achievement and their ability to reliably predict the future consequences of their actions. Deficits in executive functioning tend to lead to the following behavioral results.

- an inability to benefit from hindsight

- an impaired relationship to time, such that the individual has difficulty anticipating and positioning oneself in relation to time
- an inability to firmly establish salient goals, such that long-term goals are traded in for more immediate goal attainment
- lack of motivation, impulsivity, and difficulties with organization and in following rules

Overall, children with deficits in these areas experience difficulty organizing, analyzing, and synthesizing their responses to situations.

While the view of ADHD as an executive dysfunction disorder appears to have some merit, some have argued that such a view is limited in scope and does not adequately account for the broader impact of the disorder. Barkley's model does not account for deficits in non-executive functions that are considered to be more efficient ways of distinguishing ADHD from non-ADHD individuals. Also, since deficits in executive function are not unique to ADHD, relying solely on executive function deficits may be misleading.

In contrast to the view of ADHD as deficits in executive functioning, some view ADHD as stemming from a *deficit in motivational or reinforcement systems*. It is believed that ADHD individuals are unable to process their reward stimuli accurately due to abnormalities in the fronto-limbic, dopaminergic regions of the brain. Some ways in which these abnormalities present is in the need for relatively greater amounts of rewards to motivate behaviors or in the ineffectiveness of reward systems due to a decreased sensitivity to punishment or to the absence of rewards.

Neurocognitive dysfunctions resulting from ADHD are varied and complex, and some approaches to ADHD hypothesize about *dual or multiple pathways* to ADHD. The *dual pathway model* attributes ADHD symptoms to deficits in both executive functions *and* motivational processes. Working from a similar hypothesis, the *cognitive-energetic model* explains the disorder as a combination of two observations attributing ADHD to deficits in executive functioning and regulatory processes. According to the theory behind this model, ADHD individuals require both automatically generated emotional responses and arduous self-regulatory processes to function.

Another approach, developed by Nigg and Casey (2005), integrates neuroanatomical pathways with deficits in cognitive and emotional functioning. The *integrated affective and cognitive model* is based on the theory that deficits in three neural circuits cause ADHD symptoms and comorbid diagnoses of Oppositional Defiant (ODD) or Conduct Disorder (CD). Defeicits in these three pathways lead to:

1. top-down control processes such as problems with inattention and self-regulation (e.g., inattentive and disorganized behavior) resulting

from abnormalities in the fronto-striatal and fronto-cerebellar circuitry (Nigg, 2006; Nigg and Casey, 2005; Sonuga-Barke, 2005);

2. bottom-up processes such as problems with affective processing (e.g., affecting impulsivity and hyperactivity) and an idiosyncratic temperament-approach characteristic that shows a tendency to approach rewards but a decreased tendency to avoid punishment (often manifesting as poor self-control and impaired social skills) associated with the fronto-amygdala circuitry; and

3. problems related to emotion dysregulation including a lack of empathy and a lack of regard for social rules (e.g., fearlessness and aggression) associated with hypoactivity in the fronto-amygdala circuitry.

While these neural circuits have been identified as sources of ADHD symptoms, researchers such as Halperin and Schulz (2006) view some neural processes as involved in the cure of ADHD rather than its symptom development. Employing a developmental model, Halperin and Schulz note that deficits in executive functions appear early in life, are unrelated to cortical neural dysfunctions, and are remediated as the child develops. Paralleling the improvement in the child's functioning is the development of the prefrontal cortex circuitry and higher order cortical functions. Those brain structures, they argue, develop with time and help to compensate for the early developmental deficits (for review, see Halperin and Healey, 2011).

Psychodynamic Views on Neurological Determinants

The effects of these aberrant brain structures on the child's functioning are readily observed in the child's response to cognitive assessments and in the way the child interacts with others and functions at school. However, the meanings the child construes as a result of these physiological constraints and the child's experience of herself and others cannot be captured in brain imaging technology and cognitive assessments. The practice of psychotherapy attends to the dimension of ADHD that pertains to the mind, mental processes, and mental life of the child.

Dynamically oriented therapists believe that some behaviors are biologically determined. ADHD-like behaviors are not always the result of poor home environments or exposure to social ills such as drug abuse, physical or sexual abuse, or neglect. Therapists acknowledge that for some children, life is simply chaotic—their home environments have led to distress in their families. However, some children presenting with these behaviors come from intact families without traumatic and disruptive home environments:

> Yes, I've seen it—I've seen environmental cases where there is a chaotic environment, distress in the family, etc., but at this point in my life most of the

kids that I see tend to be kids from decent families, from parents where they want to help their kids and they find themselves unable to. So since these are the good-enough families, good-enough parents that would provide for their kids in many different ways, I cannot in good conscience go and say this is just psychological—something else is there, too, something else that kind of skews development and interactions from early on, from four-year, pre-K, kindergarten, first grade, and everything becomes, I think, a cycle of reacting to increasing problems due to impulsivity and inattentiveness. [SAP]

Some behaviors observed by therapists leave them with the belief that some children may be physiologically primed to be hyperactive or inattentive. For example, one analyst describes seeing two kids in their practice who were brothers. According to the family history, both boys were hyperactive from a very young age. One child is described as *"climbing on the refrigerator,"* while the other child was reported to have *"never slept through the night for the first year or so"* [LOM]. However, there is a third observation of children who do not fit either hyperactive or inattentive type but are "atypical." For example, other therapists hold the view that some children are "atypical" in that they present with early childhood histories of developmental delays identified during the preschool years.

Nonetheless, the impact of these behaviors goes beyond biology, adversely affecting many areas of the child's life. One may not be able to alter the biological etiology of the child's behaviors, but the therapist can intervene in these other areas. One analyst holds the view that irrespective of the biological origins of a child's behavioral symptoms, these ADHD symptoms are pervasive:

They [ADHD symptoms] immediately seem to wrap around the child's entire personality. I mean, with really profound consequences, so it immediately impacts affect control even early in life, impacts frustration tolerance, relationships, self-control, sense of mastery. . . . It also has a very deep impact on the parent–child relationship; it's probably one of the most problematic aspects. [MER]

Every aspect of the child's life and development is affected, including her cognitive functioning, her emotional functioning, her family functioning, her self-esteem, her emotional regulation, how she does in school, how she learns. All these areas of that child's life can benefit from psychodynamically oriented treatment.

THE PSYCHODYNAMIC PERSPECTIVE ON ADHD

The etiology of psychological disorders is bidirectional, such that neurological anomalies produce psychological symptoms and mental events can lead to neurological changes (Kaufman and Chaney, 2001; LeDoux, 2002; Salomonsson, 2004; Schore, 2003). With this in mind, models of ADHD that explore intrapsychic and environmental determinants of symptoms associated with ADHD may well uncover factors that lead to the very neurological differences observed in the studies discussed in the previous section. Psychoanalysts view any kind of psychological disturbance as dependent on the individual's subjective experience, even when the contributors are neurological (Damasio, 1994; Fonagy, Gergely, Jurist, and Target, 2002; LeDoux, 2002; Levin, 2002; Salomonsson, 2004; Schore, 2003). Particularly, intrapsychic conflict—or the clashing of incompatible wishes, fears, or defenses—is an underlying contributor to psychopathology, and the externalizing behaviors of children with ADHD reflect a compromise formation (Whelan, 2004). Subjective mental states can also contribute to psychiatric symptoms like those of ADHD (Fonagy, 2001; Kaufman and Chaney, 2001; Klein, 1935; Salomonsson, 2004; Whelan, 2004). Psychodynamic therapists examine and work with the subjective experience of each individual to discover the psychogenic etiologies of ADHD-related symptoms. Using an *idiographic approach* to the study of ADHD, psychodynamic therapists and researchers focus on the personal circumstances that lead to symptom manifestation. This approach is based on the belief that each child is an individual, and therefore his pathway to ADHD is individualized and unique as evidenced by the heterotopy of neurological findings related to brain and neural functions. The idiographic approach has been a hallmark of psychotherapy training and education. For example, psychotherapy case studies and individualized supervision continue to be an effective method of teaching student therapists and supporting clients' progress in psychotherapy. Although psychodynamic research methods that lend themselves to this more individualized approach are different from the quantitative methods of cognitive science, they are no less valid (Rothenberg, 2004; Rustin, 2003).

Psychodynamically oriented therapists view the categorization of ADHD as merely a list of symptoms that offers a behavioral description of the child's presentation. This "symptom checklist" contributes very little in terms of informing treatment professionals about the etiology of the child's problems or their appropriate treatment. One analyst expressed *"it's a list of symptoms that describes the child who has difficulty. . . . I'm not that interested in the symptoms except as a pathway to understanding the difficulty"* [MOL]. While some clinicians may only have limited use for the ADHD diagnosis—for example, as a handy descriptive tool—any benefit may be outweighed by the risks associated with it. The ADHD label can sometimes obscure other difficulties the child may be experiencing. It is often necessary, therefore, to clarify and confirm the child's diagnosis, since there are multiple pathways that can result in attention deficits and behavioral problems. Clinicians are urged to clarify the accuracy of the diagnosis to ensure that the reasons for the child's difficulties do not go untreated. As one analyst puts it *"there are many things in childhood that can ramp up behavioral disorders . . . so that's the first thing to figure out. . . . Is it in fact ADHD?"* [HUG]. Here we explore a psychodynamic description of ADHD patients in terms of etiology—both individualistic and environmental—and a psychodynamic approach to working with the ADHD-diagnosed child that focuses on core/intrapsychic issues.

Psychodynamic Determinants

There is a range of interpersonal, neurobiological, and environmental conditions that results in ADHD symptoms. The psychodynamic therapist recognizes and considers all potential influences on the child's symptom expressions, but some factors are uniquely considered by psychodynamic approaches. These factors will be the focus of the discussion in this section. A psychodynamic approach informed by psychoanalytic theories views environmental (including parental/caregiving environments and environmental insults) and intrapsychic issues (e.g., self-concept, conflict, and emotions) as contributors to ADHD symptoms. Although each of these factors is discussed here separately, many children diagnosed with ADHD show evidence of one or more of these contributing factors in their lives.

From the psychodynamic perspective, it is possible to view ADHD symptoms as playing a role in relieving the psychological pain and miseries of childhood. Symptoms related to ADHD may be observed in children who become *"emotionally dysregulated"* [HUG], or may be a byproduct of difficulty with *"emotional connectivity"* [LUB]. Disorders such as anxiety and depression as well as response to trauma all have some adverse effect on children's cognitive abilities to focus and pay attention. Clinicians report many examples of external impingements on the child's physical and emotional development, including *"a very seriously ill parent, or a parent with a psychiatric disorder, or an alcoholic parent . . . a lot of energy is siphoned off to the side . . . or a child who is sexually abused . . ."* [LOM]. Similarly, children who have suffered a loss can also present with the kinds of symptoms regularly attributed to ADHD. From the analyst's view, ADHD symptoms often are conduits for the child to express strong emotions such as anger or mourning.

Environmental Determinants

The Caregiving Environment: Disruptions in Early Attachments

Bowlby's (1988) *evolutionary theory of attachment* postulates about the importance of the attachment relationship between the parent and the child.

Relations during infancy serve as essential building blocks for the development of the child's mental life. It is believed that the child develops the ability to understand mental states of others and of the self within a safe environment. It is through the interactions with the parent that the child learns the world is a safe place and is uninhibited in exploring the environment and in interacting with others. The child learns that a display of his distress may elicit comforting responses in others leading to increased confidence in the parent's ability to provide comfort (Bowlby, 1973). In contrast, the child's experience of caregivers as unavailable and unsupportive can stem from disruptions in the early attachment relations caused by physical and sexual abuse or other psychologically intrusive events. Consequently, the child's experience of being impinged on, real or imagined, can lead to an environment that fosters insecurity, self-doubt, and doubts about the intentions of others. These fractures in the interpersonal world of the child force the development of *secondary strategies of affect regulation* (Mikulincer and Shaver, 2003). Secondary strategies of the attachment system include *hyperactivation* and *deactivation*, which reflect the child's efforts to gain or avoid proximity with the attachment figure. While hyperactivation strategies suggest the child wants to obtain some reassurance of the caregiver's attention and support, deactivation strategies suggest the child's efforts are aimed at discontinuing or suppressing any potential threats in their interpersonal world.

Ainsworth and colleagues (1978) also theorized about attachment relations and their importance to the developing psychological life of the child, but she identified slightly different patterns of proximity-seeking behaviors in children. These attachment categories include a *secure attachment* style that develops from supportive and responsive caregiving relationships; an *avoidant attachment* style resulting from disengaged and rejecting caregivers; and an *ambivalent attachment* style forming from inconsistent caregiver responses that range from appropriate to neglectful. A fourth attachment style was proposed by Main and Solomon (1990), the *disorganized* style, where children experienced their caregivers as frightening.

The hyperactivation process can be observed in ADHD children whose behavioral presentations are such that they cannot be ignored. Children who are hyperactive *demand* the attention of others, who are often driven to distraction by the child's behavior. Commands to *stop fidgeting, sit still, "walk, don't run," stop moving about*, and so on, are familiar refrains the hyperactive child hears from most adults with whom they interact. In contrast, the child who presents with symptoms of inattentiveness can be viewed as recruiting deactivation strategies as he withdraws into his own thoughts and fantasies, avoiding engagement with those in his environment. For these children, a struggle arises in their interpersonal interactions with others—they work to deactivate at the same time that others in their world make desperate attempts to engage and sustain their interests. Their familiar refrains, then, become *pay attention*, *focus*, and *stop daydreaming*, as the adults around them struggle to gain the child's attention.

While Bowlby's perspective informs proximity-seeking behaviors, Ainsworth and colleagues speak to the importance of caregiver experiences for the child's ability to self-regulate and how they affect the child's behavior. Depending on the child's attachment style, ADHD-related behaviors such as distractibility and hyperactivity can emerge in service of helping children to regulate their emotional states. Children with a secure attachment learn regulation strategies from their caregivers and develop a capacity to communicate and interpret nonverbal cues. Moreover, they learn whether they can rely on others for support and comfort. ADHD symptoms represent one possible behavioral presentation among children who lack the emotional experience needed to develop appropriate self-soothing capacities. Thus, symptoms such as impulsivity and hyperactivity may reflect the tendency of some children to respond promptly to their environmental triggers, signifying the marked absence or impoverished capacity to efficiently and appropriately self-soothe rather than being indicative of an ADHD pathology.

Environmental Insults: Trauma and Complex Trauma

Trauma is the occurrence of an event that threatens the individual's well-being, disrupts regular emotional capacities, and reroutes attention to the event in a way that is experienced as helping the individual to survive. Among children, a range of events can result in a trauma response including "survival of natural and man-made disasters, violent crimes, motor vehicle accidents, severe burns, exposure to community violence, war, peer suicide, and sexual or physical abuse" (Hamblen and Barnett, 2009).

As a result of a trauma experience, an individual responds to the threat with intense fear and feelings of helplessness characteristic of Post-Traumatic Stress Disorder (PTSD). Three main factors moderate the child's response to trauma including the severity of the trauma; parental reaction to the traumatic event (such that lower levels of parental distress result in less likelihood of PTSD); and proximity to the traumatic event (with less distress in those farther away). Other contributors to trauma response include the number of traumatic events in the past, gender (with a higher predisposition among girls), and, among some studies, age (younger children are more at risk) (Hamblen and Barnett, 2009).

While not every child who has been exposed to a traumatic event may meet the criteria for a PTSD diagnosis, their responses to these events are often concerning nonetheless and can be categorized as a *complex trauma response* (van der Kolk and McFarlane, 1996). Repeated traumatic experiences during childhood have a detrimental impact on a child's physical, sensory, emotional, cognitive, and social development. A child can be adversely affected by trauma on multiple dimensions of their emotional and physical functioning—for example, attachment, biology, affect regulation, dissociation, behavioral control, cognition, and self-concept.

Regarding the impact of trauma on self-concept, it is well documented that negative experiences such as abuse, over a period of time, can lead to negative views of the self (Rodriguez-Srednicki and Twaite, 2006, p. 54). Studies of women who have experienced sexual abuse found that those experiences had an adverse effect on their self-concept (Courtois, 1979); women who were abused were more likely to report feeling inferior and lacking in self-worth (DeFrancis, 1969) and were more likely to have a negative view of themselves (Herman, 1981). Children with sexual abuse histories were more likely to develop low self-esteem (Tong, Oates, and McDowell, 1987); were self-deprecating, especially if damage occurred before the development of language (Green, 1978; Orr and Downes, 1985); and felt a sense of powerlessness (Cook, Blaustein, Spinazzola, and van der Kolk, 2003). Abused children not only blamed themselves for the abuse but also experienced negative shifts in their sense of self, their ability to self-regulate, and their sense of their own competence (Durham and Conway, 2014).

More compelling than the formation of a negative self-concept due to early traumatic experiences is the psychological calisthenics children undergo to maintain an attachment to the abusive or neglectful caregiver. According to Herman (1992), children who experience abusive caregivers either dissociate the abuse from conscious awareness or construct a theory that explains the abuse. For instance, in the service of maintaining a relationship with the caregiver—upon whom the child is dependent—the child comes to believe that he is bad and the caregiver is good. This internalized, albeit distorted, view gives the child hope that if he were to become good, the abuse would cease. Over time, the child's inner sense of being bad does not only deepen but also has the potential to become a part of the child's personality (Rodriguez-Srednicki and Twaite, 2006, p. 55). Another dynamic evident among some abused children is Ferenczi's concept of *identification with the aggressor*, which postulates that the abused child knowingly or unknowingly assumes the adult's guilt (Frankel, 2002). Because the caregiver is available to the child as an object for identification and introjection, the child's self-concept becomes fused with aspects of the abuser (Kluft, 1990). For example, an abused child who identifies with her abuser may endorse violence as an appropriate way to deal with conflict or may believe that she was deserving of the abuse.

The adverse effects of trauma on children include a range of responses that may present themselves as inattention or hyperactivity but in fact are related to:

- negative affective states (fear, anxiety, depression, anger, and hostility);
- acting out behaviors (aggression, sexually inappropriate behavior, self-destructive behavior, and substance abuse);
- interpersonal difficulties (problematic relations with family and peers);
- learning-related problems (poor school performance); and
- other intrapsychic difficulties (feelings of isolation and stigma, poor self-esteem, difficulty in trusting others).

Comorbid disorders accompanying trauma exposure include substance abuse; other anxiety disorders, such as separation anxiety, panic disorder, and generalized anxiety disorder; and externalizing disorders, such as ADHD, ODD, and CD. ADHD symptoms of hyper-alertness and restricted attention can mirror trauma responses (Conway, 2012). In particular, inattention in a child could be a result of trauma exposure. For children who have been exposed to traumatic events, the expectation of danger renders them incapable of attending to matters beyond physical or psychological survival (Perry, Pollard, Blackeley, Baker, and Vigilante, 1995, in Orford, 1998).

Display of behavior modulation is another dimension of the child's functioning that represents shared symptoms between ADHD and trauma. Like ADHD children, children who have been maltreated have difficulty coping with changes in their routine. For abused children, over-controlled behavior patterns (e.g., fearfulness, sleep problems) reflect their feelings of helplessness and loss of power—they counteract these feelings with rigidity or over-compliance (Cook et al., 2003). Similarly, children with ADHD often have difficulty with transitions. Changing classes or transitioning from home to the car can be challenging. For the ADHD child, their difficulties are not necessarily protective or in response to abuse, but rather reflect difficulty with planning ahead, problem solving, and regulating emotions resulting from a tendency to become anxious, overwhelmed, or dysregulated by task demands. Like victims of childhood trauma, ADHD children also present with difficulty sleeping.

Under-controlled behavior patterns, which are harder to disentangle, are characterized by impulsive behaviors, aggression, and other oppositional behaviors. Among maltreated children, under-controlled patterns may be due to deficits in executive functioning such as planning, organization, delay of gratification, and self-control (Mezzacappa, Kindlon, and Earls, 2001). Deficits in executive functioning are hallmark symptoms for children with ADHD. It is fair to say that children presenting with ADHD or trauma are equally likely to present with these symptoms.

Like ADHD children, individuals exposed to complex trauma are more distractible, inattentive, and meet the criteria for attention-deficit disorders (Erickson, Egeland, and Pianta, 1989; Famularo, Kinscherff, and Fenton, 1992; Salzinger, Feldman, Hammer, and Rosario, 1993). Maltreatment can cause disruptions in attention that in turn may lead to hyper-attunement and reactivity to potentially dysregulating aspects of the social environment (Shields and Cicchetti, 1998).

In a school environment, both ADHD children and children with a history of trauma have learning problems and are often referred for special education services (Shonk and Cicchetti, 2001). When compared with students who did not suffer abuse, maltreated children exhibit more emotional and behavioral dysfunction in school that can lead to aggression, poor peer relations, and emotion dysregulation (Dodge, Pettit, Bates, and Valente, 1995). Children diagnosed with ADHD present with these very same issues, and both sets of children have noted difficulty engaging in academic work.

Intrapsychic Determinants

A psychodynamic approach broadens the scope of the impact of ADHD beyond impaired executive functions and neurocognitive processes to consider children's subjective experiences. Most are well aware of ADHD children's struggles at school and at home, but are less familiar with the underlying mental processes that either cause or accompany ADHD. However, consideration of the mental life of the ADHD child is within the purview of a psychodynamic psychotherapist. ADHD children present with an equally diverse range of intrapsychic issues as neurological ones. The cross section of intrapsychic issues observed in the clinical situation includes mental processes related to the self (self-concept, self-esteem); conflict; and emotion regulation, especially with regard to emotions associated with shame and aggression. It is unclear whether these issues are manifested symptoms associated with ADHD, develop as a result of the constraints a child with ADHD experiences, or reflect some combination of the two.

Intrapsychic Issues Related to the Self

Self-concept Our knowledge and views of ourselves are generally based on a combination of our talents as well as our limitations attributable to our unique identity. *Who we are* includes our beliefs about our physical and personality characteristics. However, our self-perceptions do not exist in a vacuum—they are influenced by our expectations of ourselves and others' perceptions of us (Dinkmeyer, 1965; Honess and Yardley, 1987). Beginning with early childhood, our experiences with our caregivers shape our view of ourselves. According to the child development literature, the developmental process from early childhood through adolescence is marked by the child's increasing ability to differentiate the self from others—to shift his experience of himself from the concrete, more physical attributes, possessions, and skills to a more nuanced and complex view of himself as having an internal life and a psychological world. As the child develops, his self-concept becomes increasingly more abstract, complex, and hierarchically organized into cognitive mental representations (Harter, 1998).

One model that explains the formation of one's self-concept was put forth by John Bowlby (1907–1990), who referred to the developmental process of the construction of an *internal working model*. An internal working model is our internal representation of our core beliefs about ourselves and the world around us. After repeated interpersonal experiences with a caregiver, infants begin to construct their first internal working model, which serves as a template for relationships and events (Murthi, Servaty-Seib, and Elliott, 2006). In the process of forming the internal model for others, the infant also constructs beliefs about the self. Children with a view of themselves as worthy and competent have benefited from positive early caregiving experiences that led them, as infants, to feel valued and deserving of love. On the other hand, negative experiences during infancy may result in feelings that one is not worthy of being treated well. Based on the negative feedback ADHD children receive from the world and the predominance of failed interpersonal relationships they encounter, they develop a false self that can both protect and lash out in a rage (Eresund, 2007). Children with ADHD are plagued with a poor self-concept (Cione, Coleburn, Fertuck, and Fraenkel, 2011; Eresund, 2007; Gilmore, 2005; Sugarman, 2006).

Self-esteem Generally our view of ourselves is affected by others' feedback. How we feel about ourselves is reflected in our behavior. For children with ADHD, low self-esteem is a strong predictor of both emotional and behavioral problems (Leary, Schreindorfer, and Haupt, 1995). However, the research regarding self-esteem and ADHD is mixed. On the one hand, researchers have found children diagnosed with ADHD are at greater risk for low self-esteem compared to children without this diagnosis (Slomkowski, Klein, and Mannuzza, 1995; Weiss and Hechtman, 1993). In a study of 114 boys with ADHD, Treuting and Hinshaw (2001) found that aggressive boys with ADHD reported more depressive symptoms and lower self-esteem levels compared to the reports of non-aggressive ADHD boys and boys without ADHD.

Since self-estimation is derived from our intellectual self-assessment of competency, it is not surprising that children with attention and hyperactivity problems often feel inadequate (Brownback, 1982). As a result of repeated "failure" and negative feedback from others in their interpersonal world, children diagnosed with ADHD come to believe that they are "bad"—they internalize a view of themselves as "bad" and self-identify as such. They more often than not get the message that they are "bad," "doing something wrong," or "always in trouble." As a result, these children tend to *feel* bad. Children in this situation may seek more gratifying roles: for example, *"being the class clown, because that is the most, you know, gratifying role you can play, 'cause [if] you can't control yourself, at least you'll get people to laugh"* [LUB].

On the other hand, some researchers argue that even though children with ADHD may have difficulties, they may experience an inflated sense of themselves (Gresham, MacMillan, Bocian, Ward, and Forness, 1998; Hoza, Pelham, Milich, Pillow, and McBride, 1993). Some have interpreted high self-esteem in ADHD children as attempts at positive impression management (Taylor and Brown, 1988) or, even worse, as indicative of psychopathic tendencies (Lynam, 1996). Although the research thus far is not conclusive, the findings of these studies resonate with individuals who are inclined to view ADHD children negatively. Among the professionals I interviewed, however, there was a sense that anger may play a role in any perceived link between ADHD and psychopathic tendencies. One analyst explained: *"What do you do if you are angry? You don't listen. Then guess what? You don't listen, now you are even more 'bad' and have an even worse diagnosis"* [LUB]. For example, the child now becomes perceived as a sociopath.

Intrapsychic Issues Related to Conflict

Analysts hold the view that conflict arises when, despite our best efforts, our wishes and desires are not fulfilled. Wishes are mostly unconscious, and conflict usually arises when something in our environment interferes with their fulfillment. Freud believed that the demands of the external world position the child to become aware that it exists—that there is a reality that is outside of himself. These exigencies force the child to develop higher-ordered thinking so as to obtain some relief from the mounting instinctual pressures. For example, a baby that wishes to be fed learns through delay of gratification that the act of feeding is not utterly dependent on his wish but on the participation of something external to himself. The child then gradually comes to learn that there are things she can do to facilitate the fulfillment of the wish. This process of learning and thinking directly affects behaviors and advances her development. Freud characterizes this process as the *brick wall of reality*. Freud also speaks of conflict arising out of *sexual instincts*. The child's desire for the parent of the opposite sex is a controversial idea. Non-gratification allows the child to develop appropriate relations with the parent. Consequently, growth comes from finding some way of resolving the conflict (unfulfilled desire) and accept reality. Although based on a classical model of conflict, the idea that ADHD children are experiencing a period of growth through their internal struggle to resolve conflict and in so doing become symptomatic is a useful framework when considering the source of the behaviors that led to their diagnosis.

[For example,] a child looks as if they have ADHD, but they [are] actually in mourning, or they are actually very angry about something. The behavior is a way that the child releases emotions . . . within the child himself, maybe there's emotions that are simply emerging in that way, and then you bring them to the world, like school, and that same behavior causes trouble then the child is treated as if he is a troublemaker or something is wrong with him, then that makes a spinoff in his self-image, but if you unpack the different parts it starts out with a way to express feelings. [LUB]

More contemporary analysts, such as Brenner (1994; 2002), view conflict as ubiquitous and arising out of conscious experiences of displeasure. Instead of id, ego, and superego conflict, the location of conflict occurs between wishes, defenses, prohibitions, and a range of unpleasant affects. In response to unpleasant affects such as depression and anxiety, a compromise is formed that is present in every mental activity. All three agencies of the mind—id, ego, and superego—are represented in the *compromise formation*. There is a tendency to view the compromise formation in terms of the extent to which it interferes with the individual's life. In keeping with Brenner's view of the conflict, unpleasant affect, which may result from depression or anxiety, activates conflict. It follows that in an effort to reduce this conflictual experience, the child becomes symptomatic:

> A child's best possible solution to inner and outer difficulties, inner conflict, inner emotional states, inner anxieties, outer stress, and so on and so forth . . . a symptom is the best possible solution. [DON]

This view holds for both conscious experiences of conflict (Brenner's view) and unconscious experiences due to repression (Freud's view). Although there is a lack of clarity regarding which comes first, conflict or unpleasant affect, in Brenner's view, a compromise formation is the end result and the focus of clinical intervention. Put more simply, the child's response to the unpleasant affect—her compromise formation—needs to be analyzed. A focus on what can be consciously observed in the child would be the content discussed in the therapy. Following this model, then, the analyst would centralize the child's wish rather than try to ascertain or discern the desires of the id, defenses of the ego, or punishments of the superego. The patient's verbalizations would be heard as the compromise formation that would need to be responded to. It is important to note the exponential nature of compromise formation in that every mental event is in and of itself a compromise formation; recognizing this allows us to appreciate the complexity of the mind and to free the therapist from the tendency to view mental acts in silos of id, ego, and superego components. The therapist also can appreciate that his or her own wishes, defenses, and punitive tendencies are involved in their mental activity vis-à-vis the patient. In doing so, therapists are able to recognize that they may not have an objective view of their patients' problems. But with their patients, from an intersubjective positioning, the therapists can cautiously proceed to make and test observations. The ubiquitous nature of conflict removes a tendency to pathologize and shifts the therapist's focus toward which compromise formations interfere with the patient's accomplishments of his goals or brings him pain. The goal of therapy is to help the client make adjustments so they can function.

Boesky (2000) refers to the intrapsychic in terms of what the analyst attends to—that is, the patient's associations—in listening for evidence of conflicting wishes. In therapy, the therapist works on the *edge of awareness* (Gardner, 1983), actively listening for expressions of conflict in the patient's wishes. One caution is that this approach by definition omits a focus on the more complex aspects of mental life that Brenner elucidated. In Brenner's terms, Boesky's approach to focus on a pair of conflicting wishes can be thought of as a focus on only one aspect or occurrence of compromise formation. Similar to Boesky, Gray (1996) also focuses on the analytical method, recommending that the analyst pay close attention to the processes observed in the patient's associations, giving equal attention to each of the three psychic entities. Gray's (1994) method of *close process monitoring* is accomplished through a therapist's stance of *evenly hovering attention* recommended by Freud in his 1909 report on the case of Little Hans (Smith, 2003). The analyst observes the patient and, when a conflict occurs, calls the patient's attention to the conflict. Although there is some recognition that the surface may not accurately represent what lies beneath, as is the case with defensive ego functioning, the analyst comments on material that can be easily demonstrated to the patient. Kris (1985) identifies two types of conflict: *convergent*, which is conceptualized as the expression of a wish by the id that is opposed by the ego or defense, and *divergent*, in which aspects of the conflict are paired opposites or ambivalence (e.g., love and hate). Divergent conflicts can be conscious or unconscious. Kris proposes resolving this conflict through mourning the loss and retention of one aspect of the conflict through fantasy. Whether one views conflict as a compromise formation (Brenner) or a response to incompatible wishes (Boesky), attends equally to conflict arising in the id, ego, or superego (Gray), views conflict as a defense against id wishes or ambivalence (Kris), there is an appreciation for the ubiquitous nature of conflict and its centrality to mental life. The usefulness of exploring conflict in therapy is clear.

Meanwhile, relational analysts such as Bromberg (2003) assert that conflict is due to either repression or disassociation due to trauma. He focuses on the patient's expression of different self-states during therapy. He argues for a therapeutic goal that entails moving the patient from a dissociative state to a conflict state, the assumption being that a patient who has difficulty tolerating ambivalence may end up in a dissociative state. So in this case, for the patient to be in conflict would be tantamount to an experience of wholeness. Although there is some debate about whether this process is purely conscious or unconscious, it is generally agreed that one's ability to mentally tolerate two conflicting feelings at the same time while being able to manage one's emotions is an indication of well-being. The conflict here is therefore seen as a developmental attainment.

On the other hand, the relationship between dissociation and conflict has been viewed by some relational analysts as *adversely* impacting development. Rather than viewing conflict as a developmental achievement for those who have experienced trauma and have moved beyond disassociation, conflict is seen as a divided attempt to cope with trauma. One analyst I interviewed, who was influenced by the work of Louise Kaplan, Judith Kestenberg, and Ira Brenner, endorses a view of trauma-related conflict as resulting in divided energy. Conflict is believed to provide energy to cope:

> Any given child has a standard-sized bucket of libido, of resources, and in a perfect world that child would use all of those energies to go straight up, developmentally. Well, if a child has a preoccupied parent who has a trauma for instance, or a difficulty in the family, or . . . there's some outside thing, the child then redirects some of their libidinal energy. That's energy that can't go toward their own [psychic] growth. In fact, it's counterproductive to their growth because it's being siphoned off. [MOL]

Finally, Pizer (1998) puts forth the idea that mental life is more akin to a paradox than a conflict. A paradox necessitates that the components of mental life—be they wishes, defenses, self-punishments, or unpleasant affects—are multidimensional, existing on many levels both simultaneously and sequentially. Since conflict is ubiquitous, then, the therapeutic goal is not to resolve conflict but to accommodate it.

ADHD Symptoms as a Response to Conflict ADHD children seem to be caught in cycles of negativity and reactivity. For some children, their reaction to emotionally challenging situations may present as difficulty in concentrating or as hyperactivity. One analyst gives the example of an emotional reactive response of inattention: *"The child reacts negatively to something the teacher says, for instance 'pay attention' or 'stop talking,' and becomes symptomatic—i.e., difficulty concentrating, headaches, stomach aches, and the like. The symptoms are a defensive response to feelings triggered by the teacher's response"* [SAP]. In some instances, a lack of concentration may be indicative of the child's need to avoid negative emotional experiences. A child who is distracted employs a defense of avoidance, *"dreaming out the window"* [LUB].

Movement or a lack of focus in children can also be seen as a defense against painful affect. One view is that the child's movement is in the service of avoiding difficult emotions. Similarly, daydreaming is also a way to avoid focusing on difficult emotions. From the child's point of view, *"It's a way to not feel"* [LUB]. The child takes the initiative to control her feelings, whether this is achieved through daydreaming, where she is avoidant—*"I don't want to think about this. Oh, this is boring. Oh, I'll look out the window"* [LUB]—or she becomes active—*"turn up the action . . . run the hell out of it"* [HUG].

On the other hand, children also *"seem to recruit action to deal with any internal discomfort"* [MER]. Some children lack the capacity to manage their feelings appropriately, instead converting them into *"impulsive activity or even motoric restlessness"* [MER]. These children are impelled by their feelings and *"are doing their very best to cope with something inside that is very upsetting"* [SIE]. One analyst describes such a child's defense as an inclination to "run": *"you're a screw-up, and what do you do with that? Do you split from it? Do you disavow it? Or you run? These kids . . . are runners"* [SEI]. In other words, one may say they employ the defense of avoidance: *"consider moving into action orientation as an avoidance. . . . 'This feeling is uncomfortable. What do I do with the discomfort? Whoa, make it go away'"* [LUB].

Most distressing for ADHD children is that once this cycle of negativity and reactivity is activated, it prohibits the child from accessing the more enjoyable defense mechanisms of sublimation. For latency-age children (six to twelve years old), our culture offers academic achievement as one way of receiving pleasure or gratification. For latency-age children with ADHD, this focus on the building—and celebrating—of academic prowess is not experienced as pleasurable. It is difficult for the ADHD child to succeed academically, and schools become fraught with painful emotional experiences. Another analyst explains that *"a child, when he goes to school, wants to master the basics, and wants to be seen that way . . . and when he is not able to do so, he will defend against feeling as a 'loser'"* [VAU]. In sum, defense in ADHD children emerged as the overuse of action, that is, hyperactivity. However, ADHD children lack opportunities to use the defense of sublimation where they are successfully able to transform their urges into enjoyable experiences.

A Relational View of Conflict To distinguish relational views from those informed by drive theory, it is useful to note that for relational-oriented analysts, conflict arises not from pressures related to the drives for expression, but from fantasy and "real" relations between the self and others. Relational analysts would explain the source of conflict as originating from the child's experience of the parents internalized as exciting, rejecting, or ego ideal (Fairbairn's model). From an object relations view, one may think of experiences with early significant others and how the child comes to represent these experiences internally. Through the internalization of the parent, the child develops an internal representation of himself, self-regulatory capacities, and an ability to mentally represent his experiences (Fonagy, Gergely, Jurist, and Target, 2002; Winnicott, 1967). Moreover, he is also better able to identify and regulate affective experiences (Conway, Oster, & Szymanski, 2011; Fonagy et al., 2002; Fonagy and Target, 1998; Gensler, 2011; Gilmore, 2002; Hopkins, 2000; Leuzinger-Bohleber et al., 2011; Orford, 1998; Salomonsson, 2011; Sugarman, 2006). Another area in ADHD children's lives that benefits from a healthy and positive experience within the parental relationship is their capacity to think about their own mental state as well as the mental state of others (Conway et al., 2011; Fonagy and Target, 1996; Jones, 2011).

Interpersonal conflicts with significant parental figures that occur early in a child's life may result in internal conflicts within the child. For ADHD children, typical areas of conflict in parental and family relationships and family dynamics include enmeshed relations with mother, a lack of father's presence, sibling conflict, adoption, and divorce (Cione et al., 2011; Gensler, 2011; Widener, 1998). Although these difficulties may arise in many families, the ADHD child finds it particularly challenging to cope with these complex family systems. Conflictual feelings interfere with the development of a major regulatory function that occurs early in the parent–child relationship. Relational conflict can lead to anxiety (Conway et al., 2011; Fonagy and Target, 1994; Gensler, 2011; Salomonsson, 2011); oversensitivity to words (Salomonsson, 2006); feelings of vulnerability to narcissistic injury (Gilmore, 2005); increased experiences of feeling shamed (Durham and Conway, 2014); and the impingements of a harsh superego (Gilmore, 2005).

The following is a case example of how relational issues may impinge on a child's functioning. The analyst describes the relational dynamics involved in the case of a child who began therapy when she was three years old. The child was initially brought to therapy when her parents went through a painful divorce. Six years later, the mother is remarried, and the child visits with her father on alternating weekends.

> When this divorce was going on . . . there was nowhere [for the child] to take [her feelings]. Her mother was caught up in what she was dealing with, her father was caught up in what he was dealing with, and she fell through the cracks. And so she developed a set of, sort of slightly eccentric behaviors that make her stand out from other kids. She didn't know how to negotiate her way into a group, she didn't know how to negotiate a difficulty with another child, when she got agitated she'd start snapping pencils, or breaking things, so people saw her as, you know, "What's wrong with that kid?" So immediately there was a kind of negative reaction by the school and . . . there wasn't an intuitively useful school psychologist or anybody who could help her, so as she developed, she departed from the norm more and more.
>
> The therapy is an attempt to sort of try to "pull her back in" . . . one of the questions I would say to the parents is: "Does she go on play dates?" Her mother responds: "No, we've moved too many times." [Therapist] . . . and, well, would it be possible to work out something so she could have a friend? She has no friends. So that really made a significant difference, suddenly she

had a small bit of kind of rootedness to one piece of emotion regulation—she could have a friend, she could negotiate things with the friend, they could have a little disagreement and maybe they didn't have to tear it up forever . . . she had no repair skills, no capacity to fix things, and no capacity to initiate things . . . and she did well enough. [MOL]

Intrapsychic Issues Related to Emotion and Self-Regulation

Emotion Regulation Emotion regulation refers to the ways individuals influence which emotions they have, when they have them, and how they are experienced (Gross, 1998). Emotions can be experienced as automatic or controlled, conscious or unconscious processes, and the quality of the emotional experience varies in latency, rise times, magnitude, and duration. Emotions impact a wide variety of mental processes (e.g., memory, decision making), behaviors (e.g., drug use, helping behaviors), and personality affects (e.g., whether one is cool under pressure or a volcano).

Some researchers, such as Barkley, believe emotions play a central role in the ADHD individual's functioning. Although regulating one's emotions is often experienced as automatic, for some, emotion regulation is an overwhelming task. Children with ADHD often experience difficulty with self-regulation and with regulating their emotions. According to Barkley (2005), children with these difficulties often appear less mature than their peers due to their difficulty in inhibiting their emotional responses. Emotion regulation is one of the major executive functions usually deficient in children with ADHD. Barkley describes the emotional landscape of ADHD children as having poor frustration tolerance and being easily angered, overly sensitive, and irritable.

Similar to Barkley, researcher Craig B. H. Surman, a medical doctor at the Massachusetts General Hospital Pediatric Psychopharmacology and Adult ADHD Program, in an interview with webMD Health News, refers to the difficulty ADHD individuals have with emotions as *deficient emotional self-regulation* (Surman, Biederman, Spencer, Miller, Petty, et al. 2013). In his research, Surman found a subset of ADHD individuals who have difficulty controlling their emotional reactions. This characteristic appears to be shared genetically among siblings of ADHD participants in his study.

Further complicating the child's challenges with emotion regulation is what Barkley refers to as the ADHD child's delay in developing an internal language, or *mind's voice*. The ability to internally contemplate and self-reflect plays a crucial role in self-regulation. The absence of the internal voice can lead to increased impulsivity and frustration when one is required to cope with one's emotions. It is important to note that although emotion regulation is a commonly recognized problem for children with ADHD, the clinical and physiological indices remain heterogeneous (Musser, Galloway-Long, Frick, and Nigg, 2013). Given the varying reasons for emotion-regulation deficits, an individualized approach to working with children is necessary.

Shame Among school-aged children, academic success or failure is associated with their self-development and whether they obtain their parents' approval. For a child who fails at achievement-oriented tasks, self-evaluative emotions such as shame become salient (Durham and Conway, 2014). Shame has been theorized by some to result in anxiety when standards set by harsh parental expectations are unmet (Freud, 1959) and can also lead to both harsh attacks on the self (Seligman's theory of learned helplessness—1972) and to depression due to negative self-evaluations (Beck, 1967).

Young children are especially at risk for shame experiences since they are more predisposed to making global self-evaluations (Darwin, 1965). While pride is more generally associated with success, a child who "fails" is more likely to experience guilt and shame. Developmentally, children as early as two-and-a-half years old can compare their behaviors to the expectations of others (Lewis, Alessandri, and Sullivan, 1992). For ADHD children whose experience is too often that they do not meet expectations, shame becomes a part of the emotional landscape in a way that may be inescapable. As young as preschool, negative parental feedback can result in shame (Alessandri and Lewis, 1993; Kelley, Brownell, and Campbell, 2000) and become even more demarcated as an emotional response by age four (Alessandri and Lewis, 1996).

For children who experience shame, "the self is viewed as small, helpless, frozen, and emotionally hurt when shamed" (Izard, 1977, in Durham and Conway, 2014). It is therefore not unreasonable that children who experience shame also view themselves as "bad" (Burhans and Dweck, 1995) and can be overwhelmed by these emotional experiences (Durham and Conway, 2014). One analyst comments that shame *"is a huge emotion . . . it makes you feel different and terrible, and angry, and hopeless, and outcast"* [LUB]. Not only is the shame a factor for the child but also for the parents: *"I think, when kids come to me, very often the parents are carrying the shame that goes unacknowledged"* [VAU].

Shame and Aggression According to Durham and Conway (2014), shame can be internalized, leading to hate and anger directed at the self. This in turn results in a cycle of negative views of the self as incompetent and to incapacitating experiences of contempt and disgust (Harder and Lewis, 1987, in Durham and Conway, 2014), an dfears of rejection and abandonment (Tangney, 1990). Attempts to avoid feelings of shame may also lead to an externalization or displacement of shame emotions (Lewis, 1987; Lewis, 1992; Miller, 1985) as anger and aggression (see Durham and Conway for full discussion). In some instances, the resulting aggression can also be a demand for attention. For example, one analyst recalled, *"especially with the aggressive [child], I couldn't let my mind wander in sessions. I had to be very, very present. There was a demand to be very, very present. And it was the hyper-active behavior that kind of did that because it was like pulling at you"* [LOM]. Another analyst posited a gender difference in how these emotions present themselves, reporting that *"Girls tend to not express the difficulties and impairments as much in aggression, it's more inward, and it's often very unrecognized and very undiagnosed. And that, you know, based on some of the current research, is part of what feeds and leads to much more serious psychopathology in adolescent girls"* [MAC].

SUMMARY

Researchers and clinicians have written about ADHD from a variety of per-spectives, but their views on ADHD are not limited to their discipline. In fact, there are shared views among those practicing in the medical and psychological fields. ADHD has been described as a neuropsychiatric disor-der by both psychiatrists and psychoanalysts (Barkley, 2006a; Salomonsson, 2004). Some describe ADHD as a disruptive behavioral disorder, though their views on the etiology may differ (Barkley, 2006a; Fonagy, 2004; Whe-lan, 2004). For example, while both Fonagy and Barkley describe the behav-ioral aspects of the disorder, Fonagy, a psychoanalyst, views these behaviors as being associated with infant–caregiver attachment (Fonagy and Target, 2002) while Barkley, a psychiatrist, attributes them to difficulties in execu-tive functioning (Barkley, 2006a; Crosbie and Schachar, 2001; Hinshaw, 2001; Lahey, 2001; Nigg, 2001). For some, ADHD is a developmental disor-der with both environmental and biological contributors (Carlson, Jacobvitz, and Sroufe, 1995; Gilmore, 2002; Jacobvitz and Sroufe, 1987; Salomonsson, 2004) that results in learning problems (Gilmore, 2000; 2002) and other neurocognitive challenges (APA, 2000; Levin, 2002). It is important to note that a belief in neurological/biological contributors to ADHD does not pre-clude a belief in psychogenic causes for the child's ADHD-related behavior.

The psychodynamic understanding of ADHD introduces the notion that ADHD has multiple determinants. The child's relatively observable symp-toms can be readily associated with deficits in his ego functioning, leading to executive functioning deficits. However, depending on the psychodynamic understanding of the etiology of the child's symptoms, the child not only experiences deficits in her ego functioning but also in her intrapsychic and relational world. These two psychodynamic perspectives are a focus of the next chapter. Since most of the deficits experienced by children with ADHD are located in the ego and impact their relational world, the next chapter offers a psychodynamic model for constructing the child's mental life—from ego psychology to developmental and relational perspectives—that is useful in understanding the core intrapsychic and relational issues discussed in this chapter. The next chapter also begins to set the stage for understanding the psychodynamic approach to the treatment of ADHD. Subsequent chapters focus on psychodynamic psychotherapy interventions with ADHD.

CHAPTER HIGHLIGHTS

Psychodynamic therapists refuse to categorize children based on their behaviors. Instead, they seek to understand the complexity of the child's symptoms and thereby engender compassion for the child. It is only through asking questions that go beyond the child's manifest symptoms that we can begin to appreciate the child's struggles. Rather than asking *"how can we fix this child?,"* the psychodynamic therapist is more likely to investigate questions such as *"what function do the child's symptoms serve"* and *"what is the child attempting to communicate?"* If there is a biological basis for these symptoms, *"what role does biology play in the manifestation of the child's symptoms?"* and *"how does the child negotiate these limitations?"* Finally, *"what role does the parental environment play in this disorder?"* Appreciation for the varied etiology of ADHD symptoms is a prerequisite for understanding that ADHD symptoms extend beyond inattention and hyperactivity.

Neurological Perspective on ADHD

- Neuroimaging and neurocognitive assessments have been used to identify some of the neurological determinants of ADHD.

  1. *Neuroimaging*

     - ADHD is associated with brain size and structure (i.e., immature brain structures in specific regions of the brain); brain circuitry (i.e., pathophysiology in the communication system in areas of the brain); and brain function (i.e., dysfunction in some of the brain's regions when activated).

  2. *Neurocognitive*

     - Neuropsychological assessments identified a variety of domains in which ADHD children experience deficits including general cognitive ability, attention, processing speed, executive functioning, and motor dysfunction.

  3. The prevailing *Neurological and Neurocognitive Models of ADHD Etiology* include a view of ADHD as stemming from deficits in

executive functioning *or* deficits in motivational or reinforcement systems.

4. *Psychodynamic psychotherapists view neurological determinants as important contributors to the understanding of ADHD symptoms.* Neurological determinants, such as aberrant brain structure and brain function, are observable through the child's response to cognitive assessments and interpersonal functioning at home and school. Neurological findings also support the notion that some children may be physiologically primed to be hyperactive or inattentive. Nevertheless, psychodynamic psychotherapy focuses on the resulting impact on the child's mind, mental processes, and mental life.

The Psychodynamic Perspective on ADHD

- The psychodynamic approach to understanding ADHD holds true to several tenets:

  - The etiology of psychological disorders is bidirectional, such that neurological anomalies produce psychological symptoms and mental events can lead to neurological changes
  - Psychological disturbance is dependent on the individual's subjective experience regardless of its neurological or intrapsychic origins.
  - Subjective mental states can also contribute to psychiatric symptoms like those of ADHD
  - Psychodynamic therapists examine and work with the subjective experience of each individual; this reflects their position that each child is an individual, and therefore his pathway to ADHD is individualized and unique.

- A psychodynamic approach informed by psychoanalytic theories views environmental (parental/caregiving environments and environmental insults) and intrapsychic issues (e.g., self-concept, conflict, and emotions) as contributors to ADHD symptoms.

  - Environmental determinants include disruptions in early attachments and trauma and complex trauma.
  - Intrapsychic determinants include issues related to (1) the self (i.e., self-concept, self-esteem); (2) conflict (i.e., a view of ADHD as a response to conflict—relational vs. drive theory view of conflict); and (3) emotion and self-regulation (i.e., issues of shame and aggression).

- In sum, it is important to note that a psychodynamic approach recognizes that ADHD has multiple determinants and the impact on the child goes beyond their deficits in ego functioning or the cognitive realm and equally impacts their internal experiences of themselves and their relational world.

Chapter Two

Psychodynamic Psychotherapy

A Compassionate Treatment Approach

May all beings be at ease. Whatever living beings there may be, whether they are weak or strong, omitting none . . . the seen and the unseen, those living near and far away, those born and to-be-born, may all beings be at ease! . . . Even as a mother protects with her life her child, her only child, so with a boundless heart should one cherish all living beings.
—Metta Sutta

Regardless of the etiology of their Attention Deficit Hyperactivity Disorder (ADHD) symptoms, ADHD children tend to experience impaired functioning in a range of cognitive or executive processes and interpersonal functions. In some cases, the maturation or development of these abilities has been thwarted by their interaction with their environments, neurobiological factors, or psychological disposition. Psychodynamic psychotherapists focus on this entire developmental process. The field of psychodynamic psychotherapy has many well-developed models that are useful in understanding the emergence of the psychological life of the child, each developed in response to one of the prevailing orientations of those working within it. These orientations vary according to the factors, tendencies, or relational context the analyst believes lies at the heart of the child's mental development. For some analysts, understanding the child's mental development means learning how she arrives at a sense of who she is in relation to herself and others. This curiosity about the child is central to the psychodynamic psychotherapist's approach to their work with the child and is an inherently compassionate approach that values and respects the individual. Others view the child's psychological development as emerging from her dispositional tendencies and the extent to which she can develop specific intrapsychic functions. Still others view the child's mental development as occurring within the context of her relationship with others. And finally, for some therapists, both biological and relational disposition factors are at play (Conway, 2012).

Before discussing the psychological developmental models, I wish to first discuss what I mean when I refer to the *mental life of the child*. That term embraces the child's entire psychological world, which includes consideration of the child's view of himself, how he regulates his emotions, his interactions with others, and his ability to think and contemplate ideas. It also includes a range of cognitive capacities including memory, attention, perspective taking, reality testing, and so on. Some consider these ranges of abilities as executive functions, relational/interpersonal functions, or a combination of both. This dimension of the child's functioning is positioned by some theorists in a psychic structure of the mind referred to as the ego. For others, the child's psychological life is grounded in their developing sense of self. While the terms "ego" and "self" are theoretically bound to psychodynamic orientations such as ego psychology and self psychology, I prefer to use the term "mental life of the child" since it encompasses all aspects of the child and frees the therapist to consider the possibility that both ego and self psychologies can contribute to understanding the child.

Psychodynamic therapists have observed both ego and relational deficits in ADHD children. Ego Psychological and Object Relations theories are the two predominant theories that emerged from a systematic review of the literature explaining the mental life of ADHD children (Conway, 2012). Gilmore, a prominent psychoanalyst who works psychodynamically with ADHD children, considers ADHD symptoms as indicative of disturbances in the ego, mainly reflected in executive functioning deficits (Gilmore, 2000; 2002). The child's development of the self in relation to others is within the realm of object relations theorists. Object relations theories applicable to ADHD examine the extent to which children achieve a coherent sense of self (Klein, 1952), are able to establish healthy self- and other representations through symbolization (Bion, 1959), can make emotional investments in relationships, and can achieve a unified self-identity that demonstrates coherence of self (Conway, Oster, and McCarthy, 2010). These relational dimensions are important to children's capacity to self-regulate and for the development of their personality (Conway, Oster, and Szymanski, 2011; Kernberg, 1980). Now for a closer look at two of these developmental theoretical perspectives—ego and relational—the chapter elaborates on these two models that inform psychodynamic psychotherapists' understanding of ADHD.

THE EGO DEVELOPMENTAL MODEL

To gain a compassionate understanding of ADHD, we explore the challenges faced by the ADHD child in the context of some well-established psychoanalytic developmental models. These models highlight aspects of critical ego developmental capacities that are central to the child's emotional and interpersonal functioning. Therapists and theorists have conceptualized the mental processes associated with children's abilities to perform a myriad of tasks as occurring in a psychic structure referred to as the *ego*. As such, it is a mental structure that plays a central role in the ADHD child's functioning. Think of the ego as an embodiment of the psychological processes that result from a combination of the physical brain's interaction with the environment. These interactions lead to the creation of mental processes that shape personality and other psychological processes common to the human experience. These psychological processes associated with the ego play a role in the deficits encountered by ADHD children.

Ego Psychology

> The ego is an organization of psychological processes—a coordinating and organizing system that facilitates our functioning in life or in responding to reality. For the ADHD child, disruptions in this coordinating system lead to confusion, frustration, depression, and other responses.

ADHD is a disorder that reflects a deficit in ego functioning. Therapists can list the ego's range of mental activities and equally list ways in which ADHD children are deficient in these ego functions. However, this view of ego functions and deficits offers only part of the picture needed to understand the ADHD child. What is missing is an appreciation for the process through which the child came to inherit these ego deficits.

Using Freud's model of the mind (1923), I will illustrate how ego functions in ADHD children operate in the context of the other components of the mind. Although the field of psychoanalysis has evolved beyond this model, it is still a useful illustration of the unique intrapsychic processes that compromise the ego and result in ADHD symptoms. Freud's model is useful in that it is a diagrammatic representation of a system for organizing psychological processes.

In 1923, Freud theorized about a three-part structural model of the mind comprised of the id, ego, and superego. In simple terms, the *id* is responsible for the fantasies and wishes that are instinctual. The *ego* is responsible for executive functions including reality testing, memory, and perception. The *superego* is responsible for our internalized morals and values. Although graphic representations of these aspects of the mind exist, they are not actual entities but a representation of a system of organization.

Freud supports the notion that an essential aspect of our psychological functioning is the mental coordination of psychological processes. External events are represented internally through a process that begins with our perception—influencing our thoughts, arousing our emotions, and shaping our behaviors. Think of the ego's job as a coordinating and organizing system that facilitates our functioning in life or in responding to reality (Freud, 1926). These ego processes include motivation, perception, memory, self-regulation, attention, planning, and organization. Coordination of these functions is under the auspices of the ego and is necessary for survival. It is what helps us to plan, execute our plan, and accomplish our goals. This system of coordination of these psychological processes is responsive to the environment or reality. As we encounter reality, our motivation, memory, perception, and so on, changes or adjusts to accommodate the reality of our circumstances.

For Freud, the ego's functions are conscious. However, his daughter, Anna Freud, theorized that it did not serve the ego's defense mechanism to operate consciously. She believed that the defenses would be more effective if they were unknown. In 1936, Anna Freud wrote in *The Ego and the Mechanisms of Defense* that the ego protects itself from threats posed by the id, the superego, and reality. In terms of the id, the ego could become overwhelmed by id urges—sexual or aggressive impulses that result in anxiety. In terms of reality, the life we lead also presents many opportunities that arouse fears of a sexual or aggressive nature—for example, being threatened with physical harm. The third source of threat to the ego lies in its relation to the superego. Any sense of immorality results in guilt and self-censure. It is important to note that the ego does its best work defending against anxiety undercover, or unconsciously. So the defenses are not usually in our conscious awareness.

The ego works in the context of the id and superego systems that are not bound to reality. While the ego is subject to the instinctual wishes of the id and the injunctions or admonitions of the superego, the two psychic entities are insulated from the effects of reality. The ego is subject to the pressures of the real world while the id and superego may persist unaffected by them. Thus, of the three psychological entities, the ego is especially subject to the influence of the environment or reality. Arguably, the superego is an artifact of the parental emotional environment, and the parental environment can impact the modulation/regulation of id-instinctual wishes. Nonetheless, compared to the ego, both id and superego are impervious to reality.

However, for some individuals, there are aspects of ego functioning that are unresponsive to the influence of the environment, or *encapsulated*. Many have theorized about what leads to the ego's encapsulation. Some psychoanalytic theorists believe that aspects of ego functioning operate in a conflict-free sphere—that the ego's functions are autonomous (Hartman, 1939). Yet my own observations, and those of many of the professionals I interviewed, seem to suggest that when ego functions are in conflict—that is, when the desired experience does not fit with reality—those functions can become quarantined. The ego system then makes adjustments to compensate for that particular encapsulated ego function. It is as though the ego function is in a "bubble." Freud believed that these aspects of ego functioning that become encapsulated are repressed, have failed to grow, or are immature. As such, ego functions—for example, motivation or perception—may not have developed at a pace that is consistent with the current demands of the individual's life.

Rather, the immature ego function may emerge from the encapsulated state when certain environmental requirements appropriate to the developing needs of the individual emerge. For example, there are some transition periods in children's lives during which they are more vulnerable; during these periods, the immature ego is especially susceptible to being taxed beyond its capacity to cope. For many children, these periods of increased vulnerability coincide with their transitions into sixth grade, ninth grade, or college. During these points of increased *environmental demand*, the immature ego function is more susceptible to id wishes and superego admonitions that "bleed" into the reality-testing realm of the ego. The constraints of the ego (the need to adhere to reality) do not apply to the id or superego. One may view these other exigencies of the mind as more fluid and less beholden to reality. It stands to reason that when the pressures of the id wish are in conflict with the ego, the individual's view of what is possible or realistic—that is, the reality-testing ego functioning—is compromised. As a result, ego functions—such as the capacity to perceive things clearly, to feel motivated, and to pay attention—as well as memory recall functions, may not be sufficiently mature to help cope with or appropriately integrate reality.

Why do aspects of the ego become encapsulated in the first place? Psychoanalytic assumptions of the continuity of experiences from childhood into adulthood are not unusual for most psychotherapeutic orientations. Psychoanalysts are concerned with exploring why some childhood wishes and fears persist and seem unaltered by later experiences that are expected to have an influence on these dispositions. Freud would attribute the encapsulation of some childhood experiences to *repression*. Repression prevents the conflictual wish—conflictual in the sense that it does not match with reality and has not benefited from adjustments afforded by reality—from maturing and changing. At the same time, we also know that environmental pressures such as trauma (discussed in the previous chapter), often lead to conflictual emotions that children may have difficulty organizing.

An immature ego, which cannot handle this payload of cognitive and emotional demands, is characterized by difficulties with regard to the perception of reality, to the ability to distinguish fantasy from reality, to regulate and keep at bay impulsive presses of the id, and so forth. Children with these deficits appear inattentive, impulsive, hyperactive, have difficulties with self-regulation, difficulty in keeping their fantasies from impinging on reality testing—in short: encapsulated ego functions manifest as ADHD symptoms.

Beyond the encapsulation process that results in an immature ego, ego functions can also be impinged upon by its contextual relation to the superego. Ego functioning extends into the realm of the superego through the establishment of the ego ideal into the psychic structure of the child. In children, the superego is the aspect of their personality functioning that makes up the mental awareness of their self-recriminations and harsh criticisms. The quality of the superego is shaped by parental responses. For example, the extent to which a parent responds harshly or compassionately to the child's vulnerabilities contributes to the formation of the ego ideal. The ego ideal is an extension of the ego into the superego. It represents the narcissistic expectations of the parents that become internalized by the child and is the standard-bearer for the child's behaviors. For example, a parent's investment in having a "smart" child similar to or aligned with the parent's self-perception may be unintentionally or intentionally placed on the child. The child may in turn experience parental expectations as a demand that is beyond her reach. If the child is not able to meet parental expectations, her perceived failures may inadvertently lead to difficulties in the parent–child interactions. In other words, the child had fallen short of the parent's narcissistic expectations. However, depending on the relationship between the child and the parent, her response to her experience of falling short of her parent's standards, established by her ego ideal, can lead to one of two distinct reactions: either she adopts an attitude of *"I will try again next time to do better,"* or she can become dejected and give up trying.

Problems that originate from the contextual relation between superego and ego also manifest as ADHD symptoms. For most ADHD children, regardless of the reason for their failures in ego functioning, the experience of having failed to meet their ego ideal results in their abandonment of their goals and their demoralization. They lack the motivation to make further attempts at succeeding. These behaviors are misperceived as the child lacking a conscience—established by the ego ideal—and showing a lack of remorse or motivation to do better next time. Difficulties in the realm of the ego ideal can also include ego functioning deficits such as distortions in the child's perception regarding the expectations of others. For example, the child may not understand what is expected of him, and this lack of understanding could be misinterpreted as a lack of motivation. Furthermore, children can have a range of responses to their perceived failure to measure up, including both *externalizing responses*—such as conduct and oppositional behavior problems—and *internalizing responses*—such as depression and anxiety.

In sum, the ego organizes thoughts and feelings about realistic experiences. When ego function is compromised, the child's thoughts and feelings also are compromised. So for ADHD children with ego functioning deficits, the way in which they experience the world is markedly different from the experience of children without such deficits. Some of their ego functions are encapsulated, and they lack those mental abilities to process their experiences. Moreover, immature encapsulated ego functions are forced into the open to face reality, and it is certainly not up to the task, so to speak.

Now that we know what the problems are, we can discuss how best to intervene. Behavioral approaches, such as cognitive behavioral therapy, are great at identifying and linking thoughts and feelings, but they have limitations that will be discussed more fully in the next chapter. How do we respond comprehensively to the needs of the immature ego function? How do we help the ego develop and mature appropriately to meet the demands of life? This task is within the domain of psychodynamic approaches discussed in the subsequent chapters.

Superego-related problems, such as lack of motivation stemming from the ego ideal, can be ameliorated using *behavioral approaches* that offer cognitive behavioral interventions aimed at shaping and rewarding desired behaviors. However, when these reward systems are no longer in place, the desired behaviors they inspired may disappear. Children are then left to contend with the same internal standards that they viewed as unattainable. Arguably, providing the children with an experience of success in achieving their goals (a behavioral approach) can create changes in their thoughts and feelings. The question becomes whether or not these skills are generalizable to other situations. In other words, *Does the child learn and transfer these experiences of success to novel situations?* The prevailing knowledge suggests that behavioral approaches only work for children when they are being actively supported by those around them; such approaches do not lead to lasting changes in behavior or transfer to other situations. Generalizability to other situations is impaired by the immature ego that cannot handle reality.

In contrast, *psychodynamic approaches* focus less on the children's behaviors, seeking to intervene more pointedly on the level of mental functioning where their behaviors originate—the ego ideal. Psychodynamic therapists make an effort to understand the nature of the child's internalized "measuring stick" and on how he experiences himself when he "falls short." The therapist provides the child with an alternative response to failed superego expectation that is more tempered and compassionate. A process of internalization of the therapist's responses expands the child's repertoire of psychological options—for example, the child trades abandonment and despair with motivation and hope in response to experiences of failure. These interventions are more fully developed in the chapters that follow.

Therapists using a psychodynamic approach help the immature ego meet the demands of reality. Psychodynamic therapists are also positioned to respond to children's failures empathically. Many parents report how difficult it is to get through homework with their children. One mother painfully described the homework battles with her child who daydreamed, cried, frequently got up from his seat, or rushed through the homework without attending to the instructions. These behaviors are typical of children with ego-functioning deficits. These children find it difficult to participate in academically demanding situations that require reliance on a range of ego functions—planning, organization, impulse control, and such.

Because the ego cannot meet the demands placed on the child, adults can often observe the child's immature response—inattention and a hyper-motoric response that is not age appropriate. For example, ADHD children may repeatedly be seen leaving their seats or daydreaming, may engage in conflict with their peers, and may be slow in accomplishing age-appropriate tasks. It is crucial to recognize that these children's outward behaviors merely mirror their internal frustration and sense of inadequacy.

Case Example

To illustrate the important role of the ego, I will present a vignette from my work with a seven-year-old boy I will refer to as Bernard. Bernard frequently exhibits the symptoms we have identified as representative of ADHD. During the session, he began trying to juggle some small softballs he fished out of the toy chest. After several unsuccessful efforts, he took a toy octopus out of the toy box and proceeded to wrap each tentacle around the balls. I commented to the child that sometimes he may feel like a juggler with all of the things he needs to track. He admitted he had difficulty juggling everything and stated that having eight hands would certainly help. For this child, the experience of responding to reality with a less-than-adequate ego system is akin to trying to juggle many balls without having the skills to do so.

Sometimes ego inadequacies occur in the context of superego expectations of parental figures. Bernard's mother informed me that he had crying spells when asked to do homework. After working in the psychotherapy session, Bernard was able to articulate that he often felt overwhelmed and did not know how to respond. Bernard believed his mother wanted him to be perfect, and he feared "getting things wrong." Although being demanding was not his mother's intention, Bernard had internalized his mother's expectations of him in a way that had transformed her expectations into a harsh, unrealistic superego demand. His mother confirmed that he seemed less motivated to do his work and often felt sad. Children like Bernard, who internally experience their parents' expectations as unachievable demands, are at risk of developing depression or anxiety.

RELATIONAL MODELS OF SELF-DEVELOPMENT

Some of the clinicians I interviewed talked about the mental process of children in terms of their development of the self. These psychodynamic therapists, who were concerned about the impact of impaired ego function on the child's interpersonal world, relied on models of self-development described in the next set of theoretical approaches: the interpersonal approach, and those developed by Klein, Winnicott, and Bion.

The Interpersonal Approach

> Interpersonal cues seem to be operating outside the realm of attention. The ADHD child is not rude, disrespectful, impatient, etc., but despite their best efforts, they miss these interpersonal cues.

As a brief review: the *classical approach* acknowledges the layering of early experiences that continues throughout the lifespan, impacting present behavior. The beginning personality formation resulting from these ego-encapsulated experiences (oppositional, defiant, depressive, and anxious) is relatively fixed and accessible only through the transference neurosis that may develop in the analysis. This classical developmental perspective comes with a set of interventions that may not be readily available to non-analytically trained therapists.

A complementary view of the persistence of personality tendencies throughout life is one where the responses we elicit in others support patterns of interpersonal interactions. In this view, continuity between the past and the present is maintained because the individual's way of interacting with others elicits similar responses time and time again. *Interpersonal interactions* are not limited to observable behaviors; they also include subtle interpersonal cues that are operating just outside of our attention. A child who consistently misses certain interpersonal subtleties will unwittingly continue to elicit the same erroneous, undesired interpersonal responses from others, thus repeating the pattern. One challenge faced by ADHD children is their difficulty interacting with others in socially appropriate ways. Interpersonal interactions and attention to social cues are the bases for social interactions; for the ADHD child, however, interpersonal cues seem to be operating outside of the realm of the child's attention. A child with ADHD, for whom inattention is a predominant symptom, is often faced with interpersonal challenges. Inattention to social cues is a symptom that is not unique to ADHD; it is also evident in other developmental disorders such as Autism Spectrum

Disorder. That there are shared symptoms among disorders is one of the reasons why psychodynamic approaches do not rely solely on symptom manifestation to formulate treatment or conceptualizations of children's difficulties.

Even further, to understand a child's behaviors, one must consider the role of those individuals in the child's life who inadvertently help to support and maintain those behaviors. A range of interpersonal factors interacts with the child in a consistent enough way to affirm a child's view of herself. Even during the first few sessions with a given child, a therapist may find himself wanting to respond in a way that is probably consistent with her experiences of others. Dynamic therapists refer to this process as *countertransference*. Countertransference reactions are a pull that is hard to resist—and one that shows up again in the child's approach to the therapist (in a process known as *transference*). Analyzing the child's transference process gives the therapist access to this aspect of her experience—inherent in the transference is the distorted view of the manner in which the child perceives her interpersonal world. These distortions are what learning theorists refer to as *schemas*. According to learning theorists, new experiences are assimilated into older experiences—that is, transference neurosis—leading eventually to *accommodation*, which involves an integration of the new and old. This last step in the learning process is a challenge for the ADHD child. One can say, then, that the ADHD child does not "learn," and this has grave repercussions for their interpersonal life.

The ADHD child seems to lack an appreciation of others as having a reaction to their behavior rather than to their intention. Seeing a direct connection between one's behavior and reactions in others is somewhat of a puzzle for the ADHD child, who has yet to learn that how they behave toward others shapes how others act toward them. In other words, when children interact with others in ways that do not take into account certain social cues, they receive responses that do not fit with their expectations. They then respond to these unexpected reactions from others by developing a distorted view of themselves and their social relations. As these children continue to fail in securing the desired responses in others, they become caught in an endless cycle of missed cues, distortion, and undesirable reactive responses from their interpersonal world.

Here we can see the usefulness of a *behavioral approach* that orients the child toward a focus on behavior intervention. Children who experience these kinds of interpersonal challenges could often benefit from an understanding of the connection between their thoughts and actions. However, further complicating their experiences are their wishes and fantasies about their desired social relationships along with the reasons for the conflicts they experience and how they defend against these experiences. It is in this dimension of the child's experience that a *psychodynamic approach* is helpful—in addressing the breadth of the interpersonal struggle. As children change developmentally, their dispositions/temperaments also impact their interactions with others, adding to an already complex matrix of factors involved in social interactions. After repeated failures, because ADHD children continue to miss those important social cues and hence do not learn from them, we see the emergence of other psychopathological pathways as they attempt to cope with what they experience as an unpredictably reactive interpersonal world. Depression, anxiety, oppositional behavior, and many more symptoms emerge as these children struggle to make sense of that world.

From a psychodynamic perspective, interpersonal theorists like Sullivan (1953) link the experience of children's early interpersonal worlds with their current interpersonal behaviors. Sullivan posits that infants have certain fundamental needs (food, warmth, the absence of irritation, safety, tenderness, play, stimulation) and, depending on their needs, alternate between a state of comfort and tension. This tension can be eased by a satisfying response from the parent, resulting in a tendency toward *integration*—the bringing together of infant and caregiver into a mutually satisfying interaction. In contrast, the child's needs may elicit an anxiety response in the caregiver, and the resulting interactions are *disintegrating*. As the infant develops, he begins to create a self-system that initially discriminates between an anxious (bad) and non-anxious (good) mother. The self-system works to extend attributions toward the self, crediting "good me" when the child's activities generate approval and "bad me" when it does not. This self-system develops from the child's growing awareness that he can shape his actions to influence the likelihood of a good mother appearing and decrease the probability of a bad mother emerging. During times of threat, the self-system dominates and produces interactions that have been successful in minimizing anxiety in the past. These self-system interactions, or *security operations*, make up a set of behaviors that are employed to reduce anxiety. The self-system also shapes the individual's impression of self and others. Security operations ward off anticipated threats generalized from earlier interpersonal relations. It is possible, then, that at some point in their development, some children learn that paying attention to social cues is threatening in some way, and a self-system that values inattention was established as a way of managing anxiety related to that threat. Sullivan would explain this dilemma as originating from our response to perceived stress in set ways that perpetuate certain interpersonal patterns. From this perspective, a therapist would focus on patterns of behaviors and their unintended interactions.

Often, adults who interact with an ADHD child are unable to empathize with such a child, even if they are predisposed to like the child. The child's behaviors are experienced as deceitful, lazy, and manipulative. Sometimes the child *is* being manipulative and *is* lying to the adult. It is important to realize, though, that these behaviors are in the service of trying to elicit much sought after, gratifying, interpersonal connections. On both sides—the child's and the recipients of the child's interpersonal efforts—the possibility that the child is missing social cues is seldom acknowledged. It is painful and challenging for adults in the child's world to accept the child's distorted view of social relationships or that the child has an inability to see the obvious cues that govern rules of social engagement. Moreover, the child, who has this ability but may be inconsistent in attending to social cues, is also less likely to elicit a sympathetic response to their social transgressions. An interpersonal perspective broadens the issue of attention to social cues from simply a cognitive dysfunction or behavioral response to one where patterns of interpersonal relationships stemming from inattention are maintained and perpetuated in the interpersonal realm through distortions, fantasies, and wishes.

Psychotherapy with an interpersonal orientation draws attention to the details of interpersonal interaction and empathizes with the child's "missed" efforts to connect socially.

Case Example: A Boy and His Father

An eleven-year-old boy diagnosed with ADHD has a conflictual relationship with his father, who in turn views him as manipulative and oppositional. The father has the stance that he will not be emotionally available to the child until the child's behavior conforms to his expectations. The boy becomes angry and defies his father openly. There is little recognition that in his defiance, the boy is making an effort to have some connection with the father. The boy's actions elicit an angry response from the father, and the two become locked in a familiar pattern of provocation and outburst. Both the father and the son have a need to connect, but they miss each other's interpersonal cues. From the father's perspective, "I am looking at him while he is doing [something wrong], and he continues regardless." In the father's mind, the child's lack of response signifies a direct opposition to the father's wishes, and that opposition makes the father angry. The father, not knowing or accepting the extent of the child's inattention and distractibility, misinterprets the child's behavior as defiant. It was only after working with the parent extensively that he came to accept that his cues, usually sent via "the look," were too subtle for his son. The father also came to learn and accept that even if his son were to receive his visual messages, those messages would be quickly lost because of his son's distractibility. Moreover, the child may receive the intended message but may be uncertain about how to respond, in which case the son would do nothing.

The Work of Melanie Klein

> The introjective-projective mechanism helps manage the child's terrifying anxieties. It is through this process of introjection and projection—when the ego differentiates between internal and external realities—that the internal experiences become integrated, and the child becomes more accepting of reality.

Klein's work signifies a departure in the way people thought about intrapsychic conflict. Melanie Klein (1882–1960), a psychoanalyst with a degree in teaching, was primarily concerned with developmental psychology. Most of her theorizing was about children—their psychological developmental process and the importance of play in analyzing them. Unlike many of her counterparts, Klein believed that children are born with an ego and that superego development occurred early in life, prior to the oedipal phase. Her work signifies a departure from the way in which her counterparts usually thought of intrapsychic issues. For example, Freud believed the central neurotic conflicts occurred around secrets primarily related to the oedipal phase, and a considerable time in therapy is spent unearthing those secrets. However, because Klein views these secrets, fantasies, or wishes as a pre-oedipal occurrence, her emphasis is relational—that is, the child's symptoms may be a way to have contact with others (objects).

Klein was therefore less concerned with what is happening in the oedipal stage and more concerned with what is going on in the pre-oedipal stage. For example, Klein believed that, in adults, paranoia was a reflection of childhood fantasies that were oedipal in nature and resulted in terrifying self-punishments. Of course, such "punishments" belong to the realm of the superego, which gives us our moral compass. She believed the feelings the child had about the oedipal wishes were more intense than what Freud characterized as "prohibitions"—for Klein, they were more akin to terrifying fears and anxieties. She believed that these early infantile terrors set the stage for ego maturity.

Klein's View of the Ego

Klein believes the ego is present at birth. As the child interacts with objects in their environment, such as parents, new ego abilities develop. These emerging ego skills replace functions previously performed by parents and other relationships in the child's world. Klein believes the very first relationship a child has is with the first object they encounter—the breast. Klein theorized that through a process she called *introjection*, the child creates an internal or psychological replica of attributes of the experience of being nurtured. These experiences at the breast—which signify being cared for, gratified, and loved—begin to shape the infant's inner world. The child identifies with these "good" aspects of the breast, and these experiences are incorporated into the ego, where they function to organize future intrapsychic development. A child who has experienced a nurturing caregiver has a psychological world that reflects the benefits of such nurturing—for example, the child learns to trust their environment and expects to be taken care of—whereas a child who has received inconsistent nurturing or maltreatment is less trusting and may even develop a response to others that suggests they have expectations other than being loved and cared for. Like ego psychologists, Klein believes that the ego is modifiable: it continues to develop as it encounters new experiences from interacting with other objects in the world.

Many theorists have refined the concept of introjection. For example, Sándor Ferenczi, in his 1912 essay "On the Definition of Introjection," talks about introjection being possible when repression lifts and the individual can incorporate the object into his ego (see Abraham and Torok, 1972). Object relation theorists discuss introjection as the process of creating internal representations of the external caregiver or parental figure so that those people become a part of the self or personality. Others hold a view that introjection can also be a defense (Winnicott, 1986). Still others, such as those belonging to the Gestalt school, assert that the "introject" is one way to internalize external experiences, and it is one-dimensional or indiscriminate in that there is no selection of information to "introject." Some oppose this view and propose a more discriminating process of assimilation of selective information (Wysong and Rosenfeld, 1982). In other words, depending on children's experience with their caregivers, their ability to integrate new information may be compromised. While some see this process as indiscriminate, others believe the children's inhibition against taking in new information is selective and perhaps has emotionally based determinants.

Klein also theorizes about a second process that is central to ego development—*projection*. Projection is an unconscious defense against aspects of oneself that evoke anxiety. To protect the self, an individual attributes to others fewer desirable impulses, wishes, or fantasies. Klein believes that the infant projects onto the external object terrifying fears resulting from the death instinct. It is through a combination of the process of taking in and projecting outward that the ego develops—one that consists of aspects of both the child and the caregiver.

While aspects of external objects are taken in or "introjected" by the child, the early ego or internal representations of the child consist of fragmented part-objects. As the child develops, his internal world becomes more peopled with whole-object representations. In other words, the early ego in the infant is driven by the introjection and projection processes, which are generated in response to their need to take in the "good" and get rid of their internal anxieties and fears. The mature ego, on the other hand, is less driven by instinct and more accepting of reality. The mature ego takes in whole objects that are more realistic rather than part-objects that are more representative of the favorable attributes associated with those in the external world. As the ability to perceive reality increases, a characteristic of a more mature ego, there is less reliance on the introjective–projective mechanism.

Now that we have a sense of what is occurring in the child's internal world, it is important to consider how Klein views the organization of these experiences. According to Klein, internal experiences are arranged in two positions: the paranoid-schizoid position and the depressive position. At the *paranoid-schizoid position*, the child splits their experiences into good and bad, projecting the bad experiences outward unto others. At this point, the world is peopled with dangerous objects that pose a threat to the child. At the *depressive position*, the child is capable of seeing a more realistic view of their object and can integrate both good and bad qualities.

From a therapeutic stance, Klein sees the internal life of the child as more threatening to the child's psychological well-being than external reality. The child's fantasies, anxieties, prohibitions, aggressions, and wishes to annihilate the external object elicit in the child a fear of retaliation. These inner realities affect the child's perception of external reality. Emotional experiences of frustration, discomfort, and other painful emotions are disavowed and projected outward, resulting in the experience of being visited with these emotions from the outside—in other words, the child does not recognize these experiences as coming from within but instead experiences these difficulties as hostile attacks from the objects in his external world. In this way, the child's internal experiences shape his relationships with those around him. These inner anxieties are the focus of Kleinian therapy. Through the analysis of the transference, the therapist examines the child's early relationship to objects, and to persecutory and depressive anxieties. Different part-objects—represented by the various roles of the parents—can also be projected onto the therapist as she assumes different roles during the therapeutic process.

Klein's view of the ego's maturational process calls attention to the process through which the child's ego matures, paying particular attention to the integration of the child's internal anxieties and fears with reality. From a Kleinian perspective, all experiences are internal. It is through the introjective–projective process that these inner experiences become less fragmented and terrifying and more accepting of reality.

For the ADHD child, the symptoms observed by others are merely projections of the child's internal world. To gain some insight into the child's inner experiences, those seeking to help the child need to look at the child's level of disorganization, anxiety, depression, sense of futility in accomplishing their tasks, frustration, difficulty focusing and attending, and motor animation. For therapists and parents, empathic responses to the child can be challenging because of another one of Klein's processes known as *projective identification*. Projective identification is an interpersonal process. During this process of projection and introjection we make attributions about intolerable aspects of our experiences and our interpersonal interactions position others to respond consistently to the fantasized projections. According to Klein, once the undesirable affect has been cast off, its recipient continues to be controlled through a set of interpersonal interactions that leads to that recipient unknowingly accepting the projected role. For example, it is not unusual for ADHD children to engender angry responses in their therapists, teachers, and caregivers. Klein may posit that the therapist's response is a *projected identification response* wherein the therapist unknowingly accepts the role the child has projected onto him. Ogden sees this interpersonal process as reflective of the child's functioning at a developmental level where the boundaries between the self and object representations are blurred (Ogden, 2005). The therapist has thus succumbed to the child's view of himself or herself (child) and the therapist has behaved in confirmatory ways—inadvertently providing the child with an *introjective identification* (Scharff, 1992). The therapist may experience himself as becoming frustrated with the child or having to set limits regarding the child's behaviors in ways that are uncomfortable. His response to being engaged by the child in this manner thus confirms the child's projections—for example, her view that the therapist is mean or angry. There is no acknowledgment on the child's part that the experience of anger is her own. For the therapist, recognition that these feelings—of anger, for example—are intolerable for the child and therefore need to be contained and then represented back to her is crucial to the success of the therapy. The therapist must be able to process the feelings aroused in him by the child and help her manage her struggles with these severe internal experiences.

The child's experience with the therapist will help with the maturation of her ego development as she begins to integrate reality and her internal life becomes less terrifying. In this way, the therapist helps the child to distinguish between terrifying inner anxieties and reality.

Case Example

I once worked with a child who was experiencing many difficulties in school. Like children identified as ADHD, she experienced difficulty in focusing and concentrating. However, after a long period of getting to know her, I came to realize she did not complete her assignments and projects because doing so meant she would have to interact with others. For example, she explained very clearly that when she is unsure about how to complete an assignment, she is reluctant to ask the teacher for assistance, and that interferes with her being able to complete her assignments. This child experiences a tremendous amount of emotional distress around potential social interactions with others and avoids any activities she fears will lead to having to interact with others. Her internal anxieties and fears drove her to avoid finishing her tasks.

The Work of Donald Winnicott

> The deficits associated with ADHD are due to failure of the maternal–child dyad or the child's failure to use the mother's auxiliary ego functions to shield the child from unthinkable anxiety leading to unintegrated ego and self-experiences.

Donald Winnicott (1896–1971) developed theories about the role of the environment in the development of the self. But before the formation of the "self"—that is, before the establishment of the infant as a psychologically separate person from the mother—there exists the ego. The ego refers to the organization of the infant's experiences, and this process begins at birth. Winnicott believed that the environment, particularly the "maternal environment," is critical to the infant's psychological development.

Initially, the mother is totally given over to her infant's care—in a state he refers to as *primary maternal preoccupation*—but gradually adapts to a more facilitating role. This facilitation of the environment provides the child with a sense of omnipotence. As the child matures, the mother becomes less involved in facilitating the environment, and the infant's relationship with the external world becomes more reality based. Winnicott refers to this transition as *moving from subjective object*—having fantasy-based or mental/internal views of objects or relationships—*to objective object*—perceiving relationships more accurately.

Paralleling this development is the infant's shift from the illusion of omnipotence to acceptance of reality (Winnicott, 1963). Winnicott refers to a mother who can create this facilitating environment for the child as the *good enough mother.* The good enough mother divinely intuits the needs of the child. As the child becomes more independent, the mother is less involved and withdraws. From this experience of having to let go of the illusion of omnipotence and accept the realities of the external world, the infant's *true-self* emerges with a clear knowledge of what constitutes the child as a person. This emergence of the self is necessary but inseparable from the maturation of the ego. In fact, the ability of the mother to be "good enough" in responding to her infant's needs facilitates the ego's maturation, whereas a "not-good-enough mother" can impinge on the development of the child. Since Winnicott thinks of the baby as "on the brink of unthinkable anxiety" (p. 56), the ability of those who play a role in the parental environment to anticipate the child's needs and manage the child's anxiety is essential.

Winnicott also discussed the development of the *false-self* resulting from the impingement of the (maternal) environment. Impingement on a child's development occurs when the child is forced to deal with stresses that are out of tune with his developmental level, when he is stimulated too often, or when his internal needs build to frustrating levels. Continued stresses on the child will cause a split within the self between the genuine self and a compliant "false" self (Mitchell and Black, 1995, p. 131). In comparison to the false-self, the true-self is capable of having authentic relationships with others that are vital and real. Unlike the false-self, a true-self is able to have confidence in external relationships, is mature, has a capacity to be alone, grows from a state of dependence to independence, and is capable of having relationships with whole external objects (p. 74).

Well before there is an emergence of the self, the infant's experiences are being organized. The organization of experiences, even instinctual ones, is referred to as ego. The ego exists even before children can recognize or place words on their experiences. Therefore, from Winnicott's view, the developing ego would be influenced by the caregiver's environment. The mother–child relational dyad demonstrates ego-relatedness and serves as the basis for future relationships. As such, the infant's development of a self can be viewed as inseparable from the development of the ego. In fact, the ego exists from the onset and is further developed and matured in a good-enough caregiver environment.

In the formulation of the ego, Winnicott linked aspects of infant/child care to the potential for psychopathology. One trend he refers to as *integration* has been associated with the experience of maternal holding and has particular relevance for ADHD: "The main trend in the maturational process can be gathered into the various meanings of the word integration. Integration in time becomes added to (what might be called) integration in space" (Winnicott, 1965, p. 58). When the mother–infant dyad is good enough (i.e., it achieves the goal of staving off "unthinkable anxieties"), the infant is able to successfully experience the self or personality or psychological world as *continuous* or *going on being* (Winnicott, 1956, p. 303). In contrast, maternal–infant dyads that fail to protect—and in so doing produce unthinkable anxieties—disrupt continuity and result in a more fragmented experience of the self, resulting in psychopathology.

Another pathway for the development of psychopathology is one where the child, for whatever reason, does not avail himself of the ego support offered in the maternal–child dyad, a state referred to by Winnicott as *unintegration*. It is in this early process that Winnicott locates the etiology of "restlessness, hyperkinesis, and inattentiveness (later called inability to concentrate)" (Winnicott, 1965, p. 60). Conditions in the caregiving environment as well as of the child are required to provide the organized and continuous experience of the self that results in a mature ego. The cost to the child otherwise is an experience of himself and his world that is unintegrated, leading to symptoms of inattentiveness and hyperactivity.

A therapist adopting this approach creates a holding environment for the child and offers opportunities for mirroring.

The Work of Wilfred Bion

> Ego functions are Alpha Functions: The infant develops the capacity to learn how to manage difficult emotional experiences through having repeated experiences of its distress being received and transformed successfully.

Wilfred Bion's (1897–1979) theories that are most relevant to this discussion are his views on learning/attention and projective identification. He distinguishes between two types of learning—*learning from experience* and *learning about something.* He offers projective identification as a model for learning from experience. He theorizes that the baby's early communication with the mother is such that the child signals its distress to the mother through crying, vocalizations, bodily movements, facial gestures, and such. These distressing signals are referred to as *beta elements* and represent an emotional experience that intrudes on the baby's awareness and pervades its sensory world (Bion, 1962, p. 6). The mother or a mature caregiver receives and acknowledges these signals and responds in an appropriate manner. For example, in an optimal situation, the mother can receive the signal, can tolerate what is being communicated by the baby, and can offer a compassionate response. The mother's response, which Bion refers to as the *alpha function,* reflects the construal of meaning of these distressing signals upon which she brings to bear her intuition, attention, creativity, and imagination. In so doing, she transforms the baby's beta elements into alpha elements. Through the baby's experience of the mother's response to its distress, the mother is experienced as a *containing object,* and the child begins to learn how to manage its distress on her own. It is through this process that the child develops the ability to self-soothe, reflect, and remember the ameliorative experience. This process of identification and internalization of the mother's response lays the foundation for the baby's development of alpha functions. Bion views the quality of the mother's internal world as contributing to the birth and development of the infant's emotional life. The mother is available to respond to the child. She offers a range of responses that reflect her own internal world and can be passed on to the baby, aiding in the baby's development of these alpha functions.

The process of projective identification also allows the infant to develop the capacity to learn. The child learns how to manage difficult emotional experiences through having repeated experiences with the mother of his distress being received and transformed successfully. After many such experiences, the child can then retrieve this experience from within his thoughts and trust that future pain will be attended to effectively. Bion describes this retrieval process as the infant's reverie in his emotional experience of an *internal projective identification welcoming object.*

According to Eaton (2005), Bion suggests that not all objects are welcoming—some object experiences are with what he refers to as *obstructive objects.* Conditions both internal and external to the infant and the mother may impede the development of *transformative emotional experiences.* The infant's ability to tolerate frustration or the mother's inadequate alpha functions can contribute to an experience of failed transformative experiences. It is at these times the child may experience *infantile catastrophe* or *nameless dread.* In "Attacks on Linking," Bion (1959) describes the consequences of failed transformative experiences of infant distress. In essence, the infant is not able to benefit from the projective identification process, wherein coping with overwhelming emotions can be experienced vicariously through the caregiver. Whether the infant is unable to tolerate frustration or the mother is unable to transform these feelings, the result is the infant's attack on these emotional linkages with others. In other words, the capacity to learn through a connection to the mother's emotional life is severed. The obstructive object is now thought of or experienced as an *internal projective identification rejecting object* that willfully denies the comfort sought by the infant. The infant now has developed an identification with this rejecting object who cannot meet his needs for relief from distress and rejects emotional experiences outright. The child, having internalized the rejecting object, embarks on a desperate quest to find someone to alleviate his pain—when this search fails, he may erupt in a violent rejection of the object, try to will the object to function as the need arises, or destroy the object altogether.

Bion's perspective is particularly useful in understanding the intricate family dynamics that may arise between parent and child. Often, parents report feeling attacked by their children when those children become frustrated. For children who have difficulty with self-regulation, the relationship to the object vacillates from being perceived as welcoming to rejecting and may inspire feelings of fear. One patient reports she screams at her parents when they try to speak with her about her incomplete homework assignments. She admits that she realizes after the fact that her parents were attempting to help her, but in the moment, she was frustrated and overwhelmed.

Bion's perspective is particularly relevant to the ADHD child, who has difficulties regulating emotional experiences. One may surmise that the ADHD child failed to develop the capacity to manage difficult emotional experiences. Because of this, the child has repeated experiences of failure in having her distress received and transformed successfully. Ego functions that require self-regulatory capacity are akin to Bion's alpha functions. In a dynamically oriented therapy, a therapist responds to the child's distress as a welcoming object, transforming beta elements to alpha elements. The therapist can understand both the dread of failed transformation and the child's response in attacking the primary relationship

SUMMARY

In sum, school-aged children with deficits in ego functioning find it difficult to participate in academic and interpersonal pursuits, particularly during a time in their developmental stage that requires them to rely on a range of ego functions—for example, planning, organization, impulse control, and so on. However, for some children, ego functions become encapsulated at an early stage in their development, impeding their developmental progression. In the encapsulated state, the ego does not benefit from reality, learn from experiences, or develop. This immature ego cannot meet the payload of the demands on the child, resulting in an immature response—often including a childlike and age-inappropriate attention and motoric response. For those observing a child who presents as physically developed while behaving in a seemingly immature manner, there is initially a bit of confusion that may progress to frustration and anger. There is little recognition that the child's outward behavior merely mirrors the child's internal frustration and sense of inadequacy. Moreover, the ego deficiencies occur in the context of superego expectations of parental figures. The resulting ego ideal serves as the internal measuring stick against which children judge their own behaviors and achievements. Failure to achieve the ego ideal can lead to deficits in the ego functions of motivation and perception and can therefore result in externalizing and internalizing behaviors that are problematic for the child.

The interpersonal theoretical approach focuses on how the self-system of the ADHD child incorporates the child's capacity for attention—for example, to social cues—to help reduce anxieties and shape interpersonal interactions. While both Klein and Winnicott subscribe to the notion that children engage in a process of managing terrifying anxiety, the process through which this occurs differs for each theorist. For Klein, the introjective–projective process is employed toward stress management, and the ego function at risk is the extent to which the child distorts or can distinguish inner from outer reality. Winnicott believes the child becomes embroiled with anxiety management when the mother fails to shield the child from these troubling experiences or the child is unable to rely on the mother's auxiliary ego functions. These failures lead to disruption in the child's self-development, resulting in inattention and hyperactivity—typical symptoms of ADHD. Finally, Bion speaks to the development of children's emotion regulation capacities. Through the repeated experiences of his distress being received and transformed successfully, the infant develops the ability to learn how to manage their difficult emotional experiences.

By examining these perspectives, one gets a glimpse into aspects of ego functioning as seen through the child's interpersonal world. It is my belief that by embracing one or more of the perspectives presented here, therapists will develop more compassionate ways to treat children with ADHD symptoms, and it is my hope that they will then translate this understanding to the parents and teachers of those children.

Theoretical Approach	Ego Function	Ego Development	Approach
Ego Psychology	All ego functions: reality testing, motivation, planning and organizing, reality testing	Encapsulated ego → immature ego Ego in context of the superego → ego ideal	Help immature ego meet the demands of reality Offer an alternative response to harsh superego ideal
Interpersonal	Attention Anxiety management through activation of the self-system	Interpersonal cues operating outside the realm of attention Repetition of interpersonal patterns	Draw attention to details of interpersonal interactions Display empathy toward child's missed efforts to connect socially
Klein	Management of terrifying anxieties Integration of reality	Introjective–Projective Mechanism Projective identification	Integration of reality Distinguish terrifying internal anxieties from reality
Winnicott	Anxiety management	Use of mother's ego functions as an auxiliary Disruptions in development of the self	Holding environment Mirroring
Bion	Anxiety/overwhelming emotions	Alpha functions	Transform experience of difficult emotion through the development of the alpha response

CHAPTER HIGHLIGHTS

ADHD children tend to experience impaired functioning in a range of cognitive and interpersonal functions that have been adversely impacted by diverse factors—interactions with their environments, neurobiological dispositions, or psychological dispositions. But for the psychodynamically oriented therapist, understanding the child's mental development means learning how she arrives at a sense of who she is in relation to herself and others takes precedence over the child's behaviors. This curiosity about the child is central to the psychodynamic psychotherapist's approach and is an inherently compassionate approach. The analyst's theoretical persuasions about what influences the development of the child's mental life may be governed by their understanding of (1) the child's dispositional tendencies and the extent to which she can develop specific intrapsychic functions; and (2) the context of the child's relationship with others; or (3) as a function of all of the above.

The Ego Developmental Model

- ADHD is due to a deficit in ego functioning.
- The ego is an organization of psychological processes—a *coordinating and organizing system* that facilitates our functioning in life or in responding to reality.
- This system of coordination of these psychological processes is responsive to the environment or reality.
- However, for some individuals, there are aspects of ego functioning that are unresponsive to the influence of the environment, or *encapsulated*. In other words, when ego functions are in conflict—that is, when the desired experience does not fit with reality—those functions can become quarantined.
- The ego system then makes adjustments to compensate for that particular encapsulated ego function. It is as though the ego function is in a "bubble." As such, ego functions—for example, motivation, or perception—may not have developed at a pace that is consistent with the current demands of the individual's life.
- When changes in the child's life require the child to rely on certain ego functions, for example, during some transition periods in children's lives, the immature ego is taxed beyond its capacity to cope.
- During these points of increased *environmental demand*, the immature ego now needs to function—e.g. capacity to perceive things clearly, to feel motivated, and to pay attention, as well as memory recall functions—but the ego may not be sufficiently mature to help cope with or appropriately integrate reality.

Why do aspects of the ego become encapsulated in the first place?

The continuity of experiences from childhood into adulthood are not unusual for most psychotherapeutic orientations and are due in part to internal dispositions and environmental impingements the child encounters during their development.

Ego problems can also originate from the contextual relation between superego and ego.

Problems in this domain manifest as distortions in the child's perception regarding the expectations of others and their view of themselves as having failed to measure up. Problems encountered in this psychic realm can lead to *externalizing responses*—such as conduct and oppositional behavior problems—and *internalizing responses*—such as depression and anxiety.

Relational Models of Self Development

Relational models of self-development focus on the mental process of children in terms of their development of the self and the impact of impaired ego function on the child's interpersonal world. Some of the contributing theoretical approaches include the interpersonal approach, and those developed by Klein, Winnicott, and Bion.

- *The interpersonal approach (Sullivan)*: Interpersonal cues seem to be operating outside the realm of attention. The ADHD child is not rude, disrespectful, impatient, and such, but despite their best efforts, they miss these interpersonal cues.
- The *introjective-projective mechanism (Klein)*: The child's internal experiences are marked by terrifying anxieties and several psychological processes—introjection, projection, paranoid-schizoid positions—help to manage the child's internal emotional experiences, perpetuate our emotional response to the child, and guide other interpersonal processes.
- *The importance of the mother-child relationship (Winnicott)*: Deficits associated with ADHD are due to failure of the maternal–child dyad or the child's failure to use the mother's auxiliary ego functions to shield the child from unthinkable anxiety leading to unintegrated ego and self-experiences.
- *The importance of transformative emotional experiences (Bion)*: Ego functions are Alpha Functions: The infant develops the capacity to learn how to manage difficult emotional experiences through having repeated experiences of its distress being received and transformed successfully.

Chapter Three

Psychodynamic Psychotherapy Interventions

Treating Attention Deficit Hyperactivity Disorder (ADHD) children requires a certain degree of flexibility in the therapist's disposition. While there is a plethora of psychoanalytic perspectives, analysts' tendency to show allegiances to their training lineage can present a challenge in treating ADHD children. Adherence to one's treatment orientation and the clarity and consistency it brings to interventions is crucial to the effectiveness of psychotherapy. Nevertheless, analysts must make sure they are responding in an ethical manner to the needs of each child they are treating. The etiology and symptom presentation of the children they see in treatment must be juxtaposed against their theoretical lens even if doing so requires an expansion of their therapeutic interventions beyond the repertoire of their orientation.

A defining characteristic of the psychoanalytic perspective is the therapist's ability to maintain the focus of treatment on the child's inner experiences rather than on the child's external behaviors. The therapist has to find a way to access their feelings of compassion for the plight of the child with ADHD. It is my belief that focusing on children's internal experiences—as they contend with the demands of the external—provides an opportunity for them to begin to heal and lead psychologically healthier lives.

THE PSYCHOANALYTIC FRAMEWORK

There is a plurality of theoretical approaches captured in psychoanalytic/ psychodynamic therapies. Largely, these approaches share key concepts including a belief in unconscious processes and in the notion that the past somewhat influences present and future functioning. Previous chapters provide a review of some of the major psychodynamic theorists and their views on ego development. In this section, I present some of the major approaches used by the analysts I interviewed in a way that highlights their relevance with regard to the ADHD diagnosis.

A range of theorists informs analysts' approaches to working with children diagnosed with ADHD. The major contributors are object relations theorists such as Melanie Klein and Donald Winnicott; scholars working with the intersubjective space between therapist and child influenced by the work of Wilfred Bion; and Anna Freud's work on ego psychology. Other contemporary scholars, including Peter Fonagy, Anne Alvarez, Jacques Lacan, Christopher Bollas, and Éric Laurent also contribute to analysts' clinical work.

The therapeutic approaches presented here are informed by data collected from the analysts I interviewed as well as by the theoretical perspectives discussed in the previous chapter. Three main themes emerged from those interviews: a focus on the therapist's disposition and the use of two overlapping approaches—relational and ego psychological/developmental—that guided the analysts' techniques and interventions. Although I present a summative form of the analysts' discussion about their approach, their individual approaches to working with ADHD children varied depending on their theoretical perspectives.

Given the wide range of psychodynamic interventions to choose from, it is important to offer a context for understanding and selecting interventions. In the second part of this chapter, I discuss a model of the mind that includes the relations between ego, id, and superego and depicts interventions that target specific ADHD problems. ADHD problems resulting from the conflict between these intrapsychic structures and the child's interpersonal world are a focus of this discussion.

THE PSYCHODYNAMIC THERAPIST'S DISPOSITION

A central supposition of a psychoanalytically informed therapy is a belief in the unconscious. Therefore, practitioners subscribing to this approach view the creation of therapeutic opportunities to observe the workings of the unconscious as a primary goal of their practice. As such, the therapist's disposition should be one that focuses on:

a. creating opportunities for unconscious processes to be a part of the therapeutic effort;
b. considering the role of the unconscious in her conceptualization of the child's problems; and
c. presenting herself in a manner that reveals unconscious processes.

The analyst sees one of her primary therapeutic responsibilities as creating a space for the unconscious to emerge. For example, one analyst reports *" [the] Freudian unconscious is misinterpreted as being only about repression and about sex and aggression, and it's really . . . it's about cultivating a space for the person's unconscious to surface in a much broader sense"* [MOL]. This view rings true when thinking about the work of Christopher Bollas (1992), who sees the therapist as having an awareness that achieving understanding of her client is illusory. Yet within the very nature of this illusion is the freedom to create together a view of each other. Similarly, analysts informed by Lacan (see Evans, 1996) and Annie Rogers (2007) also position themselves to allow the child's unconscious to emerge by being available to *"Get the story from the child [by positioning oneself as] an . . . object to receive the story."* This is akin to an oblique or indirect approach advocated by Lacan (Boothby, 1991), one that is *"less intrusive for the child and more patient in allowing the unconscious to emerge instead of deciding what you [the analyst] think the unconscious is"* [MOL]. In Lacan's terms, analysts are working *obliquely* when they decide to *"take your lead from the child and follow the child to where the difficulty is. [Such an approach takes] more patience to allow the child's unconscious to evolve and more attention to creating a space that has no demands"* [MOL].

The analyst's conceptualization of ADHD helps to consider the role of the unconscious in how ADHD symptoms are expressed. Analysts are not exempt from thinking about the child diagnostically, but they take into consideration both the unconscious conflicts and the child's conscious symptoms.

> When you're working as a psychoanalyst, you're much more concerned with the whole person, with impediments to growth . . . with the sources of conflict. You look at symptoms as a reflection of all of these different forces, and you're not going to look necessarily just at the person along the lines of a diagnosis. Because, of course, most people have multiple kinds of problems, and that's certainly true with kids with ADHD—comorbidity is the norm. But at the same time, I think even if you are a child psychoanalyst, you can't ignore diagnostic thinking. . . . You need to be comfortable in both [unconscious and conscious realms of expression]. [MAC]

When considering conscious contributors to symptomatology, it is recommended that the analyst consider *"symptoms and behaviors along all the different axes that may be contributing to the problematic difficulties the child is having"* [MAC]. Analysts are encouraged to consider how *"what you see in the child is produced by the context in which the child lives. How much of it is shaped by parental demand and parental difficulty or school demand and school difficulty"* [MAC]. For unconscious contributors, analysts are encouraged to examine *"unconscious conflicts reflected in family dynamics and the developmental status of the child"* [MAC]. Analysts can ask questions such as: To what extent *"are these developmental issues and [to what extent are they] conflicts?"* [MAC].

The analyst's presentation in the therapy room is important in facilitating her ability to access the child's unconscious. An analyst who was informed by Laurent Danon-Boileau encourages the therapist to adopt a disposition as a *drowsy nanny* (Danon-Boileau, 2001) or *limp puppet* (O'Loughlin, 2013). In these approaches, the analyst assumes a physical and psychological position of receptivity. For example, the analyst *"sits there and only acts when their analyst unconscious is activated by the unconscious of the child. So you sit there and become limp and receptive"* [MOL]. In a therapy session, the analyst may set the stage for this receptivity by providing the child with some instructions regarding the structure (or the lack of structure) of their time together. For example, one analyst described:

> When children come to my office, I tell them you don't have to talk. You don't have to write. You don't have to draw. You don't have to play. You don't have to do anything except be here. And I'll be here with you, and we'll see what happens. And that creates a space that has, well, some demand, but a lot less demand than children typically experience. And then I see what happens when a child decides to take that space and do something with it. [MOL]

EGO PSYCHOLOGY INTERVENTIONS

ADHD is a disorder marked by deficits in executive functioning associated with the prefrontal cortex of the brain. These include executive functioning deficits ascribed to the ego, a mental structure of the brain responsible for synthesizing, organizing, and integrating experiences (Gilmore, 2002). In children diagnosed with ADHD, clinical presentations associated with ego deficits include difficulties planning, incorporating multiple tasks, inhibiting impulses, and delaying gratification (Conway, 2012). Executive-functioning impairments (located in the brain) aligned with ego-functioning impairments (located in psychic/mental structures) are a focus of this chapter. I also discuss the psychological interventions addressing these difficulties.

Psychodynamic interest in the ego functioning of children in addition to their executive-function deficits extends the understanding of the nature of some of their ego-functioning difficulties. A nuanced approach along these lines has identified difficulties in *reality sampling* (Jones, 2011). Reality sampling is the child's ability to distinguish fantasy—an id activity—from their ability to distinguish reality—the realm of the ego. In situations where actual experiences are undersampled, children display distortions in their perception of reality and their relationship to time. Jones describes the results of these distortions as the child shifting from one task to another in the service of seeking some gratification but failing. It is almost as though the child is being pushed around by her emotions rather than feeling in control and able to make choices she finds satisfying. This is a problem not only because this search for pleasure drives the child but also because, for some children, this lack of satisfaction results in an oversampling of reality. The resulting experience for the child is overstimulation, a condition that her immature ego is unable to manage (Jones, 2011). Furthermore, failure in the normal ego-regulatory capacities can result in a motor discharge that manifests as hyperactivity (Jones and Allison, 2010). An over- or undersampling of reality therefore has consequences for children's perception of time, leads to oversensitivity toward others, and compromises development of secondary-process thinking (Conway, 2012).

The ego psychology approach focuses on ego functioning and development with attention to the ego's ability to defend against anxiety caused by primitive id impulses or superego ideal and reality. Therapist interventions include understanding how the ego defends against anxiety, integrating the child's primitive wishes into current ego functions, and the therapist's adoption of auxiliary ego functions on behalf of the child. Figure 3.1 offers a graphical representation of these ego psychology interventions.

Ego Defense

One function of the ego is to defend against anxiety that may arise from the id, superego, or reality. As I discussed in the previous chapter, the ego's defenses are psychological processes that prevent anxiety-producing impulses from entering consciousness. When a child presents with ADHD symptoms, the analyst views his behaviors as a defense employed to cope with stress resulting from inappropriate impulses and ego-ideal failings (see chapter 4). ADHD children have a defensive profile and characteristically *"recruit action to deal with any internal discomfort"* [MER]. Along with a reduced ability to manage stressful affective experiences, there is an almost immediate reactivity wherein pain is converted into *"impulsive activity or even motoric restlessness. That's the coping mechanism that develops"* [MER]. To some extent, these responses in the child call for action from his parents and teachers. Analysts should remain neutral to avoid being *"caught up in the action"* [MER]. Another aspect of the ADHD child's defensive profile is the narrow set of options available to him to sublimate his urges. Latency-aged children are thought to sublimate their urges through their academic achievement, an option not available to most ADHD children, who tend to find academic tasks such as reading and writing unpleasant.

> For the latency-age kid with ADD, there are a lot of defenses that are very desirable that could kind of get shut off. So, you know, the usual sublimation,

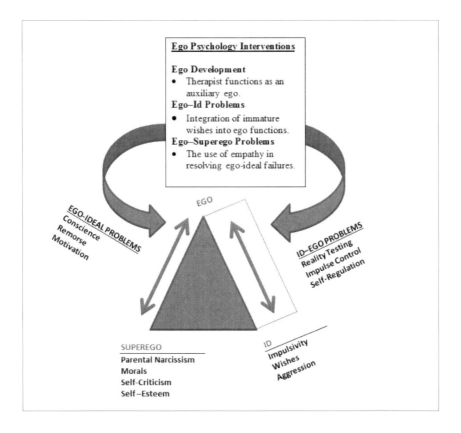

Figure 3.1.   Ego Psychology Interventions

like the myriad academic skills—reading, writing—the stuff that's so helpful for most kids, can be cut off. For ADD children, these activities are not pleasurable. They are difficult to do. They are limited. They don't get pleasure, gratification, and self-expression from the modes that our culture offers if you are between the ages of six and twelve. Things just don't come easily to those kids. [MER]

This matter of the core intrapsychic conflicts ADHD children encounter, as well as some of the reality-based threats to their sense of self, is addressed in chapter 2. Thus, it is not surprising to therapists that ADHD children often encounter difficulties with self-regulation attributed to deficits in ego functioning. As a result, they are seen as lacking in fundamental ego abilities: *"control mechanisms . . . the coping skills to regulate themselves"* [SAP; MAC]. Developmental deficits *"play a role in developing and influencing unconscious conflicts throughout life [during] the developmental stages, which in turn are going to have an impact on the way that the child nego-tiates the weaknesses that they have"* [MAC]. Even if there is a neurological basis for the child's problems, an analyst with an ego developmental approach stresses that:

> looking at children with ADHD from the framework that Anna Freud had is very very consistent with the psychoanalytic understanding of neurobiological weaknesses having an impact on and playing a role in development of and influence on unconscious conflicts throughout life, throughout the developmental stages, which in turn have an impact on the way that the child actually negotiates the weaknesses that they have. [MAC]

Working with children and giving consideration to their developmental stages does not preclude a psychoanalytic approach. One analyst who values the work of Erik Erikson explained, *"I work with ADHD kids developmentally. When I'm thinking of them psychodynamically, I'm thinking of secondary issues that come into play. These include their attempts to secure a good base or to help with their failing or flailing self-esteem"* [VAU]. These threats to self-esteem most often emerge in the context of family and school: *"Eric Erickson's stage of development for latency-age kids—an industry-versus-inferiority[-level child]—explains that the main job of a latency-age child is school. School and . . . family"* [VAU]. Children who are unsuccessful in negotiating both of these realms have little opportunity to feel good about themselves. It is also important to note that analysts' experiences have been that as children transition from one developmental stage to the next, they tend to experience some disruption in their usual regulated state. This is often when their parents seek out treatment to help them in making the necessary adjustments.

Integration of Immature Wishes into Ego Functions

A child's immature ego development has implications for her ego functioning—particularly its ability to regulate id impulses. The immature ego is insulated and impervious to the influences of reality, as described in the previous chapter. As such, primitive demands—for example, the id's wish to be loved and have its needs anticipated—are not adapted or integrated into the ego's reality functioning. This failure in integration results in immature/ineffective ego functions such as a lack of motivation or inattention. As a result, treatment is structured around shifting these naive wishes to the analyst (through transference) so they can be explored consciously, integrated into current ego functioning, and modified to be consistent with the demands of reality. Access to immature wishes occurs through the transference. Transference is used to work with id–ego issues primarily related to the ADHD child's difficulties with self-regulation and reality testing.

Not much has been written about using transference in working with children, and even less data exists with regard to using this technique with ADHD children. Conway (2012; 2013) offers a brief review of the literature on the use of transference in working with ADHD children. What research has taught us so far is that transference interpretation supports children's cognitive and affective organization in ego functions (Gilmore, 2005); aids in their development of higher-ordered mental abilities such as mentalization and self-reflection (Fonagy and Target, 1996; Jones, 2011); and stabilizes their internal affective states (Salomonsson, 2011; Sugarman, 2006). Transference interpretations tend to include commentary on the child's mental state vis-à-vis the therapist and help to contain the child's emotions (Fonagy and Target, 1996). In a session, a therapist might comment on how the child she is treating experiences her as just another adult who is inflexible and rigid. Such comments contextualize the child's experience of the therapist while providing the child an opportunity to reflect on his internal states vis-à-vis others without having to act on his building frustration. Follow-up questions, such as how the frustrating feelings may or may not occur in other situations, allow the child to improve mentalization (Fonagy and Target, 1996; Jones, 2011). The therapist should be aware that addressing negative transferences too early in the treatment has the potential for the child to experience it as an injury (Eresund, 2007; Salomonsson, 2006). Transference interpretations that focus on the mental processes of the child are most helpful. The goal is to help develop in the child a capacity to think about his own mental states and distinguish it from the mental states of others (Fonagy and Target, 1996). Children who can develop this ability to mentalize demonstrate improved self-regulation.

The transference process gives the therapist an opportunity to observe how the child represents his id wishes. For example, the child may have a desire only to participate in gratifying activities. Anyone who interferes with this immature desire may be experienced by the child as a threat to his wish fulfillment. Thus a *transference neurosis* is created, giving the analyst a glimpse of these immature desires (Wachtel, 1977, p. 36). The therapist's task is to introduce the naive desire into the session through a transference interpretation (Greenson, 1967, in Wachtel, 1977) that frees the child from having to ward off these unpleasant feelings or act out. Once introduced into the session, the therapist has an opportunity to explore these feelings with the child. Jones (2011) recommends that the therapist "act as an 'echo-chamber' for the patient, presenting the therapist's words almost simultaneously with the patient's actions" (Conway, 2012, p. 413). Explore the child's feelings (for example, feeling bored) in the context of the child's reality (doing homework) with the goal of integrating these disparate experiences. For example, over a number of sessions, the therapist may be able to help the child accept the reality that sometimes the child has to do tasks that are not as pleasurable as others may be. The therapist helps the child to find ways of soothing the self through anticipation of the next pleasurable moment. In so doing, integration is achieved, providing the child with relief as immature tendencies are transformed to more mature ones.

It is important to note that any interventions that provide relief from a child's ability to be in touch with warded-off intrapsychic pain interfere with the development of the transference neurosis and thereby interfere with the transformation of these immature cravings/inclinations into more mature reality-based ones. Therapists can unintentionally render transference work impossible by using behavioral approaches too early in the treatment. From this point of view, behavioral interventions can be seen as prematurely offering relief prior to the development of the transference neurosis. The therapist's goal is to facilitate the integration of immature wishes into the ego requiring the therapist to look together with the child at the child's discomfort.

The Use of Empathy in Resolving Ego-Ideal Failures

In the previous chapter, a discussion of the ego ideal provided some insight into a psychological process in which internalized superego edicts can leave children feeling like they fall short. These problems originate from the conflict between the superego and ego and the resulting ego ideal. Ego–superego conflict typically revolves around issues such as morals, conscience, showing remorse, and motivation.

Through the use of empathy, therapists can provide children with ADHD with an alternative response to failed superego expectations—one that is more tempered and compassionate than the responses those children may typically receive. ADHD symptoms often engender negative responses in others. Parents, teachers, or even a child's peer group may express annoyance, frustration, and anger at her ADHD-related behaviors. For example, the child may experience difficulty following instructions and completing tasks, may be overly sensitive toward others, or may not interact in socially appropriate ways. At best, she is at risk for internalizing these negative views of herself. However, external judgments are only the beginning: the child's own internal "measuring stick," which is informed by her superego, is an even harsher critic, and it can be more threatening to her psychological life. Unlike children with the ego strength to mitigate these negative self-concepts, ADHD children often succumb to self-recriminations.

In my 2013 paper on the use of transference and empathy in treating ADHD children, I discussed the important role empathy plays in engaging a client and maintaining a therapeutic alliance. Regardless of the therapist's orientation—psychodynamic or cognitive—a child who perceives her therapist as empathic has positive outcomes in treatment (Bohart, Elliott, Greenberg, and Watson, 2002; Burns and Nolen-Hoeksema, 1992; Norcross, 2002; Orlinsky, Grawe, and Parks, 1994). Through the adoption of an empathic stance toward the child's behavior, the therapist conveys to her that her perspective is important to the therapist (Conway 2013). Furthermore, through the therapist's empathic reflection on the child's internal superego struggles, the child develops the capacity to reflect on her own internal experiences (i.e., her sense of not measuring up or her feelings of anger, anxiety, or depression) (Conway, 2013; Gilmore, 2000; Nathan, 1992). These emotions could be overwhelming for the child. The therapist's empathic response helps her to organize her emotional experiences, which is referred to as the *working through* or *metabolizing* of difficult affect (Conway, 2013; Eresund, 2007). In the session, the therapist pointedly shifts the focus of the therapy from a view of the child's behavior as unacceptable to an interest in exploring and understanding the child's affective responses. The therapist strives for both *intellectual empathy*—that is, accuracy in understanding the child's perspective—and *empathic emotions*—compassionate responses toward the child's thoughts and feelings (Conway, 2013). In the use of empathy, it is important to not align with the child against her parents. ADHD children do benefit from the support and structure their parents provide, but often their feelings of frustration are magnified when they are expected to comply with the very same rules that provide them with that stabilizing framework. Indeed, Murdock (1999) cautions that children can misinterpret their therapists' empathy toward their views of their parents. In those situations, the therapist is misperceived as sanctioning disobedience. The therapist must take care to distinguish between empathy for the child's plight and communicating to the child that she does not have to follow the rules. When used appropriately, understanding helps to mitigate some of the ego-ideal issues that leave the child feeling deflated or defiant.

The Therapist as an Auxiliary Ego

ADHD children have immature egos. One approach is to consider how to treat the immature encapsulated ego. For example, one would not expect a two-year-old to have the attention span of a fifteen-year-old. So when working with a fifteen-year-old client who has the attention span of a two-year-old, we respond to the emotional needs of the two-year-old. We adjust our expectations to be consistent with the child's abilities. Then, through a nurturing approach, we titrate our expectations of the child much in the same way that mothers mirror for their children and even assume some of the auxiliary functions of their egos until they can assume those functions themselves. This approach is akin to recommendations made in *Barkley's model* (2006a) for working with clients who lack motivation. He recommended adjusting interventions closer to the *point of performance* much like one does with a child until the clients can tolerate and respond appropriately to a greater distance between the motivation and reinforcement.

The therapist assumes the function of the auxiliary ego to the child and "loans" the child her ego function. For example, if a child is having difficulty attending, the therapist assumes that function and attends for the child until he can do so independently. She starts paying attention to the child, noticing every detail and commenting on it. Jones (2011) refers to the therapist's role as one where she strives to achieve a state of fusion with the child. The therapist uses her words and gestures to represent the child's external reality back to him, *mirroring* the child's affective experiences.

The feeling the child receives from being attended to fuels his development and maturity. This has important implications for treating children with ADHD given that inattention is one of the encapsulated ego functions that typify ADHD pathology.

RELATIONAL INTERVENTIONS

From a relational perspective, ADHD is a result of interpersonal disturbances and disruptions. With a focus on interpersonal functioning, relationally oriented therapists believe children's problems stem from problematic parental and sibling interactions; parental over-involvement and abandonment; trauma; and narcissistic vulnerabilities (Cione, Coleburn, Fertuck, and Fraenkel, 2011; Conway, Oster, and Szymanski, 2011; Eresund, 2007; Hopkins, 2000; Leuzinger-Bohleber, Laezer, Pfenning-Meerkoetter, Fischmann, Wolff, and Green, 2011; Orford, 1998; Sugarman, 2006; Szymanski, Sapanski, and Conway, 2011; Widener, 1998). See chapter 2 for a full discussion of the impact of these relational factors on the child's emotional life. Also, chapter 4 offers a review of relational theories that provide a foundation for understanding the relational interventions presented here. The clinical interventions informed by relationally oriented analysts include a focus on developing a relationship with and understanding the child, holding and containing difficult affective experiences the child encounters, developing in the child the capacity to self-reflect, working with countertransference, using a narrative approach, and working with joint attention. The relational approach also endorses working with empathy and transference as these concepts were described earlier in this chapter.

Understanding and Developing a Relationship with the Child

ADHD children often have difficulties in their interpersonal relations; for these children, developing a relationship with their therapist is especially important. In order to establish a relationship with an ADHD child in his care, the therapist focuses on understanding the child. He makes himself available to the child and remains psychologically receptive and open to whatever she presents. One analyst who stressed the importance of this thera-peutic stance explained:

> So we have to sit there and let them tell us. And they will tell us in various ways through their behavior, through their drawings, and through their word-ing. Listen very carefully to what they say, how they say it, and when they say it. And the urgency behind it, or the nonchalance behind it, whatever it hap-pens to be. [SIE]

To accomplish this task, the therapist enters each session without assump-tions, much in keeping with Bion's approach: *"Do not make assumptions . . . approach each session without knowledge and desire. You are in a state of reverie or receptivity with no agenda, no purpose"* [MOL]. In establishing a relationship with the child, the analyst's goal is to attempt to understand her. From one analyst's perspective, children have a limited number of options when trying to communicate their distress to others. Therefore, it is the analyst's job to understand the child in his care. One may ask questions such as:

> "How does that make you feel better—to get up and move around?" "How does that make you feel better to scream?" "How does that make you feel better to. . . ?" So if I take an adaptive point of view that says, "You're trying to do the best you can with what you've got. Tell me about how that works for you and maybe we can, maybe we can help you rework that a little bit in a way that gets you into trouble less, helps you learn more, um, evokes love instead of fury." [DON]

Although the expectations from family and educators push for symptom reduction, it is important that the analyst value the importance of his relation-ship with the child. An analyst inspired by Anne Alvarez's *The Thinking Heart* (2012) agrees that *"an attempt to understand the kids, not manage them"* [SAP] is at the center of a psychodynamic approach. To reach this understanding, one analyst explains, *"I try to think of children as people. And not as either children or adults, but as persons with a developing perspec-tive, point of view, and integrity. We should believe children. Their experi-ences are real and should be validated"* [LOM].

Holding and Containing Difficult Affective Experiences

Mentalization leads to the development of self-regulation in the child, which allows the child to manage difficult experiences. However, this capacity may take some time to develop in the child. In the meantime, earlier on in the relationship, the therapist is tasked with creating an environment that con-tains the child's complicated emotional responses. Analysts value the relationships they form with the children they treat; these relationships—and the understanding within them—provide a context for helping the children contain their difficult affective experiences. Together, therapist and child create *"a space where things that might seem frightening become less dangerous and become less toxic"* [LOM]. This co-creation within a trusting therapeutic environment—the ability to trust what is happening in the room—and the ability to develop an individual level of comfort allows the child to explore emotions and experiences that may otherwise be more frightening. Honesty between the therapist and the child about the conflicts and difficulties he has been experiencing is necessary. A critical part of the treatment is the process of arriving at a point where he can discuss his difficulties. An analyst explained:

> I think you need to try to find a point, with a child, where you can be frank, and where you can name things that are "unnameable." So they can address the conflicts and difficulties. So they can be understood. Not only that the symptoms are manageable, but that they can be frank about the underlying pain or difficulty. That's my sense of what the core of the work is. Finding a way to speak to that "difficulty" that lies beneath. But its formulating is a very slow process. [MOL]

Countertransference

Countertransference is the psychotherapist's conscious or unconscious response, either positive or negative, to the client (Mosby's Medical Dictionary, 2009). When examined, these responses can be useful in providing insight into the client's interpersonal experiences. A therapist who examines their own countertransference response to a child with ADHD can use their countertransference response to really understand the child's perspective. It may be useful for the therapist to know that children diagnosed with ADHD may engender strong emotions in others. Individuals interacting with the child offer a variety of reasons for this. The frustration that is often felt by parents and teachers may arise from the apparent unresponsiveness of the child to instructions, from their own failed efforts to reclaim her attention and direct her behaviors, from her perceived defiance and oppositional behaviors, from her difficulty owning up to the truth—the list goes on and on. ADHD children typically accept on some level that this is the response they receive from others, and the therapist is not expected to react any differently. One may say these children have become experts at eliciting these responses in others, both adults and peers. On the other hand, they can also present to their therapists as charming and endearing. It may take some time for the analysts to see the behaviors that are being reported by the children's parents and teachers.

For the negative countertransference response in the therapist to work productively, it is important for the analyst to be able to become unstuck—to not become locked into this role. It is true that this occurs despite the best efforts of most, but being able to shake loose and not be pigeonholed is an important step in the therapy. Undoubtedly, the analyst must look within to examine whether there is something that needs further exploration in his therapeutic work. However, personal contributions aside, the analyst must seek a way out—to avoid becoming stuck in this role thrust upon him of abhorring the child's behavior:

> I was sort of locked into the same interplay that she was having with her parents, and at some point I said to her. . . . "You know, you can do this differently," and she was so grateful [laughs]. You know, it was almost as though I broke up something in myself. And so, those are the challenges. And that's the exciting part sometimes—to transcend a stalemate or transcend an impasse. [DON]

The Narrative Approach

Relationally based analysts believe each child has an inner relational story that represents how he interacts with others and how others interact with him. This representational world becomes relatively fixed as the child develops, as do the stories the child can tell to represent his experiences in the world. Another task for the analyst is to help the child "find" the words that will build an emotional vocabulary. For example, an analyst may help the child distinguish between emotions; for example, she may help him understand that *"disappointment is different from rage and different from losses"* [DON]. The goal is to help the child to begin to develop an internal narrative of his inner experiences.

Joint Attention

Joint attention is the shared interaction between mother and infant where both are attending to the same thing and are aware of their shared focus (Tomasello and Akhtar, 1995). Joint attention has implications for cognitive development and vocabulary learning (Akhtar and Gernsbacher, 2007). It also contributes to a variety of social cognitive behaviors, including social referencing and the developmental appreciation of others as intentional be-ings (Carpenter, Akhtar, and Tomasello, 1998). Joint attention can be broken down into its composite parts. These components include initiating joint attention, responding to joint attention, and mutual engagement occurring in a variety of domains (visual, auditory, tactile, or kinesthetic) (Akhtar, 2002; Tomasello and Akhtar, 1995). Joint attention is also culturally variant and determined in part by the mother's belief about the nature of care patterns.

For example, among middle-class American parents, children are expected to be able to pay attention to one thing at a time, while among Mayan children, parents expect the child to attend to multiple events or participants simultaneously (Chavajay and Rogoff, 1999; Rogoff, Mistry, Goncu, and Mosier, 1993). Given the many different possible combinations of the ways in which joint attention could occur, one can conclude that joint attention is heterotypic. Furthermore, the extent to which joint attention occurs is consistent with the parental expectations shaping the meaning the child derives from his attentional patterns. A child for whom the kinesthetic attention is predominant, but who joins in the visual attention, could theoretically leave the interaction without the experience of mutual engagement. This child could seek to ramp up his kinesthetic efforts to join with the parent while experiencing little success. Seeking this kind of joining with the parent may explain some of the attention-seeking qualities associated with ADHD that tend to elicit adverse responses in others.

For a clinical psychologist, especially those with a psychoanalytic orientation, joint attention is believed to be essential for the development of perspective or *theory of mind*. Theory of mind is a developmental attainment in the child that allows him to engage in pro-social behaviors as well as regulate the self vis-à-vis others. The belief is that the experience of the mother joining the infant in attending to whatever holds the infant's attention provides the opportunity to develop a knowledge of the self in relation to others. During this shared experience, the mother is quite active in looking, commenting, labeling, and organizing the experience for the child. The infant in turn is given a context for what they are observing. Beyond words, the child and mother are engaged in a reciprocal exchange of wonderment and affect.

This process, explains one analyst, is recreated in therapy and becomes a valued treatment technique that *"helps a child—a toddler or a very young child—connect, relate, pay attention. . . . Finding ways to be calm and regulated in connection with another"* [LUB]. Using this approach, the analyst's goal is to try to *"find out who that child is, where he lives emotionally"* [LUB]. First, the analyst observes the child, and together they pay attention to the child's emotions and share in the experience together. There is curiosity about what is being talked about in the session, what the child is doing in the session, what the therapist and the child are doing together. This analyst explains the ADHD child's experience as being alone and isolated but it is the analyst's job to find a way in and begin to develop a shared experience:

> The child in an ADHD world is "buzzing" without anyone in it. So in order to make a difference, you find your way in. The process that I use to find my way in is nonintrusive, nondirective, and nonlabeling. That gives me an opportunity to be in there as a shared player or talker, whichever of the two things the child

can do—play and/or talk. Once we are in, we are in a shared place that can be a little malleable. [LUB]

In the session, the analyst may say *"You see that doggie? I see, oh, yeah, that's that doggie, we are both looking at it"* [LUB]. There is a belief that joint attention helps focus attention: *"Otherwise you [the child] are just looking around, and nobody gets you"* [LUB] and create a shared experience for the child that is *"not just 'buzz,' I [the therapist] see what you are talking about"* [LUB]. This ability of the therapist to "join" with the child grows the attention. The analyst and the child "look" together at his experiences. The analyst expresses an interest in him, and he no longer feels alone. This compassionate experience is in stark contrast to the customary response of annoyance that the child likely receives from others in his life.

Play Therapy: Psychodynamic Supportive Expressive Play Psychotherapy

Psychodynamic Supportive Expressive Play Psychotherapy (SEPP) (Eresund, 2007) is a somewhat manualized play-therapy approach used in treating ADHD children. During the early phase of treatment, the therapist focuses on the positive transference occurring between the therapist and the child. This work with transference is an especially important goal given ADHD children's sensitivity to rejection and given its importance in developing a therapeutic alliance with the child.

SEPP is a supportive therapy that encourages children's expressiveness. The therapist provides the play materials and suggests play activities, is empathic toward the children in her care, and is an active listener and observer of their play and verbalizations. The therapist makes facilitative comments directing the children's attention during the play. An essential component of this expressive intervention is to encourage children's self-reflection. They are asked to reflect on their thoughts, feelings, and behaviors, and the therapist makes comments that illuminate the connection between the three (Conway, 2012). Using this expressive approach, the therapist provides treatment that focuses on strengthening ego functions through educative and supportive interventions (for a full discussion of this intervention technique, see Conway, 2012).

OTHER PSYCHODYNAMIC TECHNIQUES

Dynamic approaches attempt to teach children about their inner lives. A therapist may want to draw pictures with a child that depict certain fundamental psychological concepts such as conflict, the unconscious, self-defeating behaviors, and so on. The analyst can also introduce metaphors that explain psychological concepts. For example, one analyst talked about using a layered cake to represent the unconscious mind, a tug-of-war to describe conflict, or a see-saw to express ambivalence. The goal is for the therapist to *"help the child develop enough psychological mindedness to work mentally on the issues related to the behavior, not just rely on behavioral interventions and strategies"* [MAC]. In explaining self-defeating behavior to a child, an analyst may approach the session like the following therapist, who describes making a picture with one child that depicted battles between armies. The therapist asked the child, *"Now what's going to happen if this army gives the other army all its weapons—and all its ammunition. Who's going to win?"* The analyst explains:

> That image [of the army] might allow the child to begin to understand some-thing about the impact of one's behavior and choices and so forth. Is it going to change behavior in and of itself? I don't know. But I still would try to do this kind of work because I think it will be growth-promoting. [MAC]

These kinds of intrapsychic changes are evaluated through changes in the client's responses to the Rorschach tests (Rorschach, 1942). For example, the analysis of Rorschach responses, such as the ones involving human move-ment and human content, allows the analyst to glean the presence of psychot-ic distortions. An analyst recalled that the Rorschach was regularly used to assess changes in the client's psychological processes during the course of therapy—*"for example, more human movement would be an indication of less psychotic thinking"* [LOM].

Figure 3.2 offers a graphical representation of relational issues and inter-ventions.

AN INTEGRATIVE MODEL FOR ADDRESSING EGO–ID AND EGO–SUPEREGO DIFFICULTIES

Current analytic thought about ADHD acknowledges that both the ego and relational aspects of children's psychological worlds contribute to ADHD symptomatology. Leuzinger-Bohleber and colleagues (2011) have expressed that ADHD is a "syndrome" shaped by disturbances in early object relations, ego- and self-development, and interpersonal family challenges. Like Leu-zinger-Bohleber, Gilmore (2002) stresses the importance of the interpersonal contributions to the ADHD symptom presentation. Regardless of the biologi-cal contributions, Gilmore asserts, the relational aspects of children's lives rest on the extent to which they distort basic ego capacities in the service of synthesizing and integrating their experiences. Moreover, she locates deficits in interpersonal relations in the realm of disturbances in superego develop-ment. In fact, Gilmore (2002) holds the view that children's ego deficits

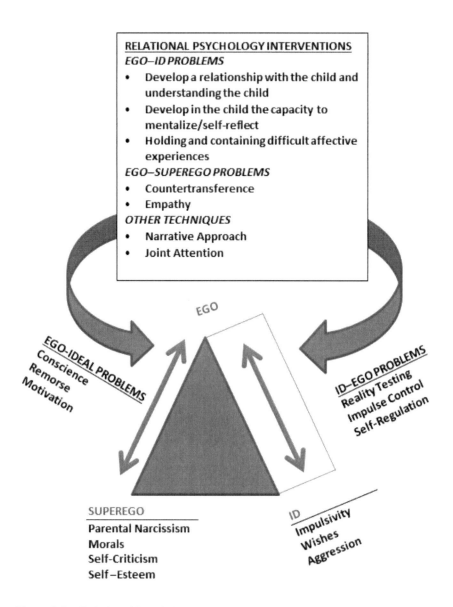

Figure 3.2. Relational Psychology Interventions

compound deficiencies in their object relations. Other notable analysts share this view that attentional difficulties originate from both ego deficits and primary object failures (Salomonsson, 2011; Sugarman, 2006). Despite this, ego functions continue to receive more attention than is typically granted to understanding the ADHD child's relational world. In this section, I will demonstrate how an integrative approach can contribute to research on both ends of that spectrum.

In brief, it appears that both ego psychologists and object relations theorists view the relationship with the primary object, usually the mother, as important. However, a central difference is in the primacy of that relationship to the child's ego and personality development. Those subscribing to an ego psychology approach believe the child is first in a state of primary narcissism, unable to differentiate the self from others, and the primary object relationship plays a secondary role in the child's development. Object relations theorists, on the other hand, believe the child's relationship with the mother is important very early on in the child's life (Ainsworth, 1969). Regardless of the stage in which children's relationships with their primary caregivers—typically their mothers—becomes necessary, both camps agree that at some point in their early development, children construct an internal representation of that external relationship that sets the template for their future relationships and psychological maturation.

Disciplinary allegiances aside, those treating children with ADHD agree that the disorder both originates and impacts both domains of children's functioning—ego development and interpersonal relations. For example, Leuzinger-Bohleber and colleagues' (2011) study of five hundred children led to the identification of seven subdomains of ADHD: organic brain problems, early emotional neglect, trauma, culture, mourning or depression, gifted child, and unavailable parent (see Leuzinger-Bohleber and Fischmann, 2010, in Conway, 2014). There are areas of overlap between relational factors—parental, familial, and peer relationships—along with biological and larger sociological contributors (Conway, 2015). Although the relational aspect of the child's functioning is not often in the forefront in relation to to concerns about academic performance and following rules, it is an important consideration even for those with an ego psychology orientation (Conway, 2015; Gilmore, 2002). If one were to ascribe the child's difficulties to the representative mental structures of the mind, one could attribute executive functioning deficits to the ego and relational challenges to the superego (Conway, 2015). Given the intricate matrix of relational and ego-developmental issues, a treatment model that address both of these aspects of the child's experience is necessary.

Fonagy refers to self-reflective abilities as having the capacity to *mentalize* (Fonagy, 2001; Fonagy and Target, 2002). The mentalization technique addresses the mostly traditional view of the ego as functioning in a way that negotiates id pressures as well as the (largely relational) ego/superego dynamics. Fonagy's research has demonstrated how relational deficits could result in ADHD-related behaviors, and he links the importance of children's relational world to ego functioning. For example, the caregiver relationship has been shown to shape the development of a range of ego–id capabilities in

children, including self-regulation of mental functions such as attention, behavior inhibition, and intensity of emotional experiences. Therefore, children
with impairments in self-regulation would benefit from treatment designed to
improve their self-reflective capacities.

Cycles of frustration and anger often characterize the ADHD child's relational world. Interacting with the ADHD child can leave one frustrated and at
times enraged at the child's seemingly impenetrable disposition. These feelings are only inflamed by the fact that the child, in what appears to be a self-
focused state, does not seem to share the same level of concern about his own
behavior. Parents, teachers, and peers are often unable to empathize with the
ADHD child's plight and may even view him as showing a lack of remorse
or as being unable to learn from his mistakes.

It is this particular dynamic that has led to my curiosity regarding the role
of empathy in the ADHD disorder and my belief that mentalization can be
useful in fostering the development of understanding. As mentioned previously, ADHD children struggle to meet their ego ideal, resulting in depression and anxiety or oppositional behaviors and conduct problems. They also
seem to struggle with other ego-ideal-related concerns such as appearing to
lack a conscience or to show remorse for their "misbehaviors." It is my belief
that empathy, which is the basis for mentalization and self-reflection, is at a
deficit in ADHD children.

In my own review of psychoanalytic case studies on ADHD, analysts
advocated the importance of empathy in the treatment of ADHD children.
Empathy was an essential component of treatment in three of the psychoanalytic approaches I reviewed in that paper (Conway, 2012; Eresund, 2007;
Gilmore, 2000; Hopkins, 2000). Analysts exhibit empathy toward the child
through mirroring and reflecting the child's feelings, techniques that have
been shown to improve children's self-regulatory capacity (Conway, Oster,
and Szymanski, 2011). In addition, analysts' expression of empathy allows
their patients to reflect and monitor affective states including short temper,
aggression, and anxiety (Gilmore, 2000; Nathan, 1992).

Technique: Developing the Child's Capacity to Mentalize/Self-Reflect

ADHD children have difficulty with self-regulation and accepting reality.
Earlier in the chapter, the concept of working to improve children's recognition and awareness of their own mental states and those of others was introduced as being possible through working with the transference process. In
this section, I will elaborate on techniques used to develop the capacity to
mentalize in the therapy session, but first, a brief introduction is warranted.
Fonagy and Target (1996) conceptualize mentalization as a psychological
process that allows individuals to be able to implicitly and explicitly interpret

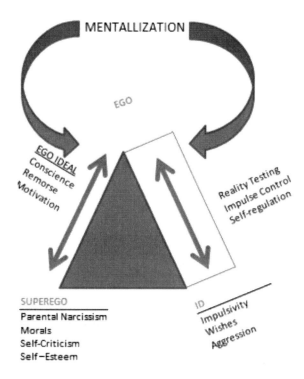

Figure 3.3. Mentalization of Ego and Object Relations Concerns

their own and others' actions in meaningful ways (Conway, Oster, and Szymanski, 2011). During the mentalization proces the individual must be able to access their own intentional mental states by reflecting on their personal desires, needs, feelings, beliefs, and reasons (Fonagy and Target, 1996; 2002). The mentalization process, albeit a complex one, is constructed through a matrix of affective and interpersonal understanding of oneself and others. This matrix serves as an internal compass for the development of a coherent sense of self and for navigating the social world effectively (see Conway, Oster, and Szymanski, 2011). Simply put, the ability to mentalize means to be able to read another's mind in order to predict that person's behavior in meaningful ways (Fonagy and Target, 1998). Figure 3.3 offers a graphical representation of mentalization's potential to address object relations concerns.

The therapist's capacity to mentalize a child, then, allows them to make transference interpretations about that child's mental state. As children learn to understand other people's behavior, they learn to adapt to different situations and be flexible in their responses. This ability to explore their experiences underlies "affect regulation, impulse control, self-monitoring, and the experience of self-agency" (Fonagy and Target, 1998, p. 92). The ability to mentalize is deficient in children diagnosed with ADHD and cannot yet be addressed fully in behavioral or pharmacological therapy.

Based on this theory, it can be deduced that children with ADHD have not developed the ability to manipulate or understand themselves or others within their environment, and these deficits result in poor emotion regulation and impulsivity. Children with poor mentalization or self-reflective abilities are literally unable to stop themselves and think rationally about the logical next move. Instead, they go about their lives using deficient tools—such as fixed attributions and fixed stereotypes—to make meaning (Conway, Oster, and McCarthy, 2010).

Case Vignettes: A Note on Methodology

Across the remaining chapters, I will present several vignettes that provide examples of analytical techniques. They are presented to give some insight into the treating analysts' thoughts. I will provide some information on the analysts' approach and the theorists that shaped their approach to therapy with ADHD children. During the interviews, analysts were asked questions about case conceptualization; they identified underlying intrapsychic issues relevant to ADHD symptoms and discussed case examples that demonstrated their interventions. I informed all analysts of Standard 4.07 of the *Code of Ethics for Psychologists*, "Use of Confidential Information for Didactic or Other Purposes." In keeping with that standard, psychologists, prior to discussing case materials for the purpose of this research study, were informed of the standard and asked to refrain from disclosing the identity of their clients. All analysts interviewed took "reasonable steps to disguise the person" they discussed with me. (More information on this standard can be found at http://www.apa.org/ethics/code.)

Case Vignette: Emma

In this vignette, an analyst [MER] describes an impulsive child with a reduced ability to self-regulate.

  Presenting Issues

> Let me tell you a little bit about a girl that I see who is now eleven, I've been seeing her since she was ten. I see her three times a week, and she has a very complicated history. She is an adopted child. She's got some special needs in addition to the ADD, so she is kind of delayed across the board, not in terms of oral self-expression, but all of her academics are delayed. Emma was brought into treatment, to put it bluntly, because she has been "driving her mother insane." This was the main referral issue.

She is a kind of a restless, overactive kid with a short fuse, but then things seemed to be getting worse around the age of ten. Her mother, a single mother, was feeling that she was very frightened about what was going to happen when Emma experienced puberty. They had tried a couple of short-term treatments, two extensive CBT treatments, and Emma was already on medication, Adderall. When she came to see me, the mother had been trying to address these issues for several years. In addition to whatever neurobiological contributions there was, Emma also had the first eighteen months of her life in pre-adoption, where she experienced some deprivation. Much of her biological history is unknown.

Part of Emma's difficulties is her problem shifting or being flexible. She'll start doing something, she'll keep doing it, you know, it does look very compulsive and obsessional after a while. I actually think a lot of ADD children use a little bit of obsessionality to sort of slow them down. It's almost like it's a self-correction act, and she comes off looking quite rigid.

Peer Relationships

Emma has had enormous problems with making friends and also just kind of regulating herself. Some of her difficulties may be due to her lack of personal space; she is very invasive. She has settled down at school. I have a lot of contact with the school. We have meetings with them a couple of times a year, and I also see the mother pretty frequently.

As Emma gets older, she has more experiences of her peers as intolerant and harsh. And it's very hard for her. She is right in the middle of that right now. She is just at that age when it is so important to have that sense of connection and wants to belong. She is having a lot of difficulties. Her teachers have described to me many times that they try to help Emma. It's a special-needs school, so they do a lot of social intervention; they try to kind of scaffold for her a little bit and arrange things where she "just happens to be" paired with a very nice girl. The other part of it is the child's personality, which is just as influential as the ADD. She is a very masochistic child, not surprisingly given her origins. She sabotages a lot of her efforts. For example, she'll start to make friends, and then she'll find herself doing something really annoying. For example, she will go after the kid a million times, or she'll pull them. She is very impulsive—recruiting ADD behavior in the service of self-sabotage. Very complicated. She is at that point where there are a lot of crucial developmental milestones that aren't quite coming together.

Relationship with Her Mother

Emma's mother works a lot and travels extensively. They have a very stimulating life, but with a lot of continuities. I see the babysitter there, the weekend babysitter, you know, everyone kind of comes in, which is, I think, helpful. In terms of her relationship with her mother, Emma is very needy, demanding of her mother, furious with the mother and bossy towards her mother. She can be very nasty at times.

Frequency of Sessions

> I initially worked with the child twice a week, and then persuaded the mother
> to get involved in an additional session, so it's more of an analytic treatment at
> this point.

Behavior in Session

> She is a very zippy young girl . . . adorable. I mean, you can barely keep your
> eyes on her because she is so all over the place motorically, very much one of
> those kids whose response to everything is zip, zip, zip.

Intervention

In the session, the analyst models this capacity to mentalize through shar-
ing reflective thoughts about the child's behavior with the child. For example, just based on observation, in a typical session with an ADHD child, the
analyst describes:

> a little girl going zip, zip, zip, from one activity to another. . . . The room is,
> like, destroyed by the end, and me [analyst] kind of active verbally, but not
> motorically active, and constantly trying to understand what the narrative here
> is? A kind of narrative building. Trying to make mentalization-type links
> between the feelings and actions, "Oh, I think you were feeling this way, and I
> think maybe that's why you all of a sudden dumped two Barbies on the floor
> and headed for the stuffed animal."

The analyst maintains a verbally active stance as attempts are made to connect feelings to behaviors.

Treatment Effectiveness

> I try to assess it partly based on what's going on in the treatment, but partly
> based on whether or not her life seems to be getting better. What has hap-
> pened? What the teachers have described to me, which, I think, has been a
> significant benefit of the treatment, is that she is learning more. She has be-
> come more available for learning. She is less distracted by her inner life and
> her neediness. She is more open to learning novel things in the classroom. So
> they are finding that she is advancing in terms of her academic levels. She is
> much more able to focus without changes in medication. She is just more
> open. She is not constantly needing reassurance or having to self-soothe. I
> think, and I don't know if this has more to do with my work with the mother or
> due to the treatment. It is probably some combination. Her mother is also
> reporting that life is better. It's a little more predictable that she can calm the
> child down at the end of the day. There is a bit more of a sense of her internal
> life. Life is somewhat less disordered. The atmosphere at home is a little
> settled down, but, you know, there are still lots of bad days.

A PSYCHODYNAMIC THEORETICAL
PERSPECTIVE ON CHANGE

Therapists usually have definite views on what helps a client to grow and change. Analysts agree that developing a relationship with the children they treat is an important first step in the children's ability to benefit from the treatment they receive (Fonagy and Target, 1994; Salomonsson, 2011). They are also likely to progress in their treatment when the therapist can work deeply to address transference occurrences in the therapeutic relationship (Cione et al., 2011). During the therapeutic session, therapists' verbalizations can be helpful in organizing the children they treat (Gilmore, 2005), and their attention to the child's mental processes (Gensler, 2011) can be transformative.

Parallel responsiveness to their therapists' efforts indicates that children are making progress. Their ability to develop a relationship with the therapist is a good first step. Another sign of progress is seen as children expand their capacity to use their experience of the therapeutic relationship both to inform other areas of their lives and to better regulate their emotions (Hopkins, 2000; Leuzinger-Bohleber et al., 2011; Orford, 1998). Being able to control their behavior and emotions positions children to make changes based on their increasing ability to mentalize—that is, to make meaning of their own and others' mental states (Conway et al., 2011; Fonagy and Target, 1996). These changes are accomplished through a long-term intensive dynamic therapy ranging from two to three years (Fonagy and Target, 1994; Hopkins, 2000). Other components of therapy facilitating change require the therapist works to develop the child's ego functions and collaborate with the family/parent to support positive psychotherapy outcomes.

Case Vignette: Analyst SAP

Analyst Background Analyst SAP's work is influenced by an ego psychologist, Rudolf Ekstein (1912–2005), author of the book *Children of Time and Space, of Action and Impulse* (1966). Ekstein's work captures a primary ego-functioning deficit in ADHD children—their relationship to time and space. Although the etiology is unclear, SAP has come to accept that some children are biologically predisposed to these difficulties in self-regulatory coping mechanisms. Heavily influenced by Fonagy, SAP believes ADHD children need to develop their capacity to reflect; thus, Fonagy's therapeutic intervention, mentalization, is a main approach implemented in SAP's work. SAP marries this object-relational view with an ego psychological one that focuses on ego functions. With regard to that ego psychology perspective, SAP's understanding of children exhibiting ADHD symptoms is that they lack the control mechanisms to regulate themselves. It is his opinion that ADHD children's main difficulties lie in their inability:

> to reflect on their experiences, draw conclusions on their experiences, use their skills to decide what they are going to do and plan ahead—that could be called executive functions, and, to use a poetic word, they cannot use their experiences in their own mind, so to speak. [SAP]

Therapeutic change occurs gradually as children develop the ability to reflect on the meaning behind their actions. Since ADHD children typically have accumulated years of frustration and years of small to relatively moderate failures by the time they come to a therapist, they are often highly reactive. The therapeutic goal is to diminish the child's reactivity and increase their ability to soothe themselves.

> Since these are kids of action, so to speak, they move, and the change gradually helps them to reflect, to see meaning in their acts. To see that their actions often reflect something more than just random acts—it's not just an empty impulse. There is something behind the impulse. [SAP]

Background SAP sees a ten-year-old boy in therapy once each week. The boy has divorced parents and has been experiencing difficulties in his academic performance. He has been held back for a year in the school he attends. The boy was referred to SAP for treatment because his mother felt that her son had become increasingly agitated, and although he was on medication and had been in therapy in the past, he did not seem to be making any progress. The boy was under the care of a neurologist, who assesses him regularly. The parents disagreed on the child's treatment needs. His father believed his son's problems were a figment of his mother's imagination. He attributes any difficulties his son may have to the mother's poor parenting. The father, who is an authoritarian and threatening parent, reports no problems when his son visits him. Although the father tried to convince the child not to participate in the treatment, the child was quickly engaged in the therapy.

Symptoms ADHD symptoms that the therapist focused on included the child's ego functions of inattention, organizing, and planning. They also worked on the most symbolic level of engagement: to create a meaningful narrative or play experience.

> [His] attention span was very low. He also displayed some other characteristics, like he would ask a question and if the response were a little long he would tune out—it was almost as if the answer didn't matter, he only wanted a quick response, "yes," "no," "you can have it." Any activity could not last more than two to three minutes. And most of the activities that would keep him somewhat involved were the activities with immediate feedback, you

know, like slamming something ten to fifteen times, playing with a ball and hitting it harder and harder and harder, but in terms of planning and thinking, and creating a play narrative, all of these pieces were missing. So in a sense I felt that this was a very confused kid who could not create meaning in a playroom. I have a very nice playroom, and he could not find anything to create a meaningful moment, a meaningful, playful moment. At the same time, this was a very sweet kid, with kind of an angelic face. So there was a stark contrast between a very sweet kid and one who was completely lost when he was left to his own devices. [SAP]

Goal of Treatment Overall the therapist was interested in the child's capacity to engage in mental processes. Developing a meaningful relationship with the therapist and moving from more impulsive and reactive play activities to play that is more organized were also therapeutic goals.

To assess his capacity to organize a little bit the room, the play, his capacity to narrate, to create a story, his capacity to reflect, his interest and curiosity in me and what I do, his capacity to engage with me—beyond the slapstick, the impulsive bantering—and I am interested to see from session to session whether I can see a change. So in the first session the kid can be much more uptight. "What happens to the next and the third and the fourth session, was he a different child?" Last, I am very keen on assessing the kid at the end or in the middle: "Can he organize the room on command?" so to speak, and that's important, meaning what? Meaning, as he is picking up one activity—the beads are on the floor and then he wants to take the strings and some clay, and I say to him, "let's put the beads away because there will be a mess in the end, and we will be stepping on things": "Can he do that?" I'm helping him—he is not by himself—but, "Can he do that?" If he can do that, there is impulsivity, but there is no overt opposition at least, and that makes for a smoother trajectory, a smoother process down the road; this is a less angry kid. [SAP]

Early Sessions During the first sessions, SAP is interested in creating opportunities to engage the child and explore with him any activities or interests he may have. SAP uses these early sessions to demonstrate to the child that in his absence, he is thought of and remembered by his therapist.

When they first come to my office, the task first is to kind of soothe them by creating a space for them, by offering a space for them, so I would not expect, I would not rely on the child to pick out the activities, but I would suggest activities to him. I would notice something about what he was interested in and I would take a plane, a paper plane, and I would make sure that next time I would say to him, "I saw that the last time you were interested in the paper plane. I brought three or four paper planes in case you were curious to see other paper planes." It was more an attempt of mine to provide him with something. To make him interested. But that's on the surface level. On a deeper level, I wanted to convey two messages. One is that he was held in my mind, that I thought of him and that what he did the previous session mattered to me. And I thought those were very important experiences for him to have. From that I could then expand and either [having him] play with his planes or play with something else. [SAP]

Behavior in Sessions This excerpt describes the child's active and impulsive behavior during the session.

> He is in the room. He cannot stop. He basically cannot play. He goes from activity to activity. He picks up whatever he picks, and he then drops it. It's a book. It's a toy. It's a puzzle. Clay. Everything becomes a mishmash. So I feel like the more he does that, the more agitated he becomes. The more I find myself trying to stop him, and he says, "Can I, can I, can I step on the door? Can I step on the table? Can I climb here? Can I pick that? O, can I break this? And I find myself one way or the other trying to stop him. The risk involved here is that I end up becoming for twenty to twenty-five minutes the person who keeps saying to him, "no, no, don't, stop, no!" And so he hears the no's that he hears everywhere else. He will also get me agitated. So the more no's he hears, the more agitated I become, and the more agitated he becomes. It's a repeat, a repeat of the same story—same old, same old. [SAP]

Intervention The main intervention was to develop the child's capacity to self-reflect through SAP's reflection to the child of what the process has been thus far in the session. Admittedly, it is challenging for analysts to themselves maintain their capacity to be reflective, especially in the face of a child presenting with ADHD symptoms. The child is experienced as demanding of the analyst's attention. SAP agrees it can be a challenge to maintain one's reflective stance, which could be easily depleted by the client's impulsivity. The inclination to respond by setting limits on the child is tempting. In order to resist this temptation, SAP is required to shift from an automatic way of responding—that is, by setting limits—to a more compassionate response.

> I think it is very challenging, and many times I find myself slipping, but what has helped me tremendously is that I have it in my mind: "Be careful. This kid will walk in, and he can sway me to the left or the right, and I have to be alert." [SAP]

SAP actively avoids directing the child toward any activity, but rather becomes more self-observant and self-monitoring so as to avoid behaving in ways that may be nonbeneficial.

> I feel like this kid needs something else. He needs the ability to reflect on what's happening because he is not aware of what he is enacting with me, what reactions he triggers from me and what reactions he causes within himself. So finally when I collect myself, I say to him, "Have you noticed that for the last twenty minutes all I'm saying to you is 'don't-don't-don't'?" He surprises me

by saying, "Yes," and then, of course joking, "No shit." And then he settles, and he offers to play a game of chess. [SAP]

SAP advocates for the importance of the analyst in maintaining a reflective stance toward the child, but he admits this is a challenge. A child's activity can distract a therapist from maintaining a therapeutic reflective stance. In those instances, the therapist fails the child, and the child experiences a failure in reestablishing how to be in the therapy.

> He is just coming back from a three-month hiatus because of the summer, so it's all new to him. He hasn't established yet his pace, his rhythm. I only see him once a week, so there is nothing ongoing. We had some projects the year before that he was working on, and he would come ready to work on them, and now there is nothing—he has to recreate that. And the second part is for me to be able to reflect much sooner the state of mind that he is in and invite him to reflect on his own act as well. Surprisingly, whenever I've done that with him . . . he responds, he responds very quickly, but it's so hard to have the presence of mind to talk like that when he is so, so active . . . through their acts, [children with ADHD] also deplete us from our own capacity to reflect. So important in working with them is kind of maintaining our, the importance of maintaining a reflective stance, which we can easily lose because of their impulsivity. [SAP]

When SAP takes an active stance toward the treatment, often the child will join the narrative and correct him if he seems off track. This process of thinking about the child's experience and verbalizing his sense of what the child may also be experiencing serves a regulatory function of containing difficult emotions the child may be experiencing. This containing function is important:

> because the child cannot do it. They need the containing—our containing functions. In this case, the containing is for us to be able to imagine them, to reflect, to think and adjust our stance. [SAP]

SAP views the child's active behavior as a defensive response to difficult interpersonal interactions that have been marked by a *cycle of negativity and reactivity* from which he has difficulty extricating himself. It is this dynamic that leads others in the child's life to attempt to manage his behaviors by seeking medication or other behavioral treatments.

> I believe this kid may have been agitated coming into the session—the father might have called, he had a fight with the Mom, or he asked for something. He is a very sensitive kid, but he never expresses his sensitivity the way another kid would express it. He would express it afterward. Like, just one statement of mine was enough for him to settle down and play chess with me. That's a tremendously sensitive response, but in terms of him coming and saying "You

know, I'm not in the mood today. Can we do something else?" or "I'm upset because of what happened," he cannot do that. He would come in agitated, and of course he would get the opposite of what he needs. He needs a soothing presence, but because he comes in a state of agitation, he gets more agitation as a response. [SAP]

Children's behaviors, even those generally thought to be problematic, can be transformed if a therapist is able to engage them, even playfully, in reflecting on their experiences. Activities they engage in can be made more *"meaningful and playful, and directed, and . . . creative"* [SAP]. SAP describes a behavior where the child locked the bathroom door repeatedly, along with his own efforts to get the child to reflect on his conduct.

When he first came, after the third or the fourth session, I am opening the waiting room, then he is coming out of the bathroom and he stares at me, and he is kind of shaken, and he has locked the bathroom door for the guests. The door is only locked from the inside, so in a sense he locked it from the inside and walked out. And no one could go in, and the water was running in the sink, and you could hear the ventilating system. And the mother was horrified, and the kid was staring at me. But I know the drill—I have a little screwdriver, and I opened it.

So the following week, as I am opening the door to welcome him in, he is coming out of the bathroom, and he pauses right there at the door, and I ask him "you are not going to do it again, are you?" And he laughs and then closes the door. And of course he has done it again. And the mother goes "No!" and I laugh with the mother and say, "Well, we'll do the screwdriver routine." And I give him the screwdriver.

Third session, as he is leaving, exiting my playroom, I lean over and say, "Don't forget your goodbye move." And he stares at me in a surprised way, and then he nods and goes quickly to the bathroom, and afterwards, he, of course, locked the bathroom. He is not doing it anymore, but it's like that, turning the moment of impulsivity, confusion, thoughtlessness, and making it into a playful encounter, so that can be reflected upon. [SAP]

Transference SAP uses the child's behavior toward him, and his own behavior toward the child, to address transference occurring in the session. SAP acknowledges the child's frustration and anger at experiencing multiple failures (even failure at interpersonal interactions).

The child's behavior:

Even the child I'm describing now—who is angelic—he tries to smack me playfully. But he is a strong kid, so his playful smacks, a little punch, a little push, and I think there is some bottled anger and frustration. [SAP]

Therapist verbalization:

Doesn't it make you mad to have a grown-up like me always say "no" to you? For twenty minutes I am saying "no." [SAP]

SAP's willingness to explore these transference processes during treatment spares the child from having to resort to *"overt acts of anger, like quitting school or not going to school, not reading, fighting with peers"* [SAP].

Conflict Conflict is viewed in an interpersonal sense as the child's difficulty in feeling a sense of belonging. Influenced by analysts such as Shirley Truckle, Catherine Mathelin, and Björn Salomonsson, SAP explained that children can feel as though they are *"of no consequence or . . . of negative consequence"* [SAP]. These feelings, compounded by the child's efforts to seek out a sense that they matter, are often conflicted and confusing for the child.

> I was never convinced by the psychodynamic literature, early literature on conflicts—you know, oedipal conflicts—it never fully clicked with me. I always felt that the conflict that these kids experience is the conflict that they have with placing themselves in the world and feeling agency, feeling kind of productive in the world. . . . But of not being wanted, of not actually being valued, of not being welcomed, if you want, by their peers, by their teachers, and they are very aware of that. So being that there is this conflict that they have from early on, they sense that something is missing, but they cannot engage with it and actively change it. And that, I think, creates even more conflicts because they seek what they miss. [SAP]

SAP was also influenced by the French analyst Renë Kaeś (2007), who centralizes three elements of psychoanalysis—the speech or the act that is desired, the symptom, and the imagination—in a way that SAP is able to draw upon in capturing the experience of the ADHD children he works with.

> We get caught in the symptom and their speech. Everything is the symptom. Even the treatment, even the way you conceptualize their classroom problems, everything, what they do and what I told them to do and what they didn't do. So what's missing almost entirely is—from their part and our part—the capacity to imagine, to kind of think in these potentials and to see that in them. And so in that sense they are really, they end up missing something that many non-ADHD kids get from us. [SAP]

SAP works to avoid becoming stuck in a view of the child as a symptom. Toward that end, the ability to "hold" the child in his imagination—to mentalize—is a crucial component of his intervention. Children who lack the capacity to mentalize are prone to difficulties in emotion regulation, which can result in depression and anxiety.

How to enable them to become more imaginative and for us to imagine them. . . . It's sad because I think it speaks of profound loneliness—which can fuel more agitation, by the way. I feel like a lot of these kids would be more agitated. And I think adolescents may become moody, and then we talk about comorbidity—ADHD and depression. And I think the more sensitive kids that I know, they may also be very anxious, and they would hide their anxiety in two ways, either by withdrawing or become more agitated. [SAP]

Progress in Therapy SAP felt that seeing the child only once each week created a disjointed experience for the child and that a twice-weekly treatment schedule would have been optimal. However, despite the constraints, after six months of treatment, there were some noticeable changes in the child's ability to be more reflective. Keeping in mind that SAP's overall goal was to change the way the child experiences himself and the world, and the way he makes sense of himself, a longer-term therapy would be appropriate. Nonetheless, in the relatively short space of time that elapsed between the beginning of SAP's sessions with the child and the time of our interview (six months), there were some observable changes in the child.

> I see changes in a sense. Before the summer break, I saw changes. He was making drawings on a blackboard, and usually it was one monster, and the monster was becoming progressively less monstrous from session to session. . . . It was his goodbye drawings, gradually less ferocious and disgusting at the same time, it was almost like a nice blob, which is how the boy I think felt—cuddly, not formless, but cuddly.
>
> And something was emerging—I see it now—that he started to ask me questions: "What do you think of that?" or "Who's the other person?" He has begun to notice changes in my office and ask me "Why?" I have a new colleague who uses an office in my suite, and he asks, "Who is this person? How long has he been here?" Now, three, four, six months ago he would never have—he would have noticed, but he wouldn't have had the presence of the mind to ask, "Why?" Because he would not have expected any answers or because he would not have felt comfortable or confident enough to ask me these questions. And, of course, the interesting question is what he asks afterward: "Do you like him?" Which is, I think, is a transference question: "Do you like me?" [SAP]

These capacities to notice others and reflect on one's experiences directly contribute to less impulsivity and hyperactivity. The child begins to take the time to consider his experiences, and there is less need to act out.

> I think I am offering them the desire, in some capacity, to make sense out of their acts, and this is something that they are missing, and this is something invaluable, and something that they really need in their lives and their exchanges with others. If I am not there for this kid, well, the side of this kid that is sensitive, that makes sense, would not be engaged and would not be advo-

cated. He needs that from me, I think. He needs that from his teachers also. [SAP]

SUMMARY

A psychodynamic approach attempts to place children's experiences at the center of their treatment. It is a compassionate approach in which therapists work respectfully with children to validate and understand their points of view. It is this process of shared and co-constructed experiences that sets the stage for the therapeutic work to occur. This chapter looked at psychodynamic interventions with ADHD children. I presented interventions orientated toward both ego psychology and object-relations approaches as well as an integrated model that addresses both ego–id and ego–superego issues. The chapter ends with a case example of an analyst's reports on therapy with a ten-year-old boy that demonstrates some of the techniques discussed in the chapter.

CHAPTER HIGHLIGHTS

A predominate characteristic of psychodynamic psychotherapy interventions is the therapist's ability to maintain the focus of treatment on the child's inner experiences rather than on external behaviors. To maintain this focus requires the therapist to be in touch with their deep sense of compassion for the plight of the child with ADHD. Such a focus on children's internal experiences—as they contend with the demands of the external—provides an opportunity for them to begin to heal and lead psychologically healthier lives.

- The first part of the chapter introduces *therapeutic interventions* informed by analysts' interviews and my clinical knowledge. Recommendations focusing on three main interventions that inform therapists on their appropriate (1) therapeutic disposition; and (2) the use of ego psychological/developmental; and (3) relational techniques and interventions are discussed.

    1. The psychodynamic *therapist's disposition* is informed by a belief in the unconscious and therefore the therapist's goal is threefold:

        - Creating opportunities for unconscious processes to be a part of the therapeutic effort;
        - Considering the role of the unconscious in her conceptualization of the child's problems; and

- Presenting herself in a manner that reveals unconscious processes.

2. *Ego psychology interventions* focus on ego functioning and development with attention to the ego's ability to defend against anxiety caused by primitive id impulses or superego ideal and reality. Therapist interventions include (see figure 3.1):

- Understanding how the ego defends against anxiety—ADHD behaviors as viewed as a defense employed to cope with stress resulting from managing inappropriate impulses and coping with ego-ideal failings.
- Integrating the child's primitive wishes into current ego functions—access immature wishes and facilitate reality through the use of transference.
- The use of empathy in resolving ego-ideal failures—the therapist strives for both *intellectual empathy*—that is, accuracy in understanding the child's perspective—and *empathic emotions*—compassionate responses toward the child's thoughts and feelings.
- The therapist's adoption of auxiliary ego functions on behalf of the child—the therapist stands in for the child in those situations where the child's abilities are limited, assuming functions such as paying attention on the child's behalf and reflecting these observations to the child when appropriate.

3. *Relational interventions* focus on developing a relationship with and understanding the child, holding and containing difficult affective experiences the child encounters, developing in the child the capacity to self-reflect, working with countertransference, using a narrative approach, and working with joint attention. Empathy and transference are also considered relational interventions.

- The second part of the chapter presents an *integrative model of the mind* that includes the relations between ego, id, and superego and depicts interventions that target specific ADHD problems.

1. Therapists must balance their therapeutic attention to the child's ego functions equally with attention to understanding the ADHD child's relational world.
2. The use of mentalization techniques addresses both aspects—ego functioning and interpersonal relations—of the child's functioning and facilitates the development of the child's capacity for empathy and self-regulation.

- The chapter concludes with a brief discussion on the psychodynamic theoretical perspective on therapeutic change in the ADHD child. Change is facilitated by the success of the therapist-child dyad in developing a therapeutic relationship and working through transference issues and increasing self-reflective capacities to achieve better self-regulation in the child, ego strengthening, and development leading to behavior change.

Chapter Four

Psychodynamic Psychotherapy of ADHD

Treatment Guidelines

While some of the analysts I interviewed expressed a preference for a particular theoretical orientation—ego psychology or relational—most recognized the need for an integration of other disciplines in order to treat Attention Deficit Hyperactivity Disorder (ADHD) adequately. The main areas of integration included neuropsychology, child-developmental theories, and psychoanalysis. According to one analyst, *"I have an integrated way of understanding people, certainly highly psychodynamic and psychoanalytically informed, but also very neuropsychologically informed and developmental, so, and I think about people from a lot of different theoretical orientations"* [HUG]. ADHD is heterogeneous in its etiology, symptom manifestation, and responsiveness to treatment. As such, therapists are challenged to cast a broad net in their assessment and treatment of the disorder. *"[ADHD] is a very complicated, multidimensional problem that requires a variety of models and an open-minded, integrative perspective"* [HUG]. Therefore, analysts working with ADHD children in a dynamic way must also fully consider the child's developmental stage along with any possible neurological contributors to their condition.

I have argued that psychoanalytic theory can make a significant contribution to the treatment of ADHD. As discussed in previous chapters, the possibilities for what ails children with ADHD are many, ranging from insults at the interpersonal level to scores of environmental, biological, and psychological factors. The current behavioral understanding of ADHD is limited, and behavioral treatments fail to address some of the broader psychological processes that have gone awry in ADHD children's experiences of themselves and others. Even within the small body of literature that focuses on treating ADHD children from a psychodynamic perspective, it is clear that analysts tend to view the symptoms and treatment of ADHD exclusively through their own particular theoretical lens. This bias among psychoanalytic treating professionals has led to certain aspects of children's problems being more or less the focus of their treatment depending not on how central those aspects are to their particular case but depending instead on their analyst's orientation.

I refer to the well-known metaphor of blind men trying to describe an elephant. Neuropsychologists, developmental theorists, behavioral theorists, nutritionists, sociologists, and yes, even psychoanalysts are all part of this phenomenon, all trying to describe the elephant as they "see" it. For the analytic part of the ADHD zeitgeist, there is an urgent need to advocate for these children and help society and all concerned with ADHD treatment understand their plight. The continued outrage and anger expressed toward ADHD children—absorbed even as treatment professionals continue to fail them—necessitates a perspective that values the child's internal functioning *as well as* their external. Indeed, work with ADHD children should be collaborative and comprehensive. Such a model highlights children's inner worlds—their experience of themselves and of themselves in the world. Taking into consideration all that these children brings to the table in terms of their biological dispositions, developmental stages, and sociocultural histories, the therapist plays a crucial role as an advocate for these children and a coordinator of *all* of their experiences of themselves.

AN INTEGRATED PSYCHODYNAMIC MODEL OF TREATMENT

Although I presented parts of this model in detail throughout this book, it is important to give the complete model in a summary form (see figure 4.1).

Symptoms of ADHD include symptoms primarily classified into two broad categories: inattention and hyperactivity. Symptoms of inattention include difficulty paying close attention, sustaining attention, and listening when spoken to; difficulty following through, finishing tasks, organizing tasks, and keeping track of things; failing to give close attention to details; avoiding tasks that require sustained mental effort; losing things; and being easily distracted and forgetful in daily activities. Symptoms of hyperactivity include fidgeting; difficulty remaining seated; excessive movement, such as running about or climbing in inappropriate situations; inability to engage in leisure tasks quietly; a tendency to be "on the go" and act as if "driven by a motor"; talking excessively; blurting out answers before questions are completed; difficulty waiting for his or her turn; and interrupting or intruding on others. Children with ADHD often present with comorbid disorders including both internalizing disorders—over-controlled behaviors resulting in depression and anxiety—or externalizing disorders—under-controlled behaviors resulting in diagnoses such as conduct disorder and oppositional defiant disorder.

A psychodynamic approach establishes the individual etiology of the child being treated for ADHD. According to Salomonsson (2004), the psychoanalytic method makes salient "the interactional experience unique to the individual" (p. 121). Unlike other approaches, the strength of this approach is the ability it gives the therapist to understand the child and the unique contributors to her particular difficulties. This approach does not seek to generalize about the experiences of all ADHD children but aims to understand the experience of the individual. For efficiency, the psychodynamic conceptualization of ADHD is presented in a summary format. It is important to keep in mind that these are lists of possible contributors and that each child has unique circumstances.

A psychodynamic conceptualization of the etiology of ADHD-related behaviors includes a view of ADHD children as having experienced disruptions in early attachment; neurobiological insults; trauma and complex trauma; and impingements in the maternal, school, and broader sociocultural environments. As a result of these circumstances, children experience many difficulties underlying their manifestations of inattention and hyperactivity. The three top areas of difficulties resulting in ADHD symptom expression are (1) intrapsychic, (2) cognitive–biological, and (3) relational. Intrapsychic issues are those conflicts that occur within the child's developing psyche. ADHD children are particularly distressed by conflict between internal urges and external demands or reality. They have a poor self-concept and poor view of themselves and have difficulty with self-regulation and with regulating their emotions—particularly with overwhelming feelings of shame and aggression. Their symptoms adversely impact their interpersonal worlds. Children with ADHD experience problematic relationships with their peers, parents, and teachers; often feel isolated in their families, and are often stigmatized. On a more cognitive level, the child experiences deficits in executive-functioning skills such as motivation, learning, reality testing, and memory, and they may demonstrate changes in brain structures and other biologically determined disorders. Many psychoanalytic theories, especially ego-developmental and relational theories, have contributed to our understanding of how the ego functions develop in children in ways that are particularly relevant for the treatment of ADHD children.

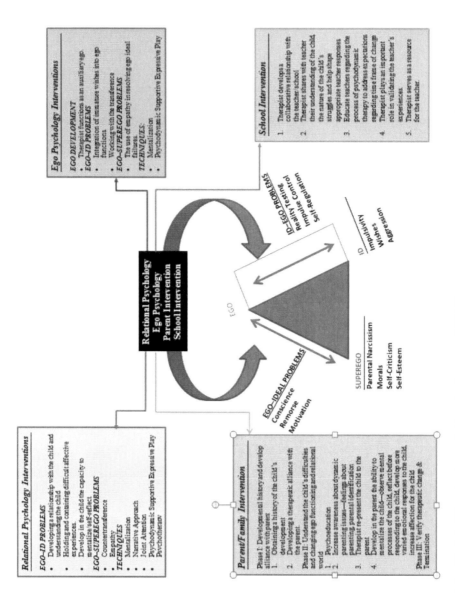

Figure 4.1.   Model of Psychodynamic Psychotherapy of ADHD

To begin to address the ADHD child's difficulties, it is necessary for her therapist to have an all-encompassing stance that takes into account her dispositional contributors (temperament, ego deficits, immature ego, and neurological vulnerabilities) as well as the impact they have on the child's interpersonal world. Psychoanalysts are interested in the child's psychological processes, which occur in the structures of the mind. Using Sigmund Freud's tripartite structure of the mind as representational of the mind's organization, the child's difficulties can be conceptualized on this unconscious level as problems resulting from ego–id and ego–superego activities. As such, therapeutic interventions must be appropriately organized to target these areas of the child's psychological experiences. Analysts also recognize that beyond the child's intrapsychic world is an external world of significant others, parents, and teachers who provide a context for the child's experience of herself. Therefore, interventions are not only directed toward the child's psychological processes but also toward her parent/family and school.

INITIAL PHASE OF TREATMENT

Developing a Therapeutic Relationship

Goal: Developing a therapeutic relationship; Creating a space for the child to feel safe
Therapist's stance: Active and empathic; Adopting the role of commentator and observer of the child's play.

Hypothetical Example of a Session

The following is an example of a session with a seven-year-old boy.

Therapist: It is nice to see you again.

Child: Can we play with the toys again today?

Therapist: Certainly.

(The child begins to play with a set of toy animals. He throws the toys onto the carpet and sits on the floor. He starts to slam the toys into each other, with one toy taking the role of the attacker.)

Therapist: I see that he is attacking the others. Is that what is happening?

Child: Yes! He is strong, and he can beat them all up.

(He says this enthusiastically and continues to smash the other toys.)

Therapist: I see.

(The child leaves all the toys lying on the floor and takes out the board game Candy Land.)

Child: Let's play. What color do you want to be?

(Therapist is about to respond, but the child cuts the therapist off.)

You can be red, and I will be yellow.

Therapist: OK. (Therapist allows the child to take the lead.)

Child: Orange!

(The child moves two orange places instead of one.)

Therapist: Oh, I see you moved two places.

Child: Yes. I have special powers! I can move to a lot of spaces.

Oh, he is going to really hurt them. (Child abandons Candy Land and turns his attention back to the toys on the floor.)

In this session, the therapist joined the child, allowing the child to take the lead. She sought to increase the positive transference the child had toward her and held off addressing any countertransference issues that may arise. During the encounter, she took note of the themes that came up in the play and began to create a formulation of the child's intrapsychic issues, paying close attention to his mental processes. For example, she took note of the child's ability to organize his play and the length of time he was able to stay with one activity before moving on to another.

It may take four to six sessions before a therapist can build an alliance with a child and develop a sense of what unique concerns pertain to him. But it is important to remember that creating a space for the child can be valuable beyond establishing a therapeutic relationship.

Case Vignette: Therapist MOL

In this case vignette, the therapist discusses his treatment of a ten-year-old boy presenting with obsessive-compulsive symptoms. The child felt compelled to open and close the toilet seat before using the bathroom. He opened and closed the closet at night because there were monsters, and he stared obsessively at his teachers' genitals in school, which made them very uncomfortable. His parents, concerned about his behavior, brought him to see a therapist. He frequently fought with his parents, and they could tell that he was very unhappy and disorganized.

Behavior in Session

> He was entertaining. . . . He'd sit on the couch next to me—I often sit next to a child rather than across from the child—and he'd talk for about fifteen minutes and then he'd say, "Let's play a game." . . . And he'd play a game, and he'd leave all very amicable, but there was nothing clearly happening. [MOL]

Relationship with His Mother The boy's mother worked in a profession with children. When the child told his mother that he loved coming to therapy because he liked to play, his mother responded,

> You're not going there to play! You can play at home. You're going there because you have problems. [MOL]

Progress in Therapy After about six months of treatment, his father asked to consult the therapist to discuss his son's progress. When MOL asked him, *"How do you feel he's doing?"* he reports that the father responded,

> "Well, we're amazed. He's changed so much we don't know what to think." I said, "Well then, fabulous. We don't have much to talk about. We're good." [MOL]

Much of the child's progress can be attributed to the space MOL provided for the child:

> It's not about doing something to a child; it's allowing a space where the child does something. He did something with me. He did it! He didn't necessarily need me to interpret it, codify it, and name it. It just happened. Between us. And for him the happening was what mattered, and clearly it was helpful to him in some way. Of course, they discontinued therapy shortly after because the symptoms went away. [MOL]

Emergence

Sometimes creating a space for the child means allowing the child to take the lead in terms of the play and other activities in a session. The therapist's stance is helpful. It allows the child to connect and relate to the therapist in ways that are meaningful to the child and that the child may not be able to verbalize. In MOL's opinion, the therapist *"creates a space where the possibility of the child's desire can emerge, and when it emerges, I'll respond to it. I won't try to do something with it, I won't try to interpret to this child . . . I'm just going to receive and work with whatever emerges"* [MOL]. This approach rests on the belief that what the child needs will "emerge" once the therapist provides a space or opportunity for the emergence. The therapist can only respond to the child's conflicts or any material relevant to the child after the emergence. Offering interpretative responses before creating a space and allowing the *material* to surface is premature.

Intersubjective Space (The Coming Together)

In the previous examples, the children could easily engage with the therapist through play or verbally. However, there are situations where the child is unable to participate spontaneously with the therapist. *How does a therapist engage this child or have a shared experience with this child?*

Case Vignette: Joe

In this next vignette, MOL describes his work to "create a space" with an autistic child with limited verbalizations. He draws parallels between his approach and the work of Stanley Greenspan—*floortime*—and Winnicott—the *squiggle game*. Here the therapist is more active and works purposely to engage the child by seeking ways to enter into the child's world.

   Background Joe is a seven-year-old boy diagnosed with autism spectrum disorder. He has limited communication, and when he does speak, he repeats what he hears—a symptom called *echolalia*. For example, if the therapist says "Hi Joe!" he responds, "Hi Joe!" He does not engage in any symbolic exchange. His parents are very concerned that Joe has been unresponsive to other forms of therapy and sought out MOL for psychotherapy.

   Frequency of treatment Once per week.

   Conceptualization Using the interactions between a mother and child as a model, the mother's attempts to engage the child and the child's responsiveness to the mother's efforts serves as an indication of both mother's and child's ability to meet each other in a shared experience.

> In a perfect world, they would meet in the middle. The child will elicit subjectivity from the mother, and the mother will elicit from the child. [MOL]

Depending on the child's and mother's dispositions, the extent to which one of the two parties strives toward the other varies. For example, in most situations, the mother is the one who:

> reaches further into the child's domain. . . . But if you have a depressed mother, then the child is burdened to reach into the mother's territory to try and engage the mother. And likewise if you have a child who is lacking the capacity to enter the subjective, intersubjective space, the adult has to reach into the child's space. [MOL]

It is the work of the therapist to enter into the intersubjective space of the child.

Intervention The therapist's goal is to engage the subjective experience of a child who resists entering the personal space.

> I have no predetermined plan for working with a fairly seriously autistic boy with fairly limited communication. . . . So I have to figure out. "How do I engage with this child?" You can't just create a freeing space and let the child use it. With a child like this you have to be interventionist in some way, so the work I do is a bit like what Stanley Greenspan would do with floortime. I have to find a way to engage the subjective experience of a child who resists entering the subjective space. [MOL]

Behavior in session The therapist creates opportunities for the child to enter into the intersubjective space and tries to extend the shared experiences as long as possible. The child may require multiple invitations from the therapist. A common experience gives the therapist an opportunity to start a dialogue with the child.

> When that child comes into my office the very first time, he doesn't take stock of the resources like other children would. He doesn't look in the drawers to see what's there, he doesn't want to take out paper and draw, and he doesn't do anything. He sort of runs around willfully and makes some vocalizations that aren't communicative to me at the moment. And so, I watch for a while.
>
> I watch for a while, and then I open a drawer that has cars, and he likes cars, so he takes out a couple of Matchbox cars, and I have a little launcher, which has a spring on it, it can trigger cars to go. And I put a car on it, and I push the button, and the car goes flying, and he gets excited about that. So I say, "Get the car." He runs off, grabs the car, and brings it back. So I do it again. And then I don't do it again. And he says, "More!" So now he's expressed a demand.
>
> Once he's shown a need, I can work with him because now he has entered the intersubjective space. And then I say, "You know, you just have to push this thing. Push!" So the next time I don't push, he pushes. That lasts, let's say five minutes. And then he'll move on. I have some magnets, and he'll take the magnets and he'll play with them with me on a board. So he'll enter the subjective space, and then he'll retreat, and then I'll find another invitation for him to enter it again.
>
> How do you engage the child in a dialogue? Once you get into a dialogue, then you get into the child's unconscious and things start to appear: anxieties, worries, conflicts and so on. [MOL]

The Use of Empathy to Develop a Therapeutic Alliance

The therapist responds empathically to the child's expression of any distress. However, some children may not immediately share their distressing feelings with the therapist. Therefore, the therapist could respond empathically to the characters in the child's play. For example, continuing with the hypothetical example introduced at the beginning of this section, the therapist provides empathetic responses to the animals in the play.

Therapist: Ouch! That must hurt. He is hurting them.

Child: (Smiling and seems delighted) That's right! He is hurting them.

The therapist should offer genuine responses and not be too concerned about which character she empathizes with since the child will either correct her or be expecting an honest answer.

When to Talk about the Child's Presenting Problems

The therapist can raise the question of why the child believes he was brought to see her in the initial session. It is often very helpful to get the child's perspective on the problem, providing a glimpse of how he sees himself in the world and also a good sense of what others have told him about his difficulties. For example, the child may say, "I am here because I don't listen," or "I am here because I do not follow instructions." Later on in the relationship, after there is trust and a therapeutic environment has been created, the child will begin to feel safe. Then the issue of honesty between the therapist and the child about the conflict and difficulties the child has been experiencing can be discussed.

Engaging with Parents and Teachers

Therapists should be aware that when children come to them, it is usually in response to a crisis or some frustration on the part of their parents or teachers. Therefore, those adults will be seeking answers and may expect to see quick results. It is important to educate them about the treatment process early on in the therapy and establish a framework for working with them. The initial contact should be focused on obtaining a history and gathering information. During that inquiry, the therapist responds empathically to the adults' experiences with and concerns for the child. She establishes consultations with the parents on a regular basis (e.g., once per month) and is available to schedule meetings should parents request them. (See table 4.1 for a summary of Developing a Therapeutic Relationship.)

Table 4.1.   Developing a Therapeutic Relationship

Working with the Child

- Create a space for the child to feel safe.
- Respond empathically to the child's expression of any distress or to the characters in the child's play.

- Get the child's perspective of the problem (depending on the child's age).
- In the initial session, ask the child why he believes he was brought to see the therapist.

Working with the Parent/Caregiver and Teachers

- Educate parents and teachers about the therapy process.
- Establish a framework for working with parents and teachers throughout the process. (Parent consultations should be held regularly—that is, once per month—and the therapist should remain available to schedule meetings should parents request them.)
- Obtain a complete history of the child's development.
- Respond empathically to the adults' experiences with and concerns for the child.

TREATMENT FORMULATION

Understanding the Child's Difficulties

By working with children, parents, and educators, therapists come to an understanding of the children's difficulties that are related to the ego's nego-tiations of id impulses and the conflict between ego and id presses (those that reside on the ego–id side of the triangle) as well as their difficulties stem-ming from the ego negotiations of superego issues such as their feelings of not being able to measure up to their ego ideal (which reside on the ego–superego side of the triangle). Figure 4.2 offers a preliminary formula-tion of the child's intrapsychic concerns. The figure shows a graphical repre-sentation of this triangular conceptualization of the psychological organiza-tion of the mind and the associated difficulties children with ADHD encoun-ter in each area.

Identifying Dynamic Issues

The next step in using the triangle is to consider the dynamic issues that arise from conflict between the psychic agencies of the mind—for example, ego–id and ego–superego (see figure 4.3). The therapist looks for evidence of ego–id conflicts or ego–superego conflicts. A therapist can observe some examples of ego–id conflict in children who have difficulty with reality testing, impulse control, and self-regulation. Children presenting with ego–superego conflicts show a lack of motivation to meet the ego ideals. They may give up on pursuing their goals or on addressing the expectations of others. In response, they may become depressed, anxious, or even opposi-tional or conduct disordered. Children with these issues may be particularly sensitive to emotions of shame and guilt.

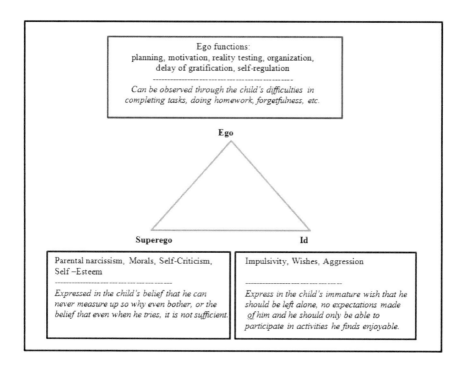

Figure 4.2.   Preliminary Formulation of Child's Intrapsychic Concerns

TREATMENT PHASE

Interventions for Ego–Id Problems

Goal: Developing a relationship with the child
Technique: Adopting a reflective stance

The therapist is available to the child and remains psychologically receptive and open to whatever the child presents. The therapist does not restrict the child but attends to whatever arises in the session—the child's words, behaviors, and drawings. On a metalevel, the therapist pays attention to *how* the child expresses himself—for example, to the tone of the child's speech.

It is also important to enter the session without assumptions and ask questions about the child's experience. For example, during a session, nine-year-old Jay explained that his teacher instructed him to let her know whether or not the other children bullied him. I asked him how he felt about this and he shrugged in an unaffected manner. As I explored with Jay his thoughts about his teacher's request, it soon became clear he had difficulty

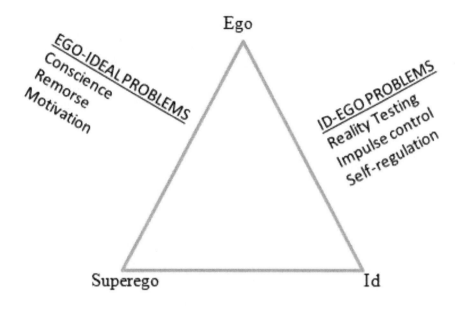

Figure 4.3.   Dynamic Issues Resulting from Conflict Between the Psychic Agencies of the Mind

imagining why his teacher asked him to let her know if he was being bullied. The possibility that she wanted to help him or intervene on his behalf was not clear to him. It was only through suspending "assumptions" that I was able to maintain a reflective stance revealing Jay's significant difficulties with reflective functioning.

Therapists adopt an adaptive point of view of the child's behaviors:

> You're trying to do the best you can with what you've got. Tell me about how that works for you and maybe we can, maybe we can help you rework that a little bit in a way that gets you into trouble less. [DON]

Goal: Ego development
Technique: Joint attention

The therapist functions as an auxiliary ego for the child by assuming ego functions that the child needs to develop. For example, if a child is having difficulty attending, the therapist assumes that function and attends for the child until the child can do so independently.

Session

In the session, the therapist and child create a shared experience to which they both attend and respond. Once the experience begins, the therapist starts paying attention to the child while noticing every detail about how the child is reacting to the experience and commenting on it. Possible joint attention activities may include gestures or mirroring the child's facial expressions while attending together. The feeling the child receives from being attended to fuels their development and maturity.

Goal: Ego development
Technique: Developing a relationship with the child

Developing the relationship with the child also serves to strengthen the ego in a way that ultimately impacts their self-esteem and other superego issues.

For example, a common complaint about ADHD children is their tendency to be the class clowns. These children strive for mastery, and when their experiences are not successful, they seek out other opportunities to stand out—such as by adopting attention-seeking roles.

> It's a gratifying role you [the ADHD child] can play because [if] you can't control yourself, at least you'll get people to laugh. The therapeutic relationship—but I also think the relationship with a "good" teacher, an admired teacher, or an admired tutor—can also serve that purpose, strengthening ego capacities and ultimately increasing superego capacities. Also, you know, having an impact on their sense of mastery and, therefore, their self-esteem. [MER]

Goal: Integration of immature wishes into ego functions
Technique: Mentalizing the transference

Therapists can access children's immature wishes through transference. Transference gives the therapist an opportunity to see how the child's id wishes are experienced. Transference interpretations are experienced near where the therapist comments on what is occurring between herself and the child in the session. The therapists' comments during transference help to contextualize children's experience of their therapists while providing them with an opportunity to reflect on their own internal states—this, in turn, helps them to develop self-regulating capacities. Transference interpretations should focus on children's mental processes with the goal of developing their reflective capabilities (Fonagy and Target, 1996).

Session

> Child: Why can't I take these toys home? I will bring them back. I promise.

> Therapist: I can see you want to take the toys home, but they must remain here. They will be here when you return for our next session.

> Child: (Pouts and begins to protest).

> Therapist: I wonder whether I remind you of other adults in your life?

> Child: Yes, you are acting like my teacher. I just wish I could take it home.

> Therapist: I can see how you may feel the way you do. We can both look forward to the next time we play together. Is it very disappointing for you when the teacher does not allow you to do certain things at school?

Goal: Holding and containing painful affective experiences
Technique: Creating a space for the child to feel safe

The therapist's task is to create an environment that can contain the complicated emotional responses of the child. The relationship and understanding of the child provides a context for helping the child hold painful affective experiences. The therapist co-creates with the child an environment where the child can trust what is happening in the room enough to explore emotions and experiences that may otherwise be more dysregulating. A more detailed discussion of this technique appears earlier in this chapter under the heading "Developing a Therapeutic Relationship," in the section titled "Initial Phase of Treatment."

Interventions for Ego–Superego Problems

Goal: Giving the child a more positive experience of himself
Technique: Working with the countertransference

Parents, teachers, peers, and others involved in children's lives often respond to them with a range of negative emotions including annoyance, anger, and frustration. Some may view ADHD-related behaviors as purposeful and defiant, and at times ascribe characteristics such as lazy, manipulative, liar, and so forth, to children with the disorder. As a result, children with ADHD can come to experience themselves in ways that can lead to anxiety, depression, and a host of other emotional problems. The therapist's role is to give them a different experience of themselves.

> The therapist monitors countertransference responses to the child and avoids being stuck in the negative countertransference.

The therapist needs to seek supervision so they can avoid being pigeonholed or trapped in a negative countertransference response to the child as well as explore ways of working with these feelings. The therapist must consider the need for further exploration of these issues in his therapy.

When asked about experiences of countertransference with ADHD clients one therapist explained:

> I'm a real believer in all of the uses of countertransference, I think it's a wonderful thing if you can put it to work. Once I am at an impasse there's something I haven't understood, there's something about myself I haven't understood, I'm stuck in my own countertransference, what was I doing? [DON]

Goal: Resolving ego ideal failures
Techniques: Empathy, Mentalization

The therapist's use of empathy, especially in the face of the child's shortcomings, provides the child with an alternative response—one that is tempered and compassionate—to his failed superego expectations. The therapist communicates with the child that his perspective is valued by providing him with an empathic response. Empathic therapist responses regarding the child's superego struggle also help the child to develop his capacity to reflect on his resulting feelings of anger and depression. Both the therapist's understanding of the child's perspective and an expression of compassion for his plight is necessary for effective empathic communications.

In the use of empathy, it is important to not align the child against their parents. ADHD children do benefit from the support and structure their parents provide. The therapist should instead explore the child's ambivalence regarding parental structure and limit setting without "taking a side."

> Therapist: I realize you find it difficult to give your parents an answer to their questions regarding whether or not you've completed your homework. Why do you suppose you find it so difficult to answer their questions?

> Child: I just wish they would leave me alone, but I know if they left me alone I would just not do anything.

Therapist: It must be very painful for you to not have successful experiences on your own.

Child: Yes, it is terrible but at the same time I know if they stop asking I will not get anything done.

Therapist: I see. So being a teenager, you want to work more independently. But realizing that you cannot causes you to feel distressed. (At this point the child begins to cry.) I am so sorry. This is so difficult for you. I can see how upsetting this is.

Child: It is just that when they ask, it feels like pressure.

Therapist: So that makes it even harder to get yourself back to doing homework.

Goal: Helping the child to develop an internal narrative of his inner experiences
Technique: Narrative approach

Each child has an inner relational narrative that represents his or her interpersonal interactions with others. The goal of therapy is to help that child express a story that describes his experiences in the world. The therapist works to "find" the words that will help him to build an affect vocabulary representative of his experience. For example, an analyst may help the child put words to their experiences and thereby develop an internal narrative. *"I try to develop an internal narrative, which has a person in it, which is a person like myself."* [DON] In time, the analyst's goal is to include the parents in developing a narrative about the child that is helpful to the parent's efforts to relate to the child. DON explains to parents *"if the child evokes responses that are the same as they always were they are still in the same rut, if the child evokes a response that is different in you, then you have a real broad possible way of responding. If your kid has only evoked hate then we find a way for him to evoke something else, right?"* [DON]

Session

With young children, therapists can make use of an emotions chart to both assess their range of emotions and teach them about other emotional responses they may have. Therapists can explore with the children other times that they may have experienced certain emotions and encourage them to give examples of how they may have felt. If a child struggles with that task, the therapist can help him to find the words to express his feelings.

Goal: Developing the child's capacity to mentalize/self-reflect
Technique: Mentalization

Mentalization is the ability "to be able to read other's minds in order to predict their behavior in meaningful ways" (see Fonagy and Target, 1998 in Conway, 2015). This technique is helpful with regard to addressing the intricate matrix of relational and ego developmental issues. It is important to note that the relational aspect of the child's functioning is not often a priority for parents and teachers when they compete with concerns about academic performance and the ability to follow rules. However, for this treatment model, the relationship that develops between the child and his therapist is significant (Conway, 2015; Gilmore, 2002).

If one were to ascribe the child's difficulties to the representative mental structures of the mind, one could attribute executive-functioning deficits to the ego (e.g., competency, reality testing, self-regulation, and the ability to complete tasks) and relational challenges to the superego (e.g., low self-esteem, depression, anxiety, oppositional behaviors, etc.) (Conway, 2011).

The therapist's capacity to mentalize The therapist's capacity to "mentalize" the child allows them to make interpretations about the child's mental state.

Child: (The child plays with an octopus toy and tries to hold several other toys with each of the octopus's tentacles.)

Therapist: Oh boy, what is the octopus doing?

Child: He is grabbing them.

Therapist: I wonder how it would feel to have as many hands as an octopus has tentacles. What would it be like to be able to have so many hands?

Child: I could hold all of these at the same time.

Therapist: I imagine you now with eight hands. You could do homework and chores and play Pokemon.

Child: (Starts laughing and joins in the imagination game).

Session

The therapist can initiate activities that convey to the child that the therapist has been *thinking* about the child. For example, the therapist may add a particular toy to the playroom that interests the child. The only caution is for the child to remember that the toys stay in the room.

Therapist must maintain a reflective stance throughout the session Maintaining a reflective capacity in the face of the child's shifting attention is not always easy for the therapist. Feeling depleted by the child's impulsiveness or activity is not unusual. The therapist must resist responding to the child with limit setting (unless the child is placing himself at risk). The analyst actively avoids directing the child toward any activity but rather becomes more self-observant and self-monitoring so as to avoid behaving in ways that may counteract treatment goals. (See table 4.2 for a summary of Treatment Formulation.)

Table 4.2.   Treatment Formulation

Understanding the Child's Difficulties	*Observations in the Child*	*Resulting Dynamic Issues*
Identify deficits in ego functions (planning, motivation, reality testing, organization, delay of gratification, self-regulation, etc.).	Difficulties in completing tasks, doing homework, forgetfulness, etc.	
Identify problems stemming from ego–id conflict (impulsivity, wishes, and aggression).	The child's immature wish that he should be left alone, with no expectations placed on him, and that he should be able to participate only in enjoyable activities	Difficulties with reality testing, impulse control, and self-regulation
Identify problems stemming from ego–superego conflict (parental narcissism, morals, self-criticism, self-esteem).	The child's belief that he can never measure up (so why even bother), or the belief that even when he tries, his efforts are not sufficient	Lack of motivation (giving up on pursuing goals or on meeting the expectations of others), depression, anxiety, oppositional or conduct disordered, sensitivity to emotions of shame and guilt

Table 4.3.   Treatment Interventions for Ego–Id Problems

Goal	*Technique*	*Effect on the Child*
Developing a relationship with the child	Adopting a stance that is open, available, receptive, attentive, nonrestrictive, and makes no assumptions; Asking questions about the child's experience; Adopting an	Creates feeling of being safe and understood

Goal	Technique	Effect on the Child
	adaptive point of view of the child's behaviors	
Ego development	Joint attention; Developing a relationship with the child	Strengthens and expands ego capacity; improves self-esteem; gives the child a sense of mastery
Integrating immature wishes into ego functions	Mentalizing the transference	Allows the child to reflect on his internal states; helps to develop self-regulating capacities
Holding and containing difficult affective experiences.	Creating a space for the child to feel safe; Developing a relationship with the child	Increases ability to self- and emotionally regulate

Table 4.4.   Treatment Interventions for Ego–Superego Problems

Goal	Technique	Effect on the Child
Giving the child a more positive experience of himself	Working with the countertransference: monitor countertransference, avoid being stuck in the negative countertransference	Reorients child's experience of himself by counteracting the negative responses he's accustomed to eliciting in others
Resolving ego ideal failures	Empathy, Mentalization	Provides the child with an alternative response to failed superego expectation that is more tempered and compassionate
Helping the child to develop an internal narrative of his inner experiences	Narrative approach	Helps the child build an affect vocabulary representative of his experiences
Developing the child's capacity to mentalize/self-reflect	Mentalization: Therapist's capacity to mentalize the child allows therapist to make interpretations about the child's mental state; Maintaining a reflective stance throughout the session	Addresses the child's feelings of anxiety and depression and mitigates oppositional and other conduct behaviors; Increases child's ability to understand the behaviors of others, adapt to different situations, and be flexible in his responses

CHAPTER HIGHLIGHTS

Amid a diversity of approaches and contributors to ADHD etiology and the perpetuation of symptoms, the analyst is an advocate for the child's inner experiences. This role is especially important given the negative responses ADHD symptoms elicit in interpersonal relationships and the tendency for all concerned with the child to focus on the child's external behaviors.

- An integrated psychodynamic model of treatment is proposed that includes interventions focusing on the child's id–ego (reality testing, impulse control, self-regulation) and ego–superego or ego–ideal issues (school, parents, family).
- During the *initial phase of treatment*, the goal of treatment is to develop a therapeutic relationship by creating a safe space for the child with attention to concepts such as emergence, intersubjective space, the use of empathy, addressing the presenting problem, and engaging the parents and teachers.
- In the *treatment formulation phase*, the therapist focuses on understanding the child's difficulties and developing a formulation of the child's intrapsychic concerns specific to the id, ego, and super-ego. The treatment phase proposes intervention in two main areas:

  - *Interventions for ego–id problems* target the following therapeutic goals—developing a relationship with the child, ego development, and containing painful affective experiences.
  - *Interventions for ego–superego problems* target the following therapeutic goals—giving the child a more positive experience of himself, resolving ego–ideal failures, helping the child to develop an internal narrative of his experience, developing the child's capacity to mentalize.

Chapter Five

Behavioral and Other Approaches

Behavioral Therapy, Cognitive Behavioral Therapy, and Parent and School Interventions

This chapter offers a review of cognitive behavioral therapy (CBT) and the limits of its clinical practice with children presenting with Attention Deficit Hyperactivity Disorder (ADHD) symptoms. Toward that end, I will provide a brief description of the central concepts associated with CBT. Based on CBT's conceptualization of psychopathology, aspects of the ADHD disorder that are amenable to CBT will be discussed. It is important to note that there are limitations to CBT treatment in that it does not seem to be successful with children under eight years old. However, this treatment appears useful for adolescent children. These developmental considerations limit the practice of CBT.

CBT successfully treats some of the comorbid disorders occurring with ADHD, but the core presenting problems associated with ADHD seem to be outside the scope of this treatment approach. In contrast, a behavioral approach that focuses on training parents and teachers to manage the child's behaviors through the establishment of contingencies has been viewed as an effective intervention with ADHD, especially if combined with stimulant medication treatment. Behavioral approaches only work as long as it is being actively applied. In other words, this form of therapy does not eliminate the child's undesirable behaviors.

Since this book focuses on the psychodynamic understanding of ADHD, it is important to understand how analysts view behavioral approaches, so I will return to my interview data for a discussion of those responses later in this chapter. Finally, given the emphasis on parent training and school inter-vention embedded within behavioral approaches, this is also a good time to look at psychodynamic perspectives on working with the parent and school to address ADHD-related problems.

BEHAVIORAL AND COGNITIVE BEHAVIORAL PERSPECTIVES ON ADHD

Models considering the individual's psychological processes guide the practice of psychotherapy. One prevailing psychotherapy approach that has received a lot of attention is the behavioral approach. I have grouped behavioral approaches into two broad categories—behavioral and cognitive behavioral. The behavioral approach to ADHD, based on a belief that ADHD behaviors stem from neurological and cognitive deficiencies, differs from the cognitive behavioral approach, which is based on a belief that ADHD behaviors arise from cognitive distortions that are secondary to neurological insults. I will begin this discussion with an exploration of the more circumscribed cognitive behavioral approach; that discussion will be followed by an engagement with the more widely known behavioral approach.

Cognitive Behavioral Therapy

A principal theorist contributing to the creation of the CBT approach is Aaron T. Beck (1920–present), who was psychoanalytically trained. A concept commonly embraced by CBT—that behaviors are motivated by an individual's thoughts and emotions—can be traced back to Alfred Adler (1870–1937), another early psychoanalyst. The credit for developing cognitive interventions, however, goes to Albert Ellis (1913–2007)—the first analyst to use cognitive theories in treating psychopathology.

CBT evolved out of a range of perspectives, including learning, cognitive, behavioral, humanistic, and biopsychosocial theories (David and Szentagotai, 2006). Since that first application by Adler, the CBT approach evolved into several distinct models, including rational emotive behavior therapy, reality therapy, person-centered approaches, self-instructional training, dialectic behavior therapy, and acceptance and commitment therapy (Gilman and Chard, 2007). Although full attention to the breadth of CBT-specific models is not a focus of this chapter, fundamental CBT concepts will be briefly introduced.

A central tenet of CBT is that thoughts about the self and others influence how one interprets external events, which in turn can influence emotions and behaviors. One's interpretation of an event is subject to a set of individual factors—including personality, history, coping strategies, and social supports—and determines positively or negatively interpreted experiences. Cognitive interpretations not only determine an individual's affective and behavioral responses, but the affect and behaviors in turn reinforce the person's perception and understanding of their experiences. CBT addresses the extent to which one's interpretations cause distress. An individual's interpretations, often distorted, can cause considerable discomfort. The goal of treatment, therefore, is to increase the individual's awareness of his or her cognitive distortions and the resulting behaviors that reinforce these misperceptions. Thus, the goal of CBT is to grow awareness, coping strategies, and problem-solving skills through the use of systematic, empirically supported techniques.

Most CBT approaches share three fundamental assumptions regarding the relationship between cognition and behavior. Specifically, that cognition, affects, and behaviors can be monitored and altered, and that those alterations can lead to behavior change (Dobson and Dozois, 2001). For the therapist using a cognitive behavioral approach, the goals of treatment are directly related to these assumptions. The therapist helps to increase the client's awareness that cognitions can both distort and impact emotions and behaviors, and that they can be modified to correct distorted thoughts and maladaptive behaviors. These changes can lead to positive changes in the way clients perceive themselves and others (Beck, Rush, Shaw, and Emery, 1979). In treating children, CBT also takes into consideration the child's level of cognitive development—including learning and memory, social cognition, and metacognitive skills—and their self-regulatory abilities.

CBT Conceptualization of ADHD

Human functioning hinges on the intersection of our internal and external worlds. That our inner experiences have a reciprocal influence on interpretations of events that are external to ourselves is the basic assumption of CBT and the focus of clinical interventions, for it is within this dimension of human functioning that things can go "wrong." For example, CBT's view of psychopathology focuses on an individual's interpretation of external events and the extent to which that interpretation becomes so "distorted" or misaligned with reality that it interferes with one's ability to function.

Given CBT's focus on the effects of cognitive misattributions on behavior and affect, aspects of ADHD where misconceptions of the child's behaviors arise are most amenable to CBT interventions (Kendall and Braswell, 1993). Adults who interact with the child, specifically parents and teachers, may often experience frustration with the child's behaviors and attribute the child's lack of response to defiance, oppositional behavior, or conduct disorder. The child may also begin to have some distortions about himself vis-à-vis others in his life. In situations like these, CBT's interventions would focus on helping the adults to identify their distortions about the child and exchange them for more helpful beliefs (Anastopoulos, Rhoads, and Farley, 2006). CBT interventions have also been helpful with children when they have focused on instructing them about the impact of ADHD on their lives and enlisting them in changing behavior patterns that do not work (Hinshaw, 2006; Ramsay and Rostain, 2008).

Cognitive behavioral therapists view their goals as:

1. restructuring cognitions to replace maladaptive cognitions with more adaptive thought patterns;
2. developing the client's ability to cope during stressful times; and
3. helping the client to develop problem-solving strategies that will both modify cognitive distortions and support positive behaviors.

A central requirement for participation in CBT is the capacity to form abstract and reflective thoughts. These higher-ordered cognitive-processing skills allow individuals to become aware of cognitive distortions and understand the relationship between those cognitions and their emotions and behaviors. Children under eight years old have not yet developed these cognitive milestones, and distorted thinking is quite typical among younger children. Therefore, the limits of CBT with young children must be kept in mind (Grave and Blissett, 2004). Children have different constitutions due in part to differences in their developmental progression along with cultural, sociological, and other factors. Furthermore, children's heterotypic make-up requires that the therapist carefully select appropriate CBT interventions (Braswell and Kendall, 2001; Kendall and Choudhury, 2003). Interventions with children that meet their developmental expectations are more symbolic and less verbal (such as play therapy). These interventions rely on parental support for implementing practice techniques and use active behavioral techniques to accomplish therapeutic goals of cognitive reframing and changing behavior patterns.

Cognitive Behavioral Therapy Techniques

Cognitive behavioral therapy sessions are structured although flexible enough to accommodate a wide variety of client's presenting problems. CBT practitioners adhere to five steps that guide the sessions: (1) set an agenda; (2) review the client's completion of homework; (3) set goals for the current session; (4) teach and practice new skills; and (5) provide feedback to the client. The therapist gives feedback to the client to further develop the therapeutic alliance, offer support and encouragement, and respond to the client's misconceptions. The session ends with the assignment of mutually agreed upon homework. At the close of treatment, the client is expected to apply the techniques to other situations through the identification of potential road blocks and to sustain the gains made in the treatment (Compton et al., 2004).

CBT therapists have some standard techniques available to them during their sessions. These techniques are used to help clients understand that their thought patterns affect their behavior. Therapists and the clients work together to identify clients' negative thoughts, question their assumptions, and develop problem-solving and appropriate coping skills. The range of techniques used to accomplish these tasks includes Socratic questioning, problem-solving, cognitive restructuring, affective education and mindfulness, relaxation training, modeling and role-playing, social-skills training, exposure therapy, and imagery and attribution retraining. When working with a child with ADHD, these techniques can be used in any combination depending on the child's individual abilities and developmental level.

Behavioral Approaches

Behavioral Determinants

Behavioral approaches subscribe to the notion that the child's difficulties stem from neurological deficits; therapists oriented toward this approach view children with ADHD as having difficulties in meeting environmental demands. For example, as a result of the difficulty they have paying attention, their environments (both school and home) hold many distractions for them and therefore require some modification to enable the children to function. Likewise, parenting styles may inadvertently conflict with the ADHD child's disposition. For example, parents who do not realize their children need time to process information may expect responses immediately instead of giving them the time they need to prepare an answer, thereby leading to conflict in their interaction. From the behavioral perspective, parents and teachers need to be instructed in how to change their approaches to children with ADHD. Such behavioral adjustments to the environment accommodate these children's deficits.

Unlike CBT, the efficacy of behavioral approaches has been well-studied; however, their effectiveness with ADHD has been inconsistent (Levine and Anshel, 2011). In particular, classroom behavior management and parent training have been most commonly used with children who are hyperactive. On the one hand, studies have found that behavioral therapy alone is not an effective intervention for ADHD (Klassen, Miller, Raina, Lee, and Olsen, 1999; Selby, Calhoun, and Johnson, 2006). Gains in ADHD symptom reduction attributable to behavioral therapy begin to attenuate after about fourteen months and seldom persist after the treatment has terminated (Chronis, Pelham, Gnagy, Roberts, and Aronoff, 2003).

However, more promising uses of behavioral therapy are apparent when used in combination with some other interventions—medication and parent training. Some researchers have shown that behavioral therapies in conjunction with medication are optimal treatments (Barkely, 2006; DuPaul and Stoner, 2003; Klassen et al., 1999; MTA Cooperative Group, 1999). However, a twenty-four-month follow-up in the MTA study did not find any support that benefits of combined treatment outweigh those of medication use alone (MTA Cooperative Group, 2004). Since, the MTA follow-up study has found that at the twenty-four-month follow-up, children in combination treatments received significantly lower doses of stimulant medication compared to those who received medication alone (Swanson et al., 2007). Furthermore, treatments that have included parent training with the combined medication and behavioral interventions are considered a relatively effective intervention for ADHD compared to behavioral therapy alone (Halperin and Healey, 2011).

Since behavioral approaches are typically used in combination with medication, it is difficult to assess whether the use of behavioral therapy alone is valuable in and of itself. Parents seem to view the combination of medication and behavioral approaches favorably, but this view was not supported by teachers in one study (Klassen et al., 1999). Also, parents who participate in their child's behavioral therapy report less stress than those who do not, although their stress levels remain higher than parents of non-ADHD children (van der Oord, Prins, Oosterlan, and Emmelkamp, 2012).

The Multimodal Treatment Study of ADHD (MTA), funded by the National Institute of Mental Health and published in 2009, examined the long-term effects of ADHD treatment, and it remains the most lauded study in the field to date despite the fact that most of its results were inconclusive (Molina et al., 2009). Here are the main points. The researchers reported their findings at a six- and eight-year follow-up of 579 children diagnosed with ADHD. The children received different treatment combinations of medication and behavioral therapy. The results showed that ADHD children who received behavioral therapy in combination with medication continued to do better than they had done, but were still worse off than their non-ADHD peers, at the conclusion of the study. Researchers found no differences between children remaining on medication after the fourteen-month trial and those who discontinued the medication at the fourteen-month period. The initial advantages noted among children taking a combination of medication and therapy compared to those receiving therapy alone dissipated. For some, this study's findings suggest the mandated course of treatment should include medication; for others, the same results suggest avoidance of medication. Also, although gains were made using behavioral therapy alone, they were not sustainable. The inconclusiveness of the research to date has led other researchers and clinicians to consider alternative approaches to treating ADHD.

Behavioral Techniques

Behavioral approaches refer to a broad group of methods—based on learning theories—that are used in collaboration with parents and teachers to change the child's behavior. Although this approach does not preclude making modifications in the child's environment, home, and school aimed at facilitating improvements in attention and organization, an essential component of behavioral therapy for children with ADHD entails training parents and teachers in using behavioral techniques to improve the child's behavior (Pelham, Wheeler, and Chronis, 1998). Over time, the desired behavior is shaped by rewards, and there are consequences for failing to meet desired goals.

The parent training has both psychoeducational and skill-development components. Parents learn about the effect of ADHD on their child's behavior and are taught skills to reinforce adaptive behaviors in their child. Components of parent training include helping parents to create a structured environment; increasing attention given to positive behaviors; learning how to give effective behavioral commands; and teaching parenting techniques and contingency management skills (Dopfner and Rothenberg, 2007). Parents receive assistance setting up a contingency management system designed to reinforce their child's behavior. They also receive training in practical techniques, such as:

- positive reinforcement, which makes use of reward systems;
- time-out, which removes access to positive reinforcement;
- response costs, which involves the use of consequences—for example, the withdrawal of privileges—in response to unwanted behavior; and
- token economy, which is a combination of positive reinforcement and response cost. (Pelham and Fabiano, 2001)

Classroom management utilizes similar techniques as those relied on by parents. In addition, the teacher structures the classroom and activities so that it becomes routine for the child. Furthermore, the teacher sends a report of the child's behaviors home to the parent, providing another opportunity for the use of positive reinforcements or consequences.

Behavioral approaches do have some limitations that are worth mentioning. Children learn limited skills during behavioral interventions that are not readily generalizable to other situations. Newly acquired skills must be reinforced in the environment in which the children are expected to use those skills (Dopfner and Rothenberg, 2007). Although this approach has been shown to improve children's ADHD-related behaviors, it has not been effective in eliminating those behaviors. In addition, behavioral approaches do not address children's emotional responses or thought patterns (Barkley, 1998; Pelham and Hinshaw, 1992). A further shortcoming of this approach is that its effectiveness seems limited to only when the intervention is being used; behavioral gains do not appear to extend beyond the implementation phase (Pelham and Fabiano, 2001).

Following is a summary of behavioral strategies that can be used with ADHD children as they are grounded by Dopfner and Rothenberg (2007). This information is condensed for ease of reference in table 5.1.

1. Classroom management techniques for ADHD should include varying the classroom structure and the child's activities. Structured classroom decisions such as having the child seated close to the teacher are recommended. Other techniques include presenting the child with shortened academic assignments and interspersing lectures with physical exercises.

2. Set up contingencies (positive and negative consequences) to target specific behaviors (e.g., when the child blurts out answers before questions are completed or leaves her seat at an inappropriate time).

3. Work with the teacher to increase attention to positive interactions with the child.

4. Token systems can be used to provide immediate feedback and, later, reinforcement for desired behaviors. For example, the teacher may give a sticker on the child's sticker chart, which is then reinforced at home or by the teacher with other rewards. Examples of other rewards at school include special playtime or a lighter homework assignment. Rewards outside the school may include individual playtime with a therapist.

5. Response-cost systems—for example, the removal of privileges—have been effective in reducing problem behaviors that frequently occur (for example, interrupting or disrupting others).

6. Use time-out from reinforcement if the child is unresponsive to the response-cost system. However, caution must be taken to ensure that the time away from the classroom is not a positive reinforcement for the child. For example, a child may be wishing to avoid a particular lesson or participation in specific class activities and could see the time-out punishment as an opportunity for relief rather than a consequence. Time-out activities should also not become extremely punitive.

7. Teaching the child to use self-instruction is encouraged for children who are motivated. Children can increase attention and reduce impulsivity in learning and social settings. Teach self-instruction in social-skills training programs where the child learns how to self-monitor and exercise socially appropriate behaviors.

8. Social-skills training helps the child develop and maintain peer relationships, solve problems that arise in social settings, and reduce aggressive behaviors with peers.

9. An assessment of the need for collateral supports that offer financial and respite resources to families may be appropriate. Also, educational interventions around curriculum adjustments may be required.

10. The use of behavioral rating scales for ongoing monitoring of the child's progress is important.

For a more comprehensive review of behavioral therapy and CBT, consider Abikoff (1987), Barkley (1989), Kendall and Wilcox (1980), Kendall and Braswell (1985), Werry and Wollersheim (1989), and Whalen and Henker (1986) (see Whalen and Henker, 1991).

What Do Psychodynamic Psychoanalysts Think about Behavioral Approaches?

Therapists aiming to incorporate behavioral techniques into their psychodynamic practice make it their goal to include or teach child behavioral strategies or self-soothing strategies in a way that capitalizes on the therapeutic relationship. For example, one analyst explains:

> I might have the child, together with me, write down a list of self-soothing strategies on an index card that can be used when they become really upset. For example, when they feel like cutting themselves . . . I would read it to them, and then I would have them read it. Basically, what I'm trying to get them to do is to hear the sound of my voice when they read that list, and I would encourage them to take it home and put it in a safe place. [VAU]

Most psychoanalysts view behavioral or cognitive approaches as regimented while still seeing them as valuable tools that could be used to manage any difficulties their clients may be experiencing. Still, analysts make a distinction between behavioral approaches and dynamic ones. For example, the goal of a behavioral intervention would be to get the child to label his feelings. On the other hand, a psychodynamic intervention's goal would be to help the child to get in touch with her feelings and be able to use those feelings creatively. A behavioral intervention that aims to get the child to just label emotions is viewed as too reductive, while a value of psychodynamic approaches is its emphasis on the child's ability to not only identify their emotions, but find ways to use those feelings in adaptive ways.

Table 5.1.   Behavioral Strategies for Treating ADHD

Structure classroom to maximize attention and decrease distraction	Revise seating arrangements such that child is seated close to the teacher
Provide breaks in attention tasks	Create opportunities for physical activity to occur between attention-demanding tasks
Set up contingencies (positive and negative consequences) to target specific behaviors	Child loses a star on a conduct board each time he blurts out an answer, interrupts someone, or gets out of his seat.
Work with parents and teachers to increase attention to positive interactions with the child	Child is given verbal acknowledgment when desired behaviors are observed.
Token systems	Child receives stickers or tokens for desired behaviors.
Response cost systems	Child loses privileges when targeted behaviors occur.
Time-out	
Self-instruction	
Social skills training	
Behavioral rating scales for ongoing monitoring of the child's progress	

Dopfner and Rothenberg, 2007.

A PSYCHODYNAMIC APPROACH TO PARENTING AND SCHOOL INTERVENTIONS

Parenting and Family Dynamics

The lives of ADHD children are contextual. The first context that shapes a child's being is the family. It is often through that lens that the child first sees himself and his relationship to others. Although parents do not cause ADHD, family situations can have either an ameliorating or exacerbating influence on the child's psychological well-being. The three vignettes presented next highlight the complexities of some of the family situations familiar to children with ADHD and associated behavioral disorders. Note that these stories, presented from the point of view of psychodynamic therapists, focus on each family's relational matrix.

Vignette 1

A school-aged boy was referred for treatment because his mother was concerned about his school adjustment and his happiness. He has mild Asperger's syndrome and is hyperactive. For example, his mother proudly described him being able to climb to the top of the refrigerator when he was two-and-a-half years old. Although he was a very sweet boy, he had problems connecting with people in ways that enriched him or satisfied him. In fact, both of his parents struggled with establishing an interpersonal connection with others due to "schizoid" problems in the family. His mother received little attention from her mother and his father was distant, spending a lot of his time engaged in solitary intellectual activities. Although there was probably a biological predisposition to the child's difficulties, there was also a compelling family history of relational problems with a distinct interpersonal style. His central struggle was how to make appropriate contact [LOM].

Vignette 2

Another school-aged boy presented with similar problems to the boy profiled in Vignette 1 with regard to connecting with others, but he also experienced difficulty in focusing and was more pervasively anxious. The two boys' family circumstances were markedly different. Most of this boy's difficulties were expressed at school—acting-out behaviors included throwing desks, hitting, and biting other kids. His mother complained that he never slept through the night for the first year or so. It was unclear whether this was a physiological state that he was in or whether these were parents with very low thresholds that were disturbed by his waking up in the night. He was outraged, and much of his anxiety stemmed from his anger. He often made physical contact with the therapist by running into the office and jumping into the therapist's lap. The mother was a school teacher who found her son's acting-out behavior in school an embarrassment.

> When children act out at home and not in school, their prognosis is usually better than when they act out at school and not at home . . . the child was too afraid of his father to act out at home, so he had to bring it out into the world with him, which was worse for him. [LOM]

An interaction between the boy's father and the therapist was illuminating. During a consultation, the father sat in a chair across from the therapist with his legs crossed. During the conversation, he suddenly uncrossed his legs and sat up in a startling manner, placing his face directly in front of the therapist's face and staring at her intently with a fixed smile on his face. The therapist experienced a mild version of the little boy's lived experience—that all of a sudden, out of nowhere, his father would attack and deny it.

> The little boy had to be on alert all of the time, because at any moment Dad could kick him in the shins or, you know, knock his feet out from under him or whatever. [LOM]

Both of these boys would make very aggressive contact with the therapist.

> You know, running into me, slamming into me, you know, there was a lot of sort of physical contact, and that's the way they connected. [LOM]

A few years after his treatment ended, the therapist had occasion to see this child again. When they met, the child said to the therapist:

> Remember when I used to come into your office and jump in your lap? I had to make sure you were there. [LOM]

Vignette 3

A therapist worked with a ten-year-old boy who threw water bottles at this teacher and propositioned his teacher. Other concerning behaviors included throwing ice at cars in the street and throwing debris out the window of the school bus, which led to police involvement. His parents were going through a divorce, and he wanted to be cared for, but he was furious and in a rage. The two parents were at war. The child was in crisis, and his father wished to send him to military school. The therapist communicated with both parents, and everybody agreed that they had to do something different. The parents' lack of coordination of the child's care and their undermining of each other was not helpful to the child. The parents were working through their rage through the child, and that had an adverse effect on the child. After the therapist's intervention with the parents:

> [The child] re-equilibrated; he's not perfect, but he's working really hard. He's in his local school, and he's going to school and he's getting decent grades, and you know, he's functional, and he's decently regulated. He can have explosions, but for the most part he's decently regulated. [MOL]

Parent Intervention

While it is common for ADHD symptoms and other childhood problems to have an impact on the family, it is often unclear whether the family has an adverse effect on the child. Nonetheless, it is almost a requirement that a therapist who is working with ADHD children also work with their parents or families. Therapists are encouraged to work with both conscious and unconscious feelings/conflicts arising in the family. This therapeutic work can help reduce parent anxiety and increase the likelihood of treatment success (Cione, Coleburn, Fertuck, and Fraenkel, 2011; Widener, 1998).

Most analysts have some contact with parents and view their interactions with parents as an important part of the treatment. During the first phase of the parenting intervention, the therapist is focused on obtaining a history of the child's development and developing a relationship with the parent. Prior to starting work with a child, the therapist meets the parents to obtain a detailed developmental history of the patient. A fundamental question that guides this assessment period is *What are you experiencing at home with your child*? Once treatment begins, therapists meet with parents regularly to continue developing a working alliance. During this process, the therapist is especially empathic toward the parents, who may be experiencing a range of emotions including *"anger, frustration, and rage because parents are constantly feeling inadequate"* [MAC].

The second phase of the work with parents focuses on helping them understand the child's problems. Parents receive psychoeducation about the nature of the treatment, their child's behaviors, and how to identify family patterns that may exacerbate the child's problems. Providing psychoeducation about the child's difficulties helps parents set realistic expectations for their child based on their child's developmental stage. Parents need to understand that their children's behaviors are not deliberate and willful. It is often helpful for parents to accept that their children may have hidden vulnerabilities that may well require allowances similar to children who have more visible weaknesses. For example, parents can advocate for a child who cannot complete his homework or get her assignments in on time. The therapist can also provide information for parents on the scope of ADHD in an attempt to normalize their experience. For example, parents may experience feelings of shame around their child's diagnosis. Parents can come together with the idea of being able to manage their child's ADHD, which alleviates some of the pressure the child may experience. The therapist attempts to normalize the ADHD diagnosis for the parent and the child in this way:

> I tell them millions of kids have ADHD. They go to grammar school every day. They go to high school. They go to college. They become doctors, lawyers, nurses, you know. But, the difference between them and you are that they have learned to manage their ADHD. [VAU]

One analyst described the intervention dynamic as one that works to disrupt *"a choreography in a family that has been established for years, and you have to kind of break that up, and parents are so relieved when you break it up because they've been caught in a rut for years"* [DON]. One goal of this intervention phase is to help parents become more in touch with their feelings about parenting. For example, one analyst begins working with parents by asking them how they came to have the idea of parenting. This exploration allows the therapist to begin to explore dynamic parenting issues—such as parental identification—that may present a challenge for both the child and the parent. Children may struggle with their identification or lack of identification with a parent. A parent may carry disappointment for the child, and the child, in turn, may identify with that position. Although acknowledging the process, the therapist may show restraint in making interpretations to the child. A therapist may say to the child *"You know, it sounds like you having the Dad you have—there's a real difficult issue for you"* [MOL]. Helping parents to recognize that this identification process may be at work in shaping some of their own intense emotions and their responses to the child will be helpful in ameliorating some of the adverse effects of ADHD on the parent–child relationship.

As the therapist continues to develop a clearer understanding of the child, he conveys to the parent his understanding of the child's experiences. The eventual goal is for the parent to develop the ability to mentalize the child. As one analyst puts it, *"[I want the mother to know that] I get her son . . . I understand his activities . . . for her to feel that her son is being understood . . . to have that experience of her son being known and liked, and validated. It's soothing for her"* [SAP]. The therapist plays a critical role in helping the parent develop the ability to mentalize the child by encouraging the parent to imagine how the child might be feeling when she is seemingly oppositional or defiant or unresponsive. A therapeutic achievement is marked by the parent's ability to overlook the child's overt behavior and consider the mental processes that may be occurring in her mind at that moment.

Another interpersonal dynamic between the child and parent that could benefit from mentalization is the tendency for parents to respond to the child in automatic ways. At times, parents are locked into a response pattern with their children. Parents can say "no" to their child without much thought to the child's request or become easily annoyed by the child's behavior. One analyst encourages parents to think about their responses to their children before responding to them; in other words, parents are asked to consider their oppositional responses. For example, in a session with a parent, an analyst likes to ask, *"Now is that going be a 'yes,' or is that going to be the big 'NO'? Which is it going to be?"* [VAU]. The goal is to get the parent to the point where he or she can respond with some self-reflection and consideration. For example, a parent at this stage may say *"I'm going to hold my 'no' back."* The parents can see that they have volition, as opposed to defaulting to the instantaneous "No." On an emotional level, parents are encouraged to have a range of responses to the emotions the child evokes in them. *"If the child elicits responses that are the same as they always do then they [the parents] are still in the same rut. . . . If the child evokes a response that is different for you, then you're not just a 'lousy' parent, you have a real broad possible way of responding"* [VAU]. Mentalization helps parents develop more varied emotional responses.

In addition to mentalizing their responses to the child, the analyst attempts to increase the affection parents have for their children. Parents can become lost in their anger and frustration with their children. Helping parents to reflect on what their child must be feeling is important in helping parents to experience empathy for their children. The therapist works to re-present the child to the parent in a way that allows the parent to accept the child's idiosyncrasies and develop a more compassionate response to the child. Parents need to understand that the child has a "hidden" condition that causes a discrepancy between what the child appears to be capable of doing and the child's internal experiences. Therapists give parents access to their child's inner world so that they can adjust their expectations and provide the appropriate level of support. Parents soon come to realize that their child is not purposefully trying to disrupt their lives but that the child's difficulties are an outward indication of the level of difficulty the child is experiencing internally. The more disruptive the child's behavior, the more internally disorganized and overwhelmed the child is with regard to how she experiences life. Parents benefit from understanding that their child is struggling not only to function (to respond to ego demands) but also to cope with an experience of herself as inadequate, insufficient, or deficient, especially when she compares herself to her peers or tries to measure herself against the expectations of her parents and teachers.

In my practice with children and parents, I find that parents of children with ADHD focus on controlling the child's behavior. Parents require that the child complete individual tasks and often become angry, resentful, and overwhelmed with stress in managing their noncompliant child. Empathy, tenderness, and kindness take a backseat in the face of all these other struggles. Parents need support in remembering to balance their interactions with their children. In these situations, the therapist reminds the parents of the other interpersonal experiences that they can share with their child and encourages them to embrace those experiences.

A psychodynamically oriented therapist discussed her work with a twelve-year-old girl and sought to understand what in her parents' backgrounds may have contributed to their lack of empathic response to their daughter's struggles. The goal of the therapist was to represent the child to the parent.

> I work with a twelve-year-old girl who is so cute and so engaging. I'm still trying to understand even how the parents became so alienated from her. There have been a lot of stressors in this family. Parents have had illnesses and

anxiety around those issues. I think their expectations of their child are beyond the child's developmental stage—they see her as an older child. I think that's a part that—a missing piece for the parents in terms of having more realistic expectations of any twelve-year-old, never mind one with ADHD. The parent's anger is thick. The mother feels so betrayed and hurt by the child's behavior. The parents say to me "Where did we go wrong, how could this be happening?" [HUG]

One approach to dealing with a case like this one is for the therapist to prescribe that the mother spend time with her daughter. For example, the therapist may recommend that the child and mother play together or spend time engaging in activities that the child suggests. These shared moments are at times void of negative interactions, and both can enjoy each other's company. After making this prescription, the therapist can expect reports of increased experiences of parents feeling connected to their child. The child is given the gift of having regained her connection with her mother—to cuddle with her mom—and for the mother, it is beautiful to see her daughter once more.

The therapist interprets for the parents the relations between the child's executive-functioning ego deficits and their impacts on the child's life. It is the therapist's responsibility to prepare parents for the progress the child will make and the rate at which the child will progress, with the goal of eventual termination.

I think parents need to learn about their child. They need to be informed and understand their child. As psychologists, we talk about executive functioning, but how does that translate to real life? How do the expectations of school life and family life intersect with that area of challenge for the child? I say to parents, "See how your child is functioning in all the different areas of their lives. That is your baseline. And then your job is to inch them up from whatever that baseline is in small steps, small increments. Keep it realistic. Think of smaller steps. Think creatively." I think you have to be a much more creative parent when you are raising a more challenging child. Think on your feet, in the heat of the moment. It's okay to buy yourself some time. You don't have to respond. You can say "I have to think about that." The worst thing that you can do is respond in the heat of the moment because you do need thinking time. You are often in the line of fire. Think a bit about how to reverse the intervention with the child, so that you are putting a more positive spin on it instead of the more negative spin. Our knee-jerk reaction as people is to find what we are doing wrong, criticize, and all of that stuff. It takes much more creativity to sort of take a deep breath, find ways to stay connected, keep your child engaged as a partner in the process. [HUG]

In the third phase of the treatment, parents can be a useful resource in validating therapeutic changes occurring in the child. The analyst may ask *What's going on? What are you seeing? Is there anything different?* Any discrepancies between the therapist's view and the parents' view are explored. For example, the analyst may note that, *"Well, it sounds like we're talking about two different kids."* This statement is designed to get parents thinking about what is creating the disparity and can lead to the parents revealing information they had not previously discussed. Once parents confirm that the gains the child has made are sustainable, the therapist can begin to plan for termination or transition to another treatment focus.

> It's very individualized. I say to parents, you have to be prepared to hang on for the ride because it's going to be a ride. It gets better, but it might not get better until their mid-twenties. And that's the frontal lobe maturity. Okay, so maturity on every level. The system gets more relaxed once they leave traditional school, like once they can pick their next step, after high school. That is a long ride for the parent, and I think they do need to know that. It's a long ride, and it's not going to be an easy one. Parents have to develop a thick skin because they are going to be judged by many people at many turns along the way. Parents need support in becoming the child's advocate, but it's not going to be easy, so that's the pattern. [HUG]

Parent and Family Interventions
Phase I: Gather a developmental history and develop an alliance with the parent

- Obtain a history of the child's development;
- Develop a therapeutic alliance with the parent.

Phase II: Understand the child's difficulties and changing ego functioning and relational world

- Psychoeducation of the parent:

  - Increase awareness about dynamic parenting issues;
  - Identify feelings about parenting;
  - Identify issues of parental identification.

- Represent the child to the parent.
- Develop in the parent the ability to mentalize the child such that they:

  - Observe the mental processes of the child;
  - Reflect before responding to the child;
  - Develop more varied emotional responses to the child;
  - Increase affection for the child.

Phase III: Verification of therapeutic change and termination of treatment

School Intervention

For some analysts, developing a collaborative relationship with the school is one way of helping parents feel supported. Most parents reach out to a therapist due to complaints from teachers regarding their child's behavior in the classroom. Therapists therefore often find themselves in a position where parents and teachers alike expect the child's actions to change ("*Change him. . . . Fix him now*" [VAU]). However, more than behavior management, achieving an understanding of the child is needed. Having a deep understanding of the child and the nature of what he is struggling with will help shape an appropriate and helpful response. It is important for parents and teachers to realize that changes in the child's behavior will take time. As the therapy begins to take hold, his internal life starts to change. The child's behavior reflects feelings of release from conflict, a strengthened ego, improved positive feelings about the self, positive interpersonal interactions, and so on.

Collaboration between the therapist and the teachers is necessary for the child, parents, and teachers. It is important in terms of validating not only the parents' experience of the child but also the school's experience as well. Teachers and parents are often at a loss as to how to help the child comply with their expectations. In fact, the child's difficulties leave the teacher feeling ineffective in her role, either in terms of being able to help the child or being able to teach the class without disruptions. One analyst explains it is important for the school to own their feelings of aggression toward the child: "*Of course you feel aggressive toward the child. The child, who spits on anybody—you're going to get pissed off*" [VAU]. The analyst normalizes the teacher's feelings of anger, allowing her to see the ways in which she was pushing the child away as a result of her anger. According to one analyst, "*[one teacher's] defense was, 'Let me put you in the corner over there and keep you safely out of the way. That way I don't have to feel guilty and we can say that you're a student'*" [VAU]. Therapists who can empathize with teachers and begin to engage them in changing their view of the ADHD children they encounter will have some success in improving the classroom experiences of the children they are treating.

The therapist can also be a valuable resource for teachers who genuinely care about their students and wish to be helpful. One analyst I spoke to noted that a valuable interaction with school personnel involves teaching them to recognize children who are at risk of developing difficulties. The therapist in this next interaction also sought to be a resource for teachers:

> [I work] to teach them to recognize the kid who can't figure out the simplest things. Some of the teachers are good, and they say, "You know there's something about this one . . ."—and that seems to be the seed, where the divergence starts. And if it doesn't get pulled back then, it can be a wider difference, and then in these severe cases you get ten- or twelve-year-olds who are refusing school or experiencing psychosis or having rageful outbursts or become conduct disordered. . . . Because then it becomes, you know, they [the children] don't know how to manage it, and I've worked with a few fairly complex conduct-type kids and found that you can actually—if there's a willingness in the family, you can actually rearrange the contingencies to use a behavioral sort of a measure so that you can actually get relief for that child so that they don't have actually to be so dysregulated. [MOL]

Though their educative function is the primary focus of teachers, there is another important role teachers could play with the child—to consider how they allow children's abilities to emerge. A central role of the therapist is to help the teachers to value and recognize that non-educative aspect of their relationships with the children they teach. *What could the teacher do—or what kind of environment could she provide—that would help a child with ADHD find his way?*

School Interventions
Therapists should:

- Develop a collaborative relationship with the teacher/school.
- Share with the teacher their understanding of the child and the nature of the child's struggles and help shape appropriate teacher responses.
- Educate teachers on the process of psychodynamic therapy to address expectations regarding time frame for change.
- Validate the teacher's experiences.
- Serve as a resource for the teacher.

SUMMARY

There are limitations to using both behavioral and cognitive behavioral approaches, and neither seems particularly useful in treating ADHD. Cognitive deficiencies are difficult to treat (Hinshaw, 2006). From the CBT perspective, ADHD symptoms associated with deficits in executive-functioning skills cannot be adequately addressed by CBT approaches in young children. Children manifesting difficulties with attention, motivation, planning, and organization and with inhibiting motor activity may require supportive environments and behavioral therapy that can address these problems (Hinshaw,

2006; Levine and Anshel, 2011). However, if the child's problems include depression and anxiety, then cognitive behavioral approaches are useful in modifying the cognitive distortions accompanying these comorbid pathologies (Kazdin and Weisz, 2003). From a behavioral perspective, adjustments must be made to the child's external environments so the child can achieve the desired behaviors and accomplish their goals.

The psychodynamically oriented therapist believes behavioral intervention is regimented. For dynamic therapists who use behavioral interventions, the therapeutic goal is to give the child a set of tools that allows the child to use their emotions in adaptive ways. Psychodynamic interventions with the family occurs in three phases:

1. obtaining the child's developmental history and developing an alliance with the parent;
2. working with the child to understand his difficulties, changing ego functioning, and relational world while providing psychoeducation to parents to increase their understanding of the child and develop positive parent–child interactions; and
3. verifying therapeutic change and preparing the child and parents for termination of treatment.

Therapists also work collaboratively with their clients' schools to support the parents and child in treatment. Therapists develop relationships with teachers and school staff and, similar to their work with the parents, share with those adults their understanding of their clients to encourage appropriate responses to the children. This collaboration includes educating teachers about the process of psychodynamic therapy, validating the teacher's experiences, and serving as a resource for the teachers.

CHAPTER HIGHLIGHTS

Cognitive Behavioral Approach (CBT)

- CBT is based on a belief that the ADHD behaviors arise from cognitive distortions that are secondary to neurological insults.
- *CBT Conceptualization of ADHD*: The child has distortions about himself vis-à-vis others in his life and CBT's interventions would focus on the child's interpretation of external events and the extent to which that interpretation becomes so "distorted" or misaligned with reality that it interferes with his ability to function.
- CBT is not recommended for children under eight years old.

Behavioral Approaches

- The behavioral approach to ADHD is based on a belief that ADHD behaviors stem from neurological and cognitive deficiencies and the child is having difficulty in meeting the demands of his environment.
- Behavioral therapy is most effective when combined with other interventions such as medication and parent training.
- *Psychodynamic therapists view behavioral approaches* as regimented yet offering children tools that allow the child to use their emotions adaptively.

Psychodynamic Approach to Parenting and School Interventions

- *Parenting interventions:*

  - *Phase I: Gather a developmental history and develop an alliance with the parent* (obtain a history of the child's development and develop a therapeutic alliance with the parent).
  - *Phase II: Understand the child's difficulties and changing ego functioning and relational world* (psychoeducation of the parent, represent the child to the parent, develop in the parent the ability to mentalize the child).
  - *Phase III: Verification of therapeutic change and termination of treatment.*

- *School interventions:*

  - Therapists develop collaborative relationships with the teacher/school, share with the teacher their understanding of the child and help shape appropriate teacher responses, educate teachers on the process of psychodynamic therapy to address expectations regarding the time frame for change, validate the teacher's experiences, and serve as a resource for the teacher.

Epilogue

Being deeply loved by someone gives you strength, while loving someone deeply gives you courage.
— Lao Tzu

Approximately 5.9 million children in the United States are diagnosed with Attention Deficit Hyperactivity Disorder (ADHD). The most frequent age of diagnosis occurs between three and seventeen years old, when 13.5 percent of boys and 5.4 percent of girls (U.S. Department of Health and Human Services, 2013) will be diagnosed with ADHD. These children experience symptoms of inattention and hyperactivity in multiple settings including at home and in school. Consequently, they display a range of behaviors including difficulty with sustaining attention or attending to details, completing tasks, following verbal and other instructions, remaining seated, and maintaining organization; an aversion to tasks requiring sustained mental effort; distractibility and forgetfulness in daily activities; fidgeting behavior; excessive motor movement or speaking; and interrupting or intruding on others (American Psychiatric Association, 2013). Members of their communities— including parents and teachers—and the broader society around them have a distinct view of these children that is mostly unsympathetic. These children are attributed with being lazy, lacking discipline, having been poorly parented, and being disruptive or oppositional. The moral indictments of these children are outgrowths of societal forces—economic and cultural—that impact the collective unconscious.

THE MORAL INDICTMENT OF ADHD CHILDREN

Economic Factors

From an economic point of view, ADHD symptoms can be thought of as outgrowths of the increasing participation of children, knowingly and unknowingly, in a market economy. When ADHD children are perceived as unsucessessful in achieving certain markers of economic success, a moral devaluing of these children occurs. An examination of children's role in our economy highlights the contrast between the child's contributions and what is valued in society. Children have always played a role in the economic world although there has been a shift from child labor to child consumerism. McNeal (1999) reports American children spend upwards of $23 billion annually and influence an estimated $188 billion of parental spending. Zelizer (2010) suggests that children's economic influence extends from consumerism and beyond to include broader economic activities related to production and distribution of goods. In terms of production, children are often engaged in some form of direct or indirect token economy. Children earn money, coupons, favors, and so on in exchange for domestic work and other informal "work-related" duties. In one very direct example of childhood engagement in productive labor, children are engaged in raising money for philanthropic endeavors at a very young age by their schools, teams, churches, and other groups.

Indeed, Zelizer's (1985) book *Pricing the Priceless Child* refutes the notion that we have been successful in insulating children from a market economy. At least in the United States, the transformation from the 1870s view of childhood to the twentieth-century view yielded classrooms, summer camps, play dates, and specialty workshops for children—educational and extracurricular activities that are believed to create a barrier for some children against economic and other abuses. In the meantime, there are employed children in other parts of the world who are expected to contribute to their households.

Ethnographic studies like those described by Zelizer (2010) point to some of the psychological implications of these vastly different economic contexts. Differences in a range of children's responses have been observed, including self-indulgence versus altruism, collaboration versus conflict, reasonable versus demanding, and inclusion versus exclusion. These responses are commentaries on some key components of children's psychological functioning that are particularly relevant to ADHD—difficulties with emotion regulation, impulsivity, lack of productivity, and impaired social relationships. The realization that children have economic lives raises important questions about how they negotiate these experiences. Some hold the view that children turn to crime, gang activity, and other antisocial behaviors to gain access to goods. The perception of children as unproductive, lazy, self-indulgent, and antisocial reflects a view of the child in economic terms associated with productivity, consumerism, and distribution. This economic context singles out children whose behaviors and ways of being seem to be inconsistent with economic productivity. Within this context, then, the moral indictment of these behaviors appears to be quite reasonable. However, such an indictment fails to take into consideration the idea that there may be ways to measure a child's potential that are *not* directly related to economic productivity.

Cultural Factors

Psychodynamic psychotherapists' respect for the individual differences in the manifestation of ADHD symptoms is supported by the culture bound manifestation of the disorder. Therapists appreciate that ADHD symptoms reflect a complex matrix of many contributing factors—including culture. Cultural manifestations of ADHD are reflected in the prevalence and course of the disorder, differences in the accompanying co-occurrence of other psychological problems, and parents' and families' views of the disorder. An examination of the culture specific ways in which ADHD is manifested gives us some insight into the heterotypic presentation of ADHD and the varied responses of parents to the child's behavioral difficulties and psychological suffering. In other words, whether the child receives an indictment (i.e., punishment) or assistance for their ADHD depends heavily on the child's culture.

A review of ADHD studies conducted in different countries begins to shed some light on cultural differences in the symptom manifestation. Culture does not cause ADHD, but contributes to differences in incidence, prevalence, and symptomatology. The prevalence of ADHD in the United States (from 9.1–12 percent to 11.4–16.1 percent) compared to non-U.S. countries (from 5.8–11.2 percent to 12–19.8 percent) appear to be within similar ranges. Iceland, Australia, Italy, and Sweden are exceptions, recording markedly lower rates (2.4 percent to 7.5 percent) (Faraone et al., 2003). Parents and teachers in non-U.S. countries—Brazil, Colombia, China, Canada, Finland, Germany, Hong Kong, India, Israel, Japan, New Zealand, Spain, The Netherlands, Taiwan, and the United Kingdom—rated ADHD symptoms in their children comparable to their counterparts in the United States (Faraone et al., 2003). Environmental adversity and psychosocial stress associated with the Chernobyl disaster likely account for the unusually high prevalence of ADHD among children in the Ukraine—19.8 percent compared to approximately 9.7 percent in the United States. Similarity and differences in prevalence rates only present one view of ADHD and its global impact.

Although many countries may share the same prevalence rates of ADHD, some aspects of the disorder are *culture-dependent*: culture determines the way ADHD manifests and its course. One useful way to think of ADHD symptoms has been to categorize symptoms as over- or under-controlled. Briefly, under-controlled behaviors include actions that reflect the child's ability to control his response to strong emotional urges, resulting in aggression, opposition, and impulsive behaviors. Over-controlled behaviors, on the other hand, tend to include actions that reflect the child's inhibitions, resulting in depression, anxiety, and over-compliance. Some therapists believe that these behaviors may develop as a consequence of the difficulties and limitations the ADHD symptoms impose on the child. For example, a child who has difficulty completing tasks may become depressed or oppositional as a result of their experiences. It is unclear whether depressed mood or difficulty with task completion comes first. Also, it is a challenge to disentangle the ADHD symptoms from the comorbid disorders. Some theorists and researchers believe that culture plays a role in determining which symptoms—over- or under-controlled—children express.

Interpretation of children's behaviors differs across cultures (Chiang, Barrett, and Nunez, 2000), and that, in turn, impacts parents' help-seeking behaviors (Johnston, Seipp, Hommersen, Hoza, and Fine, 2005; Yeh, McCabe, Hough, Lau, Fakhry, and Garland, 2005). For example, culturally variant views of ADHD symptoms—over- and under-controlled symptoms—suggest culture determines the extent to which certain behaviors are tolerated during childhood, and these differences may account for variations in the patterns of comorbid disorders found among ADHD-diagnosed children. Cultural norms thus set the stage for parental expectations and their tolerance of child behaviors. For example, compared to Euro-North Americans, Chinese immigrant parents tend to place higher demands on their children with regard to "inhibition (e.g., impulse control and suppression of aggression) and compliance (e.g., obedience without question)" (Julian, McKenry, and McKelvey, 1994, in Mah and Johnston, 2007, p. 136). Consequently, over-controlled behaviors reflected in comorbid disorders such as oppositional defiance disorder (ODD) and conduct disorders are less prevalent among that subset of children diagnosed with ADHD in the United States. Conversely, significantly higher rates of ODD, conduct disorder, anxiety disorder, and mood disorders are prevalent among ADHD-diagnosed children in Brazil compared to similar children in Germany (Roessner, Becker, Rothenberger, Rohde, and Banaschewski, 2007). However, Roessner and colleagues concluded that although there are differences between the two cultural groups, the broadband psychopathological profile of the Child Behavior Checklist (CBCL) was similar enough to suggest similar symptom presentation between both groups.

Cultural differences in tolerance also account for differences in the reporting of ADHD symptoms. For instance, in a sample of ADHD children, Russian children scored two times higher on the CBCL scale of attention problems compared to children in the United States (Carter, Grigorenko, and Pauls, 1995). This figure implies that many children who are diagnosed with ADHD in the United States would not have symptoms strong enough to be seen as meeting the criteria for diagnosis in Russia. Using a similar scale, researchers found a tendency for Brazilian parents to over-report compared to German parents (Achenbach, Bird, Canino, Phares, Gould, and Rubio-Stipec, 1990; Cury and Golfeto, 2003; Goodman, Neves dos Santos, Robatto Nunes, Pereira de Miranda, Fleitlich-Bilyk, and Almeida Filho, 2005). Other sociodemographic factors contributing to cultural differences include socioeconomic status and higher symptom thresholds needed to qualify for services (Office of the Surgeon General; Center for Mental Health Services; National Institute of Mental Health, 2015).

Some patterns of symptom presentation and parental response to ADHD appear to be culturally dependent—depending on the child's social and societal origins, there is an increased likelihood of the child exhibiting one set of comorbid symptoms over the other. Within North America, for example, non-Caucasian parents differ from their Caucasian counterparts in their tendency to be less tolerant of oppositional behaviors and misconduct (under-controlled behaviors) and to experience more guilt and a heightened sense of responsibility for the child's actions. These sentiments may explain why, among children of non-Caucasian parents, there are relatively more incidences of and tolerance for comorbid symptoms of anxiety and depression (over-controlled behaviors) with ADHD. Studies that focus on specific minority groups rather than a generalized Caucasian/non-Caucasian classification provide even more robust information with regard to the tendency of different cultures to attribute mental health problems to a range of external and uncontrollable factors. For example, Asian/Pacific Islander-American parents tend to blame their children's mental health concerns on their acculturation challenges, and many non-Hispanic Caucasian parents believe their children's problems stem from a range of factors such as physical and personality dispositions, family conflict, and trauma (Yeh et al., 2005).

Comparing mothers in China with mothers in the United States provides a transglobal perspective on ADHD symptom attribution. Among Caucasian North American mothers, children are credited for positive behaviors, while negative behaviors are seen to stem from factors external to the child and beyond their control (Gretarsson and Gelfand, 1988). The opposite holds true for the Chinese mothers. Chinese children are more likely to be held personally responsible for negative actions, which parents attribute to internally controllable factors, and they receive less credit for positive behaviors, which parents are more likely to attribute to external factors (Chiang, Barrett, and Nunez, 2000; Hess, Chih-Mei, and McDevitt, 1987). Thus, among Caucasian North Americans, a population in which children do not tend to be held responsible for their problem behaviors, there is an acknowledgment that the child's actions are due to the ADHD "disorder" and that she could therefore benefit from behavioral management and medication. In comparison, Chinese mothers and other minorities attribute problem behaviors in children to a range of factors including "spiritual, moral, somatic, psychological, and metaphysical" ones (Flaskerud, 1984).

In addition to differences with regard to the external attributions for problem behaviors and mental health issues in children, cultural differences are also reflected in how parents choose to address these issues. Among Chinese parents, there was more guilt and parental blame for the child's behaviors and more belief in medication and psychological causes/treatments. Canadian-Caucasian mothers meanwhile were more likely to express confidence in treatments that included behavior management and diet or vitamins.

Different cultures may make similar attributions about which symptoms indicate mental health challenges among their children, but their interpretation of the causes and treatment for those challenges can vary widely. We have seen that, while prevalence rates of ADHD tend to hold across cultures, parental attributions about ADHD behaviors seem to be culturally determined. When compared with parents from Germany, Brazil, and China, Caucasian North American parents attribute ADHD behaviors more often to external and uncontrollable factors. However, these parents differ in their knowledge about the disorder, their beliefs about its causes, and treatment preferences. Culture mediates both the parents' understanding of the problematic behavior and the treatment choices they make.

The research on the role of culture on ADHD is limited, and more research is needed to have a more comprehensive understanding of the role of culture in ADHD diagnosis and treatment. But to the extent that children's behaviors occur within the context of their families and a larger society, it is clear that culture shapes parental understanding and interventions pertaining to ADHD. Historically, the constellation of ADHD behaviors has been regarded as "misconduct" and consistent with a medical-disease model. As a result, peers, parents, and educators view children presenting with ADHD symptoms as problems in need of a cure.

Societal contributors to ADHD—both economic and cultural—are not often appreciated as we consider other factors contributing to the etiology and perpetuation of ADHD symptoms. This book highlights the complex and diverse factors contributing to ADHD, but the child and all occurrences of psychopathology occur in a societal context. The idea that society contributes to psychopathology is not new to psychoanalysis. Psychoanalysts have written about this topic for quite some time. While it is hard to disentangle whether community impacts ADHD or ADHD impacts society, it is clear that the society and ADHD intersect and have a shared effect. Some noteworthy analysts have contemplated the role of the unconscious in society. For example, during the first half of the twentieth century, Freud treated patients who presented with neurotic anxieties that he attributed to the sexual repression characteristic of the society (Freud, 1908/1959). In keeping with the location of patients' symptoms within a broader societal context, Otto Fenichel, Wilhelm Reich, Erich Fromm, Theodor Adorno, Herbert Marcuse, Christopher Lasch, and Tod Sloan wrote about how patients' symptoms might relate to larger systems such as the capitalist economy or the socioeconomic aspects of culture (Layton, 2007). Layton offers an overview of this idea of internalized societal norms and encourages the analyst to adopt a view of *mutual recognition*—one that acknowledges the impact that intrapsychic symptoms and social factors have on each other. Given the inextricable influence of society on psychopathology, consideration of how ADHD symptoms intersect with societal factors broadens our understanding of the ADHD phenomenon.

CULTIVATING COMPASSION FOR THE ADHD CHILD

A Social Construction View

Contemporary therapists question the practice of treatment professionals, parents, and educators of viewing children who present with ADHD-like symptoms as pathological. Rather, dynamically oriented therapists acknowledge that ADHD is a social construction indicative of society's views and expectations of children's behaviors. Appreciating the social constructivist process that fuels ADHD symptomatology allows for a more compassionate response to ADHD. These expectations may lead ADHD children to feel poorly about themselves: *"Kids are being made to feel like they are bad or that they are terrible, that something is wrong with them"* [DON]. ADHD-like behaviors do not occur in a vacuum, immune from the influences of the larger society. The question regarding whether ADHD is "real" or whether it is created by society is one that plagues those treating the disorder.

Societal expectations of children to be more sedentary are not syntonic with the natural tendencies of those children who require more active lifestyles. For example, one therapist explained that *"the demands of our society . . . to create a more sedentary-focused existence [are in conflict with] a child who needs a more interactive way of learning"* [HUG]. Observations in school settings confirm that those settings feature more teacher-directed activities rather than free play, a shift in focus that one therapist lamented upon: *"There used to be more time for free play, for learning at your pace, for moving around"* [LUB]. Unfortunately, children are now expected to sit still, while adults, faced with a litany of data on rising obesity levels (Centers for Disease Control, 2015), are expected to increase their activity levels after years of being trained or medicated to subdue the urge to move. One analyst commented, *"movement is a language, movement expresses things, and movement is also an essential biological force"* [LUB].

Recognizing the influence of society on our views of children's actions compels us to acknowledge that children whose behaviors differ from our expectations risk being pathologized. ADHD has thus taken on cultural meaning. As a result, the job of therapists, researchers, and others in the field is to *"separate those [ADHD children] out from the children who have difficulties produced from the things we're asking children to do"* [MOL]. Analysts view ADHD-like symptoms as representative of the child's response to his environment—a byproduct or a disguise for different kinds of feelings. For example, one analyst reports:

> I would greatly prefer if people who were going to talk about ADHD talked [instead] about sorting out the ones who seem to have some organic, genuine PDD-type origin from those who are under unreasonable teachers, who are under unreasonable pressure in unreasonable schools, or who have unreasonable demands in their family because of divorce or conflict or other difficulties. . . . Because I see both, and one of them I would certainly see as quote "ADHD" in some class sense and the other one, while they might meet the criteria if you checked off the diagnostic criteria . . . they don't have an attention disorder so much as a need for therapy because they have anxiety or some response to a difficulty—anxiety being a typical one, aggression being another one, or hyperactivity being another one—because of the demands of life is unreasonable for that child. [MOL]

While there are discrete factors that co-occur with the ADHD presentation, some analysts believe the symptoms are reflective of a constellation of inter-generational factors. Neurobiological factors, interpersonal dynamic issues, socioeconomic resources, and sociocultural views can all transmit across generations with limited variability. As such, the analyst must consider that the child is not in a vacuum and is subject to other influences, asking questions such as these, suggested by one respondent: *"What are the parents bringing to the table in terms of their neurobiology, in terms of their own psychodynamic and family background? And then in our society, what pressures are being placed on that child and on that parent?"* [HUG].

Similarly, the practicing analyst has to take into account that the child does not come into treatment with a simple list of presenting symptoms. The child brings with him the weight of his symptoms—a burden that is multilayered in its meaning. The child's behaviors have meanings that function within and are reflective of the parental relationship, the broader family system, his learning environment, and the cultural and societal communities that surround him. Each entity presses on the child with both its spoken and unspoken expectations and articulated and unarticulated judgments about what ought to be done to correct the problem created when those expectations are not met. Meanwhile, what the child may be attempting to communicate through his behaviors appears to be less important. Parents feel caught in a juxtaposition of holding their child responsible for his "problematic" behaviors while also feeling guilt related to their lack of a clear sense of how to help him. The attention the child's behavior receives is itself distracting. As we are increasingly distracted by the child's actions, we become less attentive to the child's efforts to communicate or have meaningful contact. Our own distraction places our focus on stopping the child's behavior rather than on understanding what is being shared.

ADHD symptoms are thus perpetuated by our own preoccupation with symptom elimination and our limited *"capacity to imagine"* the child as otherwise. As one analyst put it,

> When we talk about kids with ADD, and when we see these kids we are caught up [with] the symptom. . . . Everything is the symptom, even the treatment, even the way you conceptualize them in the classroom—what they do, what I told them to do, and what they didn't do. . . . So what's missing almost entirely is—from their part and our part—the capacity to imagine, to kind of think in these potentials and to see that in them. [SAP]

Because there are multiple pathways that serve as possible explanation of ADHD-like symptoms, analysts are reluctant to categorize children as ADHD or view every child with these symptoms as alike. For example, one analyst explains,

> It depends on the child. So if I'm going to understand the child's behavior [based] on the diagnosis, then I would end up having to understand all the children with that diagnosis in the same way. And, of course, you can't do that because they're individual people, and they have different things going on. [LOM]

Therapists working with children who present with ADHD-like symptoms need to remain open to the idea that each child is different and comes to the treatment with a unique set of circumstances. A range of individual, developmental, and environmental issues may shape the child's response to her environmental demands. ADHD is better conceptualized as the child's response to her biological and environmental—maternal/parental, institutional, and cultural—factors that come to bear upon her. Therapists are urged not to foreclose on a child's presentation by simply categorizing the child but to instead develop their *"capacity to imagine"* the child's potential. If we cultivate compassion for the ADHD child, we would be able to shift our stance from one of moral indictment to empathy.

A VISION FOR ALL CHILDREN

In ending, I will share a story about my experience in Paris, France, with an inclusive school—a school that welcomes all children, with and without a range of disabilities. While visiting Paris, I had the opportunity to interview Ms. Cecile Herrou, the director and founder of APARTE, an association of five inclusion pre-kindergarten and kindergarten programs in Paris. Ms. Herrou is a Freudian-trained analyst with an interest in applying her training to institutional functioning. Her inspiration for the school comes from a movement led by two French psychiatrists, Jean Oury and Felix Guattari, who in the mid-twentieth-century established and operated La Borde, a revolutionary adult psychiatric clinic in France that continues to operate today. According to Ms. Herrou, Oury and Guattari believed that *"we should think of the institution as a pathogenic environment,"* and that institutional systems could evolve with the needs of their clients. Ms. Herrou explains that a central question posed by this movement is *"How can we get over our alienation?"* From this perspective, hierarchical relationships are discouraged; instead, *"individuals are 'healed' by the entire institution working together, not just through the doctor/patient relationship. Doctors can do the dishes, and patients can call meetings."* Borrowing from this philosophy, in the inclusion school, each child is free to build a relationship with anyone, regardless of his or her primary responsibilities. *"The child is free to choose. The idea is that we live in the here and now, and you can be who you are, in a 'situation of disability,' and have a life."*

Ms. Herrou believes the learning institution should be set up to accommodate all children. In her schools, children with and without disabilities are enrolled at a ratio of three to one respectively. The setting is unusual in that all of the children learn together. Children without disabilities learn and play with children who have a range of disabilities. For example, her school has various types of children, ages one to six years old. She describes that children may have learning disabilities, extreme learning difficulties, autism, visual impairments, and medical needs such as feeding tubes, rare genetic diseases, or multiple disabilities. These children present with behavioral and emotional needs and are treated as individuals. Sometimes the children without disabilities can demand as much or more attention than the children with disabilities.

One foundational principle of the school is the perspective that each child is an individual. *"We try to take each child individually with their singularity,"* Ms. Herrou reports. *"We are aware of each child's uniqueness, and at times we can be equally surprised by a child or parent's behavior regardless of whether or not they are persons with disabilities."* The educators make it their priority to give each child equal attention. Although the training of the teachers varies, Ms. Herrou believes the environment is the most therapeutic agent. The child is encouraged, first and foremost, to be a child.

I was curious about the motivation of parents without children with particular needs to place their children in the APARTE schools. Ms. Herrou explained that parents are interested for many reasons, including their political orientations, ethical convictions, and interest in diversity. The most compelling reason for parents is a belief that a school equipped to meet the needs of children with disabilities would be qualified to handle the needs of their children. I was curious about the school's ability to meet all of the children's needs. Ms. Herrou explained that her team was oriented to think about the needs of the child rather than thinking about the disability. Like every other child, children with disabilities are, first, children. This philosophy allows each educator to provide all that the child needs to make learning and social interactions possible.

During my visit, I observed a child who was in a motorized wheelchair playing with ambulatory children. Children with visual impairments played with sighted children. Children with emotional problems played with children without these challenges. Even the names of the schools are suggestive of the values the schools embrace. The first school was called Dagobert, after a Merovingian French King who was considered odd. He did not seem to adhere to the norms of his station. He was a "goofy" king—the subject of many children stories and songs. The second school is called Gulliver, after the many European stories about Gulliver's travels. It offers a commentary on the relativity of big and small—how they can exist together. The third school, located in a community with North African and Arab families, is named Ali Baba. Ms. Herrou thought it necessary to have a reference related to the Arab world and the cultural diversity of the area. The part of the Ali Baba story that is relevant here is the concept of a poor child finding a world of treasure: if this school sounds like a utopia, it is—for a child. Every child deserves to be educated and socialized in a receptive environment. While visiting Paris, I met another educator, Albert Prevost, president of the *Conseil Francais des Personnes Handicapees pour les Questions Européennes*, or French Council for the Disabled in European Issues, who noted that schools are a commentary on society. The APARTE schools are a metaphor for what society could become.

CONCLUSION

One might think of ADHD as a perfect storm of factors that lead to a characteristic presentation of symptoms, a perception that lends itself to a medical context for diagnosis and treatment. But the context in which we perceive children is economically and culturally determined. Fortunately, there is yet another context to consider—one that intersects with all of these—the psychological one. Psychoanalysis can be instrumental in helping to understand how societal factors such as culture and economics combine with the child's psyche to produce ADHD-like symptoms and shape society's indictment of these children.

Developmentally, children are either advantaged or disadvantaged in negotiating and navigating the situations they encounter in their lives. Whatever the child's dispositions may be, children are living and functioning in a societal context that has real influence on shaping their behaviors. Children are not insulated and protected from these influences despite the best efforts of adults. Their varying predispositions eventually succumb to the societal forces bearing down on them, producing a distinctive response in each child. Think of ADHD symptoms as a unique behavioral response reflective of intrapsychic pressures generated in response to a set of specific sociocultural factors. The constellation of ADHD-like behaviors is a stereotypic response that occurs among children with particular dispositions who live in certain economic and cultural contexts. Likewise, the societal context, that is, economic and cultural, shapes the response of parents, families, teachers, and broader society to the child's behavior.

A psychoanalytic approach that appreciates the social construction of psychopathology, encompasses a view of ADHD children's unique psychological world juxtaposed to the societal context in which they live—a view that is sorely missing from most current, behaviorally focused treatment strategies. Psychodynamic theories and approaches to ADHD seek to reinsert the humanity and individualism into the treatment of the ADHD child who is often lost in the morass of societal demands. The practice of psychodynamic therapeutic approaches that allows the child the space for their sense of self to emerge and develop is the process of cultivating compassion for the child.

Bibliography

Abikoff, H. (1987). An evaluation of cognitive behavior therapy for hyperactive children. In B. B. Lahey and A. E. Kazdin (Eds.), *Advances in clinical child psychology* (Vol. 10, pp. 171–216). New York: Plenum Press.

Abraham, N., and Torok, M. (1972). Mourning of Melancholia; Introjection versus incorporation. In Rand, N. T. (Ed). *The shell and the kernel: Renewals of psychoanalysis* (pp. 125–38). Chicago: University of Chicago Press.

Achenbach, T. M., Bird, H. R., Canino, G., Phares, V., Gould, M. S., and Rubio-Stipec, M. (1990). Epidemiological comparisons of Puerto Rican and U.S. mainland children: Parent, teacher, and self-reports. *Journal of the American Academy of Child and Adolescent Psychiatry, 29,* 84–93.

Ainsworth, M. D. (1969). Object relations, dependency and attachment: A theoretical review of the infant-mother relationship. *Child Development, 40,* 969–1025.

Ainsworth, M., Blehar, M., Waters, E., and Wall, S. (1978). *Patterns of attachment.* Hillsdale, NJ: Erlbaum.

Akhtar, N. (2002). Relevance and early word learning. *Journal of Child Language, 29,* 677–86.

Akhtar, N., and Gernsbacher, M. A. (2007). Joint attention and vocabulary development: A critical look. *Language and Linguistics Compass, 1,* 195–207.

Alessandri, S. M., and Lewis, M. (1996). Differences in pride and shame in maltreated and nonmaltreated preschoolers. *Child Development, 67*(4), 1857–69.

Alvarez, A. (2012). *The thinking heart: Three levels of psychoanalytic therapy with disturbed children.* London: Routledge.

American Psychiatric Association. (1968). *Diagnostic and statistical manual of mental disorders (DSM-II)* (2nd ed.). Washington, DC: American Psychiatric Association.

American Psychiatric Association. (1980). *Diagnostic and statistical manual of mental disorders (DSM-III)* (3rd ed.). Washington, DC: American Psychiatric Association.

American Psychiatric Association. (1987). *Diagnostic and statistical manual of mental disorders (DSM-III-R)* (3-R ed.). Washington, DC: American Psychiatric Association.

American Psychiatric Association. (1994). *Diagnostic and statistical manual of mental disorders (DSM-IV)* (4th ed.). Washington, DC: American Psychiatric Association.

American Psychiatric Association. (2000). *Diagnostic and statistical manual of mental disorders (DSM-IV-TR)* (4-TR ed.). Washington, DC: American Psychiatric Association.

American Psychiatric Association. (2013). *Diagnostic and statistical manual of mental disorders (DSM-5)* (5th ed.). Washington, DC: American Psychiatric Association.

Anastopoulos, A. D., Rhoads, L. H., and Farley, S. E. (2006). Counseling and training parents. In R. A. Barkley (Ed.), *Attention-deficit hyperactivity disorder.* (3rd Ed.) (pp. 453–79). New York: Guilford Press.

Andreasen, Nancy C. (2006). DSM and the death of phenomenology in America: An example of unintended consequences. *Schizophr Bull, 33*(1), 108–12. doi: 10.1093/schbul/sbl054.

Ashtari, M., Kumra, S., Bhaskar, S. L., Clarke, T., Thaden, E., Cervellione, K. L., Rhinewine, J., Kane, J. M., Adesman, A., Milanaik, R., Maytal, J., Diamond, A., Szeszko, P., and Ardekani, B. A. (2005). Attention-deficit/hyperactivity disorder: A preliminary diffusion tensor imaging study. *Biological Psychiatry, 57*, 448–55.

Aylward, E. H., Reiss, A. L., Reader, M. J., Singer, H. S., Brown, J. E., and Denckla, M. B. (1996). Basal ganglia volumes in children with attention-deficit hyperactivity disorder. *Journal of Child Neurology, 11*, 112–15.

Barkley, D. (2008). Barkley model. *Scholarpedia, 3*(11), 1877.

Barkley, R. A. (1989). Attention-deficit hyperactivjty disorder. In E. J. Mash and R. A. Barkley (Eds.), *Treatment of childhood disorders* (pp. 39–72). New York: Guilford Press.

Barkley, R. A. (1990). *Attention deficit-hyperactivity disorder: A handbook for diagnosis and treatment.* New York: Guilford.

Barkley, R. A. (1997). Behavioral inhibition, sustained attention, and executive function: Constructing a unified theory of ADHD. *Psychological Bulletin, 121*, 65–94.

Barkley, R. A. (1998). *Attention-deficit hyperactivity disorder: A handbook for diagnosis and treatment.* New York: Guilford Press.

Barkley, R. A. (2005). *ADHD and the nature of self-control.* New York: Guilford.

Barkley, R. A. (2006a). *Attention deficit-hyperactivity disorder: A handbook for diagnosis and treatment.* New York: Guilford.

Barkley, R. A. (2006b). The relevance of the Still lectures to attention deficit/hyperactivity disorder: A commentary. *Journal of Attention Disorders, 10*(2), 137–40.

Barkley R. A., and Biederman, J. (1997). Toward a broader definition of the age-of-onset criterion for attention-deficit hyperactivity disorder. *American Academy of Child Adolescent Psychiatry, 36*, 1204–10

Barkley, R. A., DuPaul, G. J., and McMurray, M. B. (1990). Comprehensive evaluation of attention deficit disorder with and without hyperactivity as defined by research criteria. *Journal of Consulting and Clinical Psychology, 58*, 775–89.

Barkley, R., Fischer, M., Edelbrock, C., and Smallish, L. (1990). The adolescent outcome of hyperactive children diagnosed by research criteria: I. An 8 year prospective follow-up study. *Journal of the American Academy of Child and Adolescent Psychiatry, 29*(4), 456–557.

Battle, E. S., and Lacy, B. (1972). A context for hyperactivity in children, over time. *Child Development*, (43), 757–73.

Baumeister, A., and Hawkins, M. (2001). Incoherence of neuroimaging studies of attention deficit/hyperactivity disorder. *Clinical Neuropharmacology, 24*(1), 2–10.

Baumgardner, T. L., Singer, H. S., Denckla, M. B., Rubin, M. A., Abrams, M. T., Colli, M. J., and Reiss, A. J. (1996). Corpus callosum morphology in children with Tourette syndrome and attention deficit hyperactivity disorder. *Neurology, 47*(2), 477–82.

Bax, M., and MacKeith, R. (1963). *Minimal cerebral dysfunction (little club clinics in developmental medicine).* London: National Spastics Society/Heinemann Medical Books.

Beck, A. T. (1967). *Depression: Clinical, experimental, and theoretical aspects.* Philadelphia: University of Pennsylvania Press.

Beck, A. T., Rush, A. J., Shaw, B. F., and Emery, G. (1979). *Cognitive therapy of depression.* New York: Guilford Press.

Berquin, P., Giedd, J., Jacobsen, L., Hamburger, S., Krain, A., Rapoport, J., et al. (1998). Cerebellum in attention-deficit hyperactivity disorder: A morphometric MRI study. *Neurology, 50*, 1087–93.

Berwid, O. G., Curko Kera, E. A., Marks, D. J., Santra, A., Bender, H. A., and Halperin, J. M. (2005). Sustained attention and response inhibition in young children at risk for attention deficit/hyperactivity disorder. *Journal of Child Psychology and Psychiatry, 46*, 1219–29.

Biederman, J. et al. (1992). Further evidence for family-genetic risk factors in attention deficit hyperactivity disorder. Patterns of comorbidity in probands and relatives psychiatrically and pediatrically referred samples. *Archives of General Psychiatry, 49*(9), 728–38.

Bigelow, B. J. (1987). A few pointers for parents with children having learning disabilities. *Panel Discussion Presented at the Meeting of the Sudbury Association for Children and Adults with Learning Disabilities.*

Bion, W. (1959). Attacks on linking. *International Journal of Psycho-Analysis, 40*, 308.

Bion, W. (1962). The theory of thinking. *International Journal of Psycho-Analysis, 8*, 43.

Birch, H. G. (1964). *Brain damage in children: The biological and social aspects.* Baltimore: The Williams and Wilkins Company.

Boesky, D. (2000, December 16). Panel on "What Do We Mean By Conflict in Contemporary Clinical Work?" Fall Meeting, Amer. Psychoanal. Assn., New York .

Bohart, A. C., Elliott, R., Greenberg, L. S., and Watson, J. C. (2002). Empathy. In J. C. Norcross (Ed.), *Psychotherapy relationships that work: Therapist contributions and responsiveness to patients* (pp. 89–108). New York: Oxford University Press.

Bollas, C. (1992). *Being a character: Psychoanalysis and self experience.* London: Routledge.

Boothby, R. (1991). *Death and desire: Psychonalytic theory in Lacan's return to Freud.* New York and London: Routledge.

Bowlby, J. (1973). *Attachment and Loss, Vol. 2: Separation: Anxiety and Anger.* London: Hogarth Press and Institute of Psychoanalysis.

Bowlby, J. (1988). *A secure base: Parent-child attachment and healthy human development.* New York: Basic Books.

Braswell, L., and Kendall, P. C. (2001). Cognitive-behavioral therapy with youth. In K. S. Dobson (Ed.), *Handbook of cognitive-behavioral therapies* (pp. 246–94). New York: Guilford Press.

Brenner, C. (1994). The mind as conflict and compromise formation. *Journal of Clinical Psychoanalysis.*

Brenner, C. (2002). Conflict, compromise formation, and structural theory. *The Psychoanalytic Quarterly.*

Bromberg, P. M. (2003). Something wicked this way comes: Trauma, dissociation, and conflict: The space where psychoanalysis, cognitive science and neuroscience overlap. *Psychoanalytic Psychology, 20*, 558–74.

Brownback, P. (1982). *The danger of self-love.* Chicago: Moody Press.

Burd, L., and Kerbeshian, J. (1988). Historical roots of ADHD. *Journal of the American Academy of Child and Adolescent Psychiatry, 27*, 262.

Burhans, K. K., and Dweck, C. S. (1995). Helplessness in early childhood: The role of contingent worth. *Child Development, 66*, 1719–38.

Burns, D. D., and Nolen-Hosekema, S. (1992). Therapeutic empathy and recovery from depression in cognitive-behavioral therapy: A structural equation model. *Journal of Consulting and Clinical Psychology, 60*(3), 441–49.

Bush, G., Frazier, J. A., Rauch, S. L., Seidman, L. J., Whalen, P. J., Jenike, M. A., Rosen, B. R., and Biederman, J. (1999). Anterior cingulate cortex dysfunction in attention-deficit/hyperactivity disorder revealed by fMRI and the counting stroop. *Biological Psychiatry, 45*(12), 1542–52.

Cameron, J. R. (1977). Parental treatment, children's temperament, and the risk of childhood behavioral problems: I. relationships between parental characteristics and changes in children's temperament over time. *American Journal of Orthopsychiatry, 47*, 568–76.

Cao, Q., Zang, Y., Zhu, C., Cao, X., Sun, L., Zhou, X., and Yufeng, W. (2008). Alerting deficits in children with attention deficit/hyperactivity disorder: Event-related fMRI evidence. *Brain Research, 1219*, 159–68.

Carlson, L. W. (1999). *A fever in Salem: A new interpretation of the New England witch trials.* Chicago: Ivan R. Dee.

Carlson, E., and Sroufe, L. A. (1995). Contribution of attachment theory to developmental psychopathology. In Cicchetti, D., and Cohen, D. J. (Eds.), *Developmental psychopathology vol. 1: Theory and methods* (pp. 581–617). New York: Wiley.

Carlsson, E. A., Jacobvitz, D., and Sroufe, L. A. (1995). A developmental investigation of inattentiveness and hyperactivity. *Child Development, 66*(1), 37–54.

Carpenter, M., Akhtar, N., and Tomasello, M. (1998). Fourteen-eighteen month-old infants differentially imitate intentional and accidental actions. *Infant and Behavioral Development, 21*(2), 315–30.

Carter, A. S., Grigorenko, E. L., and Pauls, D. L. (1995). A Russian adaptation of the child behavior checklist: Psychometric properties and associations with child and maternal affective symptomatology and family function. *Journal of Abnormal Child Psychology, 23,* 661–84.

Casey, B. J. (2005). Frontostriatal and frontocerebellar circuitry underlying cognitive control. In Mayr, U., Awh, E., and Keele, S. W. (Eds.), *Developing individuality in the human brain: A tribute to Michael I. Poser* (pp. 141–66). Washington, DC: American Psychological Association.

Casey, B. J., Castellanos, F. X., Giedd, J. N., Marsh, W. L., Hamburger, S. D., Schubert, A. B., Vauss, Y. C., Vaituzis, A. C., Dickstein, D. P., Sarfatti, S. E., and Rapoport, J. L. (1997). Implication of right frontostriatal circuitry in response inhibition and attention-deficit/hyperactivity disorder. *Journal of the American Academy of Child and Adolescent Psychiatry, 36,* 374–83.

Casey, B. J., Epstein, J. N., Buhle, J., Liston, C., Davidson, M. C., Tonev, S. T. et al. (2007). Frontostriatal connectivity and its role in cognitive control in parent-child dyads with ADHD. *American Journal of Psychiatry, 164,* 1729–36.

Casey, B. J., Nigg, J. T., and Durston, S. D. (2007). New potential leads in the biology and treatment of attention deficit-hyperactivity disorder. *Current Opinions in Neurology, 20,* 119–24.

Castellanos, F. X. (2001). Neural substrates of attention-deficit hyperactivity disorder. *Advances in Neurology, 85,* 197–206.

Castellanos, F. X., Giedd, J. N., Marsh, W. L., Hamburger, S. D., Vaituzis, A. C., Dickstein, D. P., et al. (1996). Quantitative brain magnetic resonance imaging in attention deficit hyperactivity disorder. *Archives of General Psychiatry, 53*(7), 607–16.

Castellanos, F. X., Lee, P. P., Sharp, W., Jeffries, N. O., Greenstein, D. K., Clasen, L. S., et al. (2002). Developmental trajectories of brain volume abnormalities in children and adolescents with attention-deficit/hyperactivity disorder. *Journal of the American Medical Association, 288*(14), 1740–48.

Castellanos, F. X., and Tannock, R. (2002). Neuroscience of attention-deficit/hyperactivity disorder: The search for endophenotypes. *Nature Reviews Neuroscience, 3,* 617–28.

Centers for Disease Control and Prevention (2015). Adult Obesity Facts. Division of Nutrition, Physical Activity, and Obesity. http://www.cdc.gov/obesity/data/adult.html. Retrieved October 15, 2015.

Chavajay, P., and Rogoff, B. (1999). Cultural variation in management of attention by children and their caregivers. *Developmental Psychology, 35*(4), 1079–90.

Chiang, T., Barrett, K. C., and Nunez, N. N. (2000). Maternal attributions of Taiwanese and American toddlers' misdeeds and accomplishments. *Journal of Cross Cultural Psychology, 31,* 349–68.

Chronis, A. M., Pelham Jr., W. E., Gnagy, E. M., Roberts, J. E., and Aronoff, H. R. (2003). The impact of late-afternoon stimulant dosing for children with ADHD on parent and parent-child domains. *Journal of Clinical Child and Adolescent Psychology, 32,* 118–26.

Cione, G. F., Coleburn, L. A., Fertuck, E. A., and Fraenkel, P. (2011). Psychodynamic play therapy with a six-year- old African American boy diagnosed with ADHD. *Journal of Infant, Child and Adolescent Psychotherapy, 10,* 130–43.

Clements, S. D., and Peters, J. E. (1962). Minimal brain dysfunctions in the school-age child diagnosis and treatment. *Archives of General Psychiatry, 6*(3), 185–97. doi:10.1001/archpsyc.1962.01710210001001.

Compton, S. N., March, J. S., Brent, D., Albano, A. M., Weersing, R., Curry, J. et al. (2004). Cognitive- behavioral psychotherapy for anxiety and depressive disorders in children and adolescents: An evidence- based medicine review. *Journal of the American Academy of Child and Adolescent Psychiatry, 43*(8), 930–59.

Conners, C. K. (2000). Attention-deficit/hyperactivity disorder: Historical development and overview. *Journal of Attention Disorders, 3,* 173–91.

Conrad, P. (1976). *Identifying hyperactive children: The medicalization of deviant behavior.* Lexington, MA: Lexington Books.

Conrad, P., and Potter, D. (2000). From hyperactive children to ADHD adults: Observations on the expansion of medical categories. *Social Problem, 47*(4), 559–82.

Conway, F. (2012). Psychodynamic psychotherapy of ADHD: A review of the literature. *Psychotherapy, 49*(3), 404–17. doi: 10.1037/a0027344.

Conway, F. (2013). The use of empathy and transference as interventions in psychotherapy with attention deficit hyperactive disorder latency-aged boys. *Psychotherapy, 51*(1), 104–9.

Conway, F. (Ed.). (2014). *Attention deficit hyperactivity disorder: Integration of cognitive, neuropsychological and psychodynamic theoretical perspectives in psychotherapy.* New York: Routledge.

Conway, F. (2015). Current research and future directions in psychodynamic treatment of ADHD: Is empathy the missing link? *Journal of Infant, Child, and Adolescent Psychotherapy, 14*(3), 280–87.

Conway, F., McLaughlin, K., Tyler-Best, C., and Minutella, S. (2015). Experiences of college students with ADHD: Supports and services. In Antony, P., and Shore, S. (Eds.). *Successes and challenges faced by individuals with disabilities in higher education: Do we belong?* London, England: Jessica Kingsley Publishers.

Conway, F., Oster, M., and McCarthy, J. (2010). Exploring object relations in hospitalized children with caregiver loss. *Journal of Infant, Child, and Adolescent Psychotherapy, 9,* 108–17.

Conway, F., Oster, M., and Szymanski, K. (2011). ADHD and complex trauma: A descriptive study of hospitalized children in an urban psychiatric hospital. *Journal of Infant, Child, and Adolescent Psychotherapy, 10*(1), 60–72.

Cook, A., Blaustein, M., Spinazzola, J., and van der Kolk, B. (2003). *Complex trauma in children and adolescents: White paper from the National Child Traumatic Stress Network complex trauma task force.* Los Angeles: National Child Traumatic Stress Network.

Corbetta, M., Patel, G., and Shulman, G. L. (2008). The reorienting system of the human brain: From environment to theory of mind. *Neuron, 58,* 306–24.

Cortese, S., Kelly, C., Chabernaud, C., Proal, E., Di Martino, A., Milham, M. P., and Castellanos, F. X. (2012). Toward systems neuroscience of ADHD: A meta-analysis of 55 fMRI studies. *American Journal of Psychiatry, 169*(10), 1038–55. doi: 10.1176/appi.ajp .2012.11101521.

Courtois, C. (1979). The incest experience and its aftermath. *Victimology: An International Journal, 4,* 337–47.

Crichton, A. (1978). An inquiry into the nature and origin of mental derangement: Comprehending a concise system of the physiology and pathology of the human mind and a history of the passions and their effects. *Journal of Attention Disorders, 12,* 200–204.

Crosbie, J., and Schachar, R. (2001). Deficient inhibition as a marker for familial ADHD. *American Journal of Psychiatry, 158,* 1884–90.

Cury, C. R., and Golfeto, J. H. (2003). Strengths and difficulties questionnaire (SDQ): A study of school children in Ribeiro presto. *Revista Brasileira Psiquiatria, 25,* 139–45.

Damasio, A. R. (1994). *Descartes' error: Emotion, reason, and the human brain.* New York: Grossett/ Putnam.

Danon-Boileau, L. (2001). *The silent child: Bringing language to children who cannot speak.* New York: Oxford.

Darwin, C. (1965). *The expression of emotion in animals and man.* Chicago: University of Chicago Press.

David D., and Szentagotai, A. (2006). Cognitions in cognitive-behavioral psychotherapies; toward an integrative model. *Clinical Psychology Review, 26*(3), 284–98.

DeFrancis, V. (1969). *Protecting the child victim of sex crimes committed by adults.* Denver, CO: American Humane Association.

Dinkmeyer, D. C. (1965). *Child development: The emerging self.* Prentice Hall.

Dobson, K., and Dozois, D. (2001). Historical and philosophical basis of cognitive- behavioral therapy. In K. Dobson (Ed.), *Handbook of cognitive-behavioral therapies* (pp. 3–39). New York: Guilford.

Dodge, K. A., Pettit, G. S., Bates, J. E., and Valente, E. (1995). Social information-processing patterns partially mediate the effect of early physical abuse on later conduct problems. *Journal of Abnormal Psychology*, *104*, 632–43.

Dopfner, M., and Rothenberger, A. (2007). Behavior therapy in tic-disorders with co-existing ADHD. *European Child and Adolescent Psychiatry*, *1*, 89–99.

Douglas, V. I. (1972). Stop, look and listen: The problem of sustained attention and impulse control in hyperactive and normal children. *Canadian Journal of Behavioral Sciences*, *4*, 259–82.

Doyle, R. (2004). The history of adult attention-deficit/hyperactivity disorder. *Psychiatric Clinics of North America*, *27*(2), 203–14.

DuPaul, G. J., and Stoner, G. (2003). *ADHD in the schools: Assessment and intervention strategies* (2nd ed.). New York: Guilford.

Durham, J., and Conway, F. (2014). Shame as an accelerator for the cycle of underachievement of African American latency age boys. In K. Vaughans and W. Speilberg (Eds.), *The psychological world of black boys and adolescents* (pp. 241–56). Santa Barbara, CA: Praeger Press.

Durston, S., Davidson, M. C., Mulder, M. J., Spicer, J. A., Galvan, A., Tottenham, N., et al. (2007). Neural and behavioral correlates of expectancy violations in attention deficit hyperactivity disorder. *Journal of Child Psychology and Psychiatry*, *48*, 881–89.

Durston, S., Hulshoff Pol, H. E., Schnack, H. G., Buitelaar, J. K., Steenhuis, M. P., Minderaa, R. B., et al. (2004). Magnetic resonance imaging of boys with attention deficit/hyperactivity disorder and their unaffected siblings. *Journal of the American Academy of Child and Adolescent Psychiatry*, *43*, 332–40.

Durston, S., Tottenham, N. T., Thomas, K. M., Davidson, M. C., Eigsti, I. M., Yang, Y., et al. (2003). Differential patterns of striatal activation in young children with and without ADHD. *Biological Psychiatry*, *53*, 871–78.

Eaton, J. (2005). The obstructive object. *Psychoanalytic Review*, *92*(3), 355–72.

Edelbrock, C., Rende, R., Plomin, R., and Thompson, L. (1995). A twin study of competence and problem behavior in childhood and early adolescence. *Journal of Child Psychology and Psychiatry*, *36*(5), 775–86.

Ekstein, R. (1966). *Children of time and space of action and impulse; Clinical studies on treatment of severely disturbed children.* East Norwalk, CT: Appleton-Century-Crofts.

Eme, Robert. "Male life-course persistent antisocial behavior: A review of neurodevelopmental factors." *Aggression and Violent Behavior* 14.5 (2009): 348–58.

Eresund, P. (2007). Psychodynamic psychotherapy for children with disruptive disorders. *Journal of Child Psychotherapy*, *33*(2), 161–80.

Erickson, M. F., Egeland, B., and Pianta, R. (1989). The effects of maltreatment on the development of young children. In D. Cicchetti and V. Carlson (Eds.), *Child maltreatment: Theory and research on the causes and consequences of child abuse and neglect* (pp. 647–84). New York: Cambridge University Press.

Evans, D. (1996). *An introductory dictionary of lacanian Psychoanalysis.* New York: Routledge.

Famularo, R., Kinscherff, R., and Fenton, T. (1992). Psychiatric diagnoses of maltreated children: Preliminary findings. *Journal of the American Academy of Child and Adolescent Psychiatry*, *31*, 863–67.

Faraone, S. V. (2000). Genetics of childhood disorders: XX. ADHD, part 4: Is ADHD genetically heterogeneous? *Journal of the American Academy of Child and Adolescent Psychiatry*, *39*, 1455–57.

Faraone, S. V., Sergeant, J., Gillberg, C., and Biederman, J. (2003). The worldwide prevalence of ADHD: is it an American condition? *World Psychiatry, 2*(2), 104–13.

Fassbender, C., and Schweitzer, J. B. (2006). Is there evidence for neural compensation in attention deficit hyperactivity disorder? A review of the functional neuroimaging literature. *Clinical Psychology Review*, *26*, 445–65.

Felton, R. H., Wood, F. B., Brown, I. S., Campbell, S. K., and Harter, M. R. (1987). Separate verbal memory and naming deficits in attention deficit disorder and reading disability. *Brain and Language*, *31*, 171–84.

Filipek, P. A., Semrud-Clikeman, M., Steingard, R. J., Renshaw, P. F., Kennedy, D. N., and Biederman, J. (1997). Volumetric MRI analysis comparing subjects having attention-deficit hyperactivity disorder with normal controls. *Neurology, 48*, 589–601.

Flaskerud, J. H. (1984). A comparison of perceptions of problematic behavior by six minority groups and mental health professionals. *Nursing Research, 33*, 190–97.

Fonagy, P. (2001). *Attachment theory and psychoanalysis.* New York: Other Press.

Fonagy, P., Gergely, G., Jurist, E., and Target, M. (2002). *Affect regulation and mentalization.* New York: Other Press.

Fonagy, P., and Target, M. (1994). The theory and practice of resilience. *Journal of Child Psychology and Psychiatry, 35*(2), 231–57.

Fonagy, P., and Target, M. (1996). Playing with reality: I. Theory of mind and the normal development of psychic reality. *International Journal of Psycho-Analysis, 77*, 217–33.

Fonagy, P., and Target, M. (1998). Mentalization and the changing aims of child psychoanalysis. *Psychoanalytic Dialogues, 8*, 87–114.

Fonagy, P., and Target, M. (2002). Early intervention and the development of self-regulation. *Psychoanalytic Inquiry: A Topical Journal for Mental Health Professionals, 22*(3), 307–35.

Fonagy, P., Target, M., Steele, H., and Steele, M. (1998). Reflective-functioning manual, version 5, for application to adult attachment interviews. Unpublished manuscript, University College London.

Foucault, M. (1991). Nietzsche, genealogy, history. In P. Rabinow (Ed.), *The Foucault Reader.* New York: Pantheon.

Frankel, J. (2002) Exploring Ferenczi's concept of identification with the aggressor: Its role in trauma, everyday life and the therapeutic relationship. *Psychoanalytic Dialogues, 12*(1), 101–39.

Frazier, T. W., Demaree, H. A., and Youngstrom, E. A. (2004). Meta-analysis of intellectual and neuropsychological test performance in attention-deficit/hyperactivity disorder. *Neuropsychology, 18*, 534–55.

Freud, A. (1992). *The ego and the mechanisms of defence.* London: Karnac Books.

Freud, S. (1908/1959). "Civilized" sexual morality and modern nervousness. In E. Jones (Ed.), *Sigmund Freud. Collected papers* (2nd ed., pp. 76–99). New York: Basic Books.

Freud, S. (1923). The ego and the superego. *Standard Edition, 19*, 1926.

Freud, S. (1926). Inhibitions, symptoms and anxiety. Standard edition of the collected works of Sigmund Freud.

Freud, S. (1959). Repression. In E.Jones (Ed.) and J. Riviere (Trans.), *Collected Papers, 4*, 84–97. London: Hogarth.

Galves, A., and Walker, D. (2002). *Debunking the science behind ADHD as a "brain disorder." A letter to Dr. Rubenstein is the director of the brochure project, a joint effort of division 29 (psychotherapy) of the APA and celltech pharmaceuticals to publish and distribute brochures on attention deficit-hyperactivity disorder (ADHD).* Retrieved 11/15, 2013, from http://www.academyanalyticarts.org/galvesealker.htm.

Garcia-Sanchez, C., Estevez-Gonzalez, A., Suarez-Romero, E., and Junque, C. (1997). Right hemisphere dysfunction in subjects with attention-deficit disorder with and without hyperactivity. *Journal of Child Neurology, 12*, 107–15.

Gardner, M. R. (1983). *Self Inquiry.* Hillsdale, NJ: Analytic Press.

Gensler, D. (2011). Trouble Paying Attention. *Journal of Infant, Child and Adolescent Psychotherapy, 10*, 103–15.

Gilmore, K. (2000). A psychoanalytic perspective on attention-deficit/hyperactivity disorder. *Journal of the American Psychoanalytic Association, 48*, 1258–93.

Giedd, J. N., Castellanos, F. X., Casey, B. J., Kozuch, P., King, A. C., Hamburger, S. D., et al. (1994). Quantitative morphology of the corpus callosum in attention deficit hyperactivity disorder. *American Journal of Psychiatry, 151*, 665–69.

Gilbert, D. L., Isaacs, K. M., Augusta, M., Macneil, L. K., Mostofsky, S. H. (2011). Motor cortex inhibition: A marker of ADHD behavior and motor development in children. *Neurology, 76*, 615–21.

Gillis, et al. (1992). Attention-deficit disorder in reading disabled twins: Evidence for a genetic etiology. *Journal of Abnormal Child Psychology, 20*, 303–15.

Gilman, R., and Chard, K. (2007). Cognitive-behavioral and behavioral approaches. In T. Prout and D. Brown (Eds.), *Counseling and psychotherapy with children and adolescents: Theory and practice for school and clinical settings*. Hoboken, NJ: Wiley & Sons.

Gilmore, K. (2000). A psychoanalytic perspective on attention-deficit/hyperactivity disorder. *Journal of the American Psychoanalytic Association, 48*, 1258–93.

Gilmore, K. (2002). Diagnosis, dynamics, and development: Considerations in the psychoanalytic assessment of children with ADHD. *Psychoanalytic Inquiry, 22*(3), 371–90.

Gilmore, K. (2005). Play in the psychoanalytic setting: Ego capacity, ego state, and vehicle for intersubjective exchange. *Psychoanalytic Study of the Child, 60*, 213–38.

Goldstein, K. (1942). *After-effects of brain injuries in war*. New York: Grune and Stratton.

Goldstein, S., and Goldstein, M. (1998). *Managing attention deficit-hyperactivity disorder in children: A guide to practitioners*. New York: John Wiley & Sons.

Goodman, R., Neves dos Santos, D., Robatto Nunes, A. P., Pereira de Miranda, D., Fleitlich-Bilyk, B., and Almeida Filho, N. (2005). The Ilha de Maré study: A survey of child mental health problems in a predominantly African-Brazilian rural community. *Social Psychiatry and Psychiatric Epidemiology, 40*, 11–17.

Goodman, R., and Stevenson, J. (1989). A twin study of hyperactivity–II. the aetological role of genes, family relationships and perinatal adversity. *Journal of Child Psychology and Psychiatry, 30*(5), 691–709.

Gopin, C. B., and Healey, D. M. (2011). *The neural and neurocognitive determinants of ADHD*. Unpublished PhD., The Zucker Hillside Hospital, North Shore-Long Island Jewish Health System, New York; Department of Psychology, University of Otago, New Zealand.

Grave, J., and Blissett, J. (2004). Is cognitive behavior therapy developmentally appropriate for young children? A critical review of the evidence. *Clinical Psychology Review, 24*(4), 399–420.

Gray, P. (1994). On helping analysands observe intrapsychic activity. In: The Ego and Analysis of Defense (pp.63–86). Northvale, NJ: Jason Aronson.

Gray, P. (1996). Undoing the lag in the technique of conflict and defense analysis. *The Psychoanalytic Study of the Child, 51*, 87–101.

Green, A. H. (1978). Psychopathology of abused children. *Journal of American Academy of Child Psychiatry, 17*, 92–103

Gresham, F. M., MacMillan, D. L., Bocian, K., Ward, S., and Forness, S. (1998). Comorbidity of hyperactivity-impulsivity-inattention + conduct problems: Risk factors in social, affective, and academic domains. *Journal of Abnormal Child Psychology, 26*, 393–406.

Gretarsson, S. J., and Gelfand, D. M. (1988). Mothers' attributions regarding their children's social behavior and personality characteristics. *Developmental Psychology, 24*, 264–69.

Gross, J. J. (1998). The emerging field of emotion regulation: an integrative review. *Review of General Psychology, 2*(3), 271.

Halperin, J. M., and Healey, D. M. (2011). The influences of environmental enrichment, cognitive enhancement, and physical exercise on brain development: Can we alter the developmental trajectory of ADHD? *Neuroscience & Biobehavioral Reviews, 35*(3), 621–34. doi: 10.1016/j.neubiorev.2010.07.006.

Halperin, J. M., and Schulz, K. P. (2006). Revisiting the role of the prefrontal cortex in the pathophysiology of attention-deficit/hyperactivity disorder. *Psychological Bulletin, 132*, 560–81.

Hamblen J., and Barnett, E. (2009). PTSD in children and adolescents. Retrieved May 1, 2015 from http://www.ptsd.va.gov/professional/treatment/children/ptsd_in_children_and_adolescents_overview_for_professionals.asp.

Hamilton, L. S., Levitt, J. G., O'Neill, J., Alger, J. R., Luders, E., Phillips, O. R. et al. (2008). Reduced white matter integrity in attention-deficit hyperactivity disorder. *Neuroreport, 19*, 1705–8.

Harborne, A., Wolpert, M., and Clare, L. (2004). Making sense of ADHD: A battle for understanding? Parents' views of their children being diagnosed with ADHD. *Clinical Child Psychology and Psychiatry, 9*, 327 –39.

Bibliography 159

Harder, D. W., and Lewis, S. J. (1987). The assessment of shame and guilt. In Butcher, J. N., and Spielberger, C. D. (Eds.), *Advances in personality assessment* (6th ed., pp. 89–114). Hillsadale, NJ: Erlbaum.

Harter, S. (1998). The development of self-representation. In W. Damon and N. Eisenberg (Eds.), *Handbook of child psychology: Social, emotional and personality development* (5th ed., pp. 553–617). New York: Wiley.

Hartmann, H. (1939) . Psycho-analysis and the concept of mental health. *International Journal of Psycho-Analysis, 20*, 308–21 .

Heilman, K. M., Voeller, K. K. S., and Nadeau, S. E. (1991). A possible pathophysiologic substrate of attention deficit hyperactivity disorder. *Journal of Child Neurology, 6*, S76–S81.

Helenius, P., Laasonen, M., Hokkanen, L., Paetau, R., and Niemivirta, M. (2011). Impaired engagement of the ventral attention pathway in ADHD. *Neuropsychologia, 49*, 1889–96.

Herbert, M. (1964). The concept and testing of brain damage in children: A review. *Journal of Child Psychology and Psychiatry, 5*, 197–217.

Herman, J. L. (1981). *Father-daughter incest*. Cambridge, MA: Harvard University Press.

Herman, J. L. (1992). Complex PTSD: A syndrome in survivors of prolonged and repeated trauma. *Journal of Traumatic Stress, 5*(3), 377–91.

Hess, R. D., Chih-Mei, C., and McDevitt, T. M. (1987). Cultural variations in family beliefs about children's performance in mathematics: Comparisons among People's Republic of China, Chinese-American, and Caucasian-American families. *Journal of Educational Psychology, 79*, 179–88.

Hill, D. E., Yeo, R. A., Campbell, R. A., Hart, B., Vigil, J., and Brooks, W. (2003). Magnetic resonance imaging correlates of attention-deficit/hyperactivity disorder in children. *Neuropsychology, 17*, 496–506.

Hinshaw, S. P. (2001). Is the inattentive type of ADHD a separate disorder? *Clinical Psychology: Science and Practice, 8*, 498–501.

Hinshaw, S. P. (2006). Attention-deficit hyperactivity disorder. In P. C. Kendall (Ed.), *Child and adolescent therapy: Cognitive-behavioral procedures* (3rd ed., pp. 46–68). New York: Guilford.

Honess, T., and Yardley. K. (1987). Self and social structure: An introductory review. In K. Yardley and T. Honess (Eds.), *Self and Identity: Psychosocial Perspectives*. New York: Wiley.

Honos-Webb, L. (2005). *The gift of ADHD: How to transform your child's problems into strengths*. Oakland, CA: Newharbinger.

Hopkins, J. (2000). Overcoming a child's resistance to late adoption: How one new attachment can facilitate another. *Journal of Child Psychotherapy, 26*(3), 335–47.

Hoza, B., Gerdes, A. C., Mrug, S., Hinshaw, S. P., Bukowski, W. M., Gold, J. A., et al. (2005). Peer-assessed outcomes in the multimodal treatment study of children with attention deficit hyperactivity disorder. *Journal of Clinical Child and Adolescent Psychology, 34*, 74–86.

Hoza, B., Pelham, W. E., Milich, R., Pillow, D., and McBride, K. (1993). The self-perceptions and attributions of attention deficit hyperactivity disordered and nonreferred boys. *Journal of Abnormal Child Psychology, 21*(3), 271–86.

Hynd, G. W., Hern, K. L., Novey, E. S., Eliopulos, D., Marshall, R., Gonzalez, J. J., et al. (1993). Attention deficit-hyperactivity disorder and asymmetry of the caudate nucleus. *Journal of Child Neurology, 8*, 339–47.

Hynd, G. W., Semrud-Clikeman, M., Lorys, A. R., Novey, E. S., and Eliopulos, D. (1990). Brain morphology in developmental dyslexia and attention deficit disorder/hyperactivity. *Archives of Neurology, 47*, 919–26.

Hynd, G. W., Semrud-Clikeman, M., Lorys, A. R., Novey, E. S., Eliopulos, D., and Lyytinen, H. (1991). Corpus callosum morphology in attention deficit-hyperactivity disorder: Morphometric analysis of MRI. *Journal of Learning Disabilities, 24*, 141–46.

Jacobvitz, D., and Sroufe, A. (1987). The early care-giver relationship and attention-deficit disorder with hyperactivity in kindergarten: A prospective study. *Child Development, 58*, 1488–95.

Johnston, C., Seipp, C., Hommersen, P., Hoza, B., and Fine, S. (2005). Treatment choices and experiences in attention-deficit/hyperactivity disorder: Relations to parents' beliefs and attributions. *Child: Care, Health, and Development, 31*, 1–9.

Jones, B. (2011). The reality-sampling deficit and ADHD: Indication for an active technique. *Journal of Infant, Child and Adolescent Psychotherapy, 10*, 73–86.

Jones, B., and Allison, E. (2010). An integrated theory for attention-deficit hyperactivity disorder [ADHD]. *Psychoanalytic Psychotherapy, 24*, 279–95.

Joseph, J. (2003). *The gene illusion: Genetic research in psychiatry and psychology under the microscope.* Ross-on-Wye, UK: PCCS Books.

Julian, T. W., McKenry, P. C., and McKelvey, M. W. (1994). Cultural variations in parenting: Perceptions of Caucasian, African-American, Hispanic, and Asian-American parents. *Family Relationships, 43*, 30–37.

Kaës, R. (2007). *Linking, alliances, and shared space: Groups and the psychoanalyst.* London: International Psychoanalytic Association.

Kates, W. R., Frederikse, M., Mostofsky, S. H., Folley, B. S., Cooper, K., Mazur-Hopkins, P., et al. (2002). MRI parcellation of the frontal lobe in boys with attention deficit hyperactivity disorder or Tourette syndrome. *Psychiatry Research, 116*, 63–81.

Kaufman, J., and Chaney, D. (2001). Effects of early stress on brain structure and function: Implications for understanding the relationship between child maltreatment and depression. *Developmental Pscychopathology, 13*(3), 451–71.

Kazdin, A. E., and Weisz, J. R. (Eds.). (2003). *Evidence-based psychotherapies for children and adolescents.* New York: Guilford Press.

Kelley, S. A., Brownell, C. A., and Campbell, S. B. (2000). Mastery, motivation, and self-evaluative affect in toddlers: Longitudinal relations with maternal behavior. *Child Development, 71*, 1061–71.

Kendall, P. C., and Braswell, L. (1985). *Cognitive-behavioral therapy for impulsive children.* New York: Guilford Press.

Kendall, P. C., and Braswell, L. (1993). Cognitive-behavioral therapy for impulsive children. *The Guilford clinical psychology and psychotherapy series.* New York: Guilford Press.

Kendall, P. C., and Choudhury, M. S. (2003). Children and adolescents in cognitive-behavioral therapy: Some past efforts and current advances, and the challenges of our future. *Cognitive Therapy and Research, 27*, 89–104.

Kendall, P. C., and Wilcox, L. E. (1980). Cognitive-behavioral treatment for impulsivity: Concrete conceptual training in non-self-controlled problem children. *Journal of Consulting and Clinical Psychology, 48*, 80–91.

Kernberg, O. F. (1980). Neurosis, psychosis and the borderline states. *Comprehensive textbook of psychiatry, 1*, 1079–92.

Kessler, J. W. (1980). History of minimal brain dysfunctions. In Rie, H. E. and Rie, E. D. (Eds.), *Handbook of minimal brain dysfunctions: A critical view* (pp. 18–51). New York: Wiley and Sons.

Kiley, M., and Esiri, M. M. (2001). A contemporary case of encephalitis lethargica. *Clinical Neuropathology, 20*, 2–7.

Klassen, A., Miller, A., Raina, P., Lee, S., and Olsen, L. (1999). Attention-deficit hyperactivity disorder in children and youth: A quantitative systematic review of the efficacy of different management strategies. *Canadian Journal of Psychiatry, 44*(10), 1007–16.

Klassen, R. M., Bong, M., Usher, E. L., Chong, W. H., Huan, V. S., Wong, I. Y. F., Georgiou, T. (2009). Exploring the validity of a teachers' self-efficacy scale in five countries. *Contemporary Educational Psychology, 34*, 67–76.

Klein, M. (1935). Contribution to the psychogenesis of manic depressive states. *Contributions to psycho-analysis* (pp. 1921–1945). London: Hogarth.

Klein, M. (1952). The origins of transference. *The International journal of psycho-analysis, 33*, 433.

Kluft, R. P. (1990). Incest and subsequent revictimization: The case of the therapist-patient sexual exploitation, with a description of the sitting duck syndrome. In R. P. Kluft (Ed.), *Incest-related syndromes of adult psychopathology* (pp. 263–87). Washington, DC: American Psychiatric Press.

Konold, T. R., and Glutting, J. J. (2008). ADHD and method variance: A latent variable approach applied to a nationally representative sample of college freshmen. *Journal of Learning Disabilities*, *41*(5), 405–16.

Kris, A. O. (1985). Resistance in convergent and in divergent conflicts. *Psychoanalysis Quarterly*, *54*(4), 537–68.

Kutchins, H., and Kirk, S. (1997). *Making us crazy: DSM—the psychiatric bible and the creation of mental disorders*. New York : Simon and Schuster.

Lahey, B. B. (2001). Should the combined and predominantly inattentive types of ADHD be considered distinct and unrelated disorders? Not now, at least. *Clinical Psychology: Science and Practice*, *8*, 494–97.

Lahey, B. B., Applegate, B., McBurnett, K., Biederman, J., Greenhill, L., Hynd, G. W., et al. (1994). DSM-IV field trials for attention deficit hyperactivity disorder in children and adolescents. *American Journal of Psychiatry*, *151*, 1673–85.

Lambert, N. M. (1982). Temperament profiles of hyperactive children. *American Journal of Orthopsychiatry*, *52*(3), 458–67.

Lambert, N. M., and Harsough, C. S. (1984). Contribution of predispositional factors to the diagnosis of hyperactivity. *American Journal of Orthopsychiatry*, *54*(1), 97–109.

Lange, K. A., Reichl, S., Lange, K. M., Tucha, L., and Tucha, O. (2010). The history of attention deficit hyperactivity disorder. *Attention Deficit Hyperactivity Disorder*, *2*(4), 241–55.

Laufer, M. W., Denhoff, E., and Solomons, G. (1957). Hyperkinetic impulse disorder in children's behavior problems. *Psychosomatic Medicine*, *19*, 38–49.

Layton, L. (2007). What psychoanalysis, culture and society mean to me. *The Academia-Industry Symposium MSM 2007: Medical Practice and the Pharmaceutical Industry and Ever the Duo Shall Meet*, *5*(1), 146–57.

Leary, M. R., Schreindorfer, L. S., and Haupt, A. L. (1995). The role of low self-esteem in emotional and behavioral problems: Why is low self-esteem dysfunctional? *Journal of Social and Clinical Psychology*, *14*(3), 297–314.

LeDoux, J. (2002). *Synaptic self: How our brains become who we are*. New York: Viking.

Leuchter, A. F., Cook, I. A,, Witte, E. A., et al. (2002). Changes in brain function of depressed subjects during treatment with placebo. *American Journal of Psychiatry*, *159*, 122–29.

Leuzinger-Bohleber, M., Laezer, K. L., Pfenning-Meerkoetter, N., Fischmann, T., Wolff, A., and Green, J. (2011). Psychoanalytic treatment of ADHD children in the frame of two extraclinical studies: The Frankfurt prevention study and the EVA study. *Journal of Infant, Child, and Adolescent Psychotherapy*, *10*, 32–50.

Levin, F. M. (2002). Attention deficit disorder: A neuropsychoanalytic sketch. *Psychoanalytic Inquiry*, *22*(3), 336–54.

Levine, E. S., and Anshel, D. J. (2011), "Nothing works!" A case study using cognitive-behavioral interventions to engage parents, educators, and children in the management of attention-deficit/hyperactivity disorder. *Psychology in the Schools*, *48*, 297–306. doi: 10.1002/pits.20554.

Lewis, H. B. (1987). Shame and the narcissistic personality. *The many faces of shame*, 93–132.

Lewis, M. (1992). *Shame: The exposed self*. New York: The Free Press.

Lewis, M., Alessandri, S. M., and Sullivan, M. W. (1992). Differences in shame and pride as a function of children's gender and task difficulty. *Child Development, 63*(3), 630–38.

Lewis, T., Amini, F., and Lannon, R. (2000). *A general theory of love*. New York: Random House.

Li, Q., Sun, J., Guo, L., Zang, Y., Feng, Z., Huang, X., Yang, H., Lv, Y., Huang, M., and Gong, Q. (2010). Increased fractional anisotropy in white matter of the right frontal region in children with attention-deficit/hyperactivity disorder: A diffusion tensor imaging study. *Activas Nervosa Superior Redivida*, *52*, 193–99.

Loeber, R., Keenan, K., Lahey, B. B., Green, S. M., & Thomas, C. (1993). Evidence for developmentally based diagnoses of oppositional defiant disorder and conduct disorder. *Journal of Abnormal Child Psychology, 21*(4), 377–410.

Loge, D. V., Staton, R. D., and Beatty, W. W. (1990). Performance of children with ADHD on tests sensitive to frontal lobe dysfunction. *Journal of the American Academy of Child and Adolescent Psychiatry, 29*, 540–45.

Lynam D. R. (1996). Early identification of chronic offenders: Who is the fledgling psychopath? *Psychological Bulletin, 120*, 209–34.

Lyoo, I. K., Noam, G. G., Lee, C. K., Lee, H. K., Kennedy, B. P., and Renshaw, P. F. (1996). The corpus callosum and lateral ventricles in children with attention-deficit hyperactivity disorder: A brain magnetic resonance imaging study. *Biological Psychiatry, 40*, 1060–63.

Mah, J. W., and Johnston, C. (2007). Cultural variations in mothers' attributions: Influence of child attention-deficit/hyperactivity disorder. *Child Psychiatry and Human Development, 38*(2):135–53.

Main, M., and Solomon, J. (1990). Procedures for identifying disorganized/disoriented infants during the Ainsworth Strange Situation. In M. Greenberg, D. Cicchetti, and M. Cummings (Eds.), *Attachment in the preschool years* (pp. 121–60). Chicago: University of Chicago Press.

Makris, N., Buka, S. L., Biederman, J., Papadimitriou, G. M., Hodge, S. M., Valera, E. M., et al. (2007). Attention and executive systems abnormalities in adults with childhood ADHD: A DT-MRI study of connections. *Cerebral Cortex, 18*, 1210–20.

Mash, E. J., and Barkley, R. A. (2003). *Child psychopathology* (2nd ed.). New York: The Guilford Press.

McMahon, S. A., and Greenburg, L. M. (1977). Serial neurologic examination of hyperactive children. *Pediatrics, 59*, 584–87.

McNeal, J. (1999). *The kids market: Myths and realities*. Ithaca, NY: Paramount Market.

Mezzacappa, E., Kindlon, D., and Earls, F. (2001). Child abuse and performance task assessments of executive functions in boys. *Journal of Child Psychology & Psychiatry & Allied Disciplines, 42*, 1041–48.

Mikulincer, M., and Shaver, P. R. (2003). The attachment behavioral system in adulthood: Activation, psychodynamics, and interpersonal processes. In M. P. Zanna (Ed.), *Advances in experimental social psychology* (Vol. 35, pp. 53–152). San Diego, CA: Academic Press.

Miller, S. (1985). *The shame experience*. Hillsdale, NJ: Erlbaum.

Mitchell, S., and Black, M. (1995). *Freud and beyond: A history of modern psychoanalytic thought*. New York: Basic Books.

Molina, B. S. G., Hinshaw, S. P., Swanson, J. M., et al., (2009). MTA at 8 years: Prospective follow-up of children treated for combined-type ADHD in a multisite study. *Journal of the American Academy of Child and Adolescent Psychiatry, 48*, 484–500.

Mosby's Medical Dictionary. 8th edition. (2009). Elsevier. http://www.merriam-webster.com/dictionary/diagnosis.

Mostofsky, S. H., Cooper, K. L., Kates, W. R., Denckla, M. B., and Kaufmann, W. E. (2002). Smaller prefrontal and premotor volumes in boys with attention deficit/hyperactivity disorder. *Biological Psychiatry, 52*, 785–94.

Mostofsky, S. J., Reiss, A. L., Lockhart, P., and Denckla, M. B. (1998). Evaluation of cerebellar size in attention-deficit hyperactivity disorder. *Journal of Child Neurology, 13*, 434–39.

MTA Cooperative Group. (1999). A 14-month randomized clinical trial of treatment strategies for attention-deficit/hyperactivity disorder. The MTA Cooperative Group. Multimodal Treatment Study of Children with ADHD. *Archives General Psychiatry, 56*(12), 1073–86.

MTA Cooperative Group (2004) National Institute of Mental Health Multimodal Treatment Study of ADHD follow-up: 24-month outcomes of treatment strategies for attention-deficit/hyperactivity disorder. *Pediatrics, 113*, 754–61.

Murdock, T. B. (1999). The social context of risk: Status and motivational predictors of alienation in middle school. *Journal of Educational Psychology, 91*(1), 62–75.

Murthi, M., Servaty-Seib, H. L., and Elliott, A. N. (2006). Childhood sexual abuse and multiple dimensions of self-concept. *Journal of Interpersonal Violence, 21*(8), 982–99.

Musser, E. D., Galloway-Long, H. S., Frick, P. J., and Nigg, J. T. (2013). Emotion regulation and heterogeneity in attention-deficit/hyperactivity disorder. *Journal of the American Academy of Child and Adolescent Psychiatry, 52*(2), 163–71.

Nathan, W. A. (1992). Integrated multimodal therapy of children with attention-deficit hyperactivity disorder. *Bulletin of the Menninger Clinic*, *56*(3), 283–312.

Nigg, J. T. (2001). Is ADHD an inhibitory disorder? *Psychological Bulletin, 125*, 571-596.

Nigg J. T. (2006). Temperament and developmental psychopathology. *Journal of Child Psychology and Psychiatry, and Allied Disciplines*, *47*, 395–422. doi: 10.1111/j.1469-7610.2006.01612.x.

Nigg, J. T., and Casey, B. J. (2005). An integrative theory of attention-deficit/hyperactivity disorder based on the cognitive and affective neurosciences. *Development and Psychopathology*, *17*, 785–806.

Norcross, J. C. (2002). *Psychotherapy relationships that work*. New York: Oxford University Press.

Norvilitis, J. M., Sun, L., and Zhang, J. (2010). ADHD symptomatology and adjustment to college in China and the United States. *Journal of Learning Disabilities*, *43*(1), 86–94.

Office of the Surgeon General (US and Center for Mental Health Services). (2001). Culture counts: The influence of culture and society on mental health.

Ogden, T. H. (2005). *Projective identification & psychotherapeutic technique*. London: Karnac.

Okie, S. (2006). ADHD in adults. *New England Journal of Medicine*, *354*, 2637–41.

O'Loughlin, M. (2013). Introduction. In O'Loughlin, M. (Ed.), *Psychodynamic perspectives on working with children, families, and schools*. Lanham, MD: Jason Aronson.

Orford, E. (1998). Wrestling with the whirlwind: An approach to the understanding of ADHD. *Journal of Child Psychotherapy*, *24*, 253–66.

Orlinsky, D. E., Grawe, K., and Parks, B. K. (1994). *Handbook of psychotherapy and behavior change* (4th ed.). New York: Wiley.

Orr, D. P., and Downes, M. C. (1985). Self-concept of adolescent sexual abuse victims. *Journal of Youth and Adolescence*, *14*, 401–10.

Palmer, E., and Finger, S. (2001). An early description of ADHD (inattentive subtype): Dr. Alexander Crichton and "Mental restlessness" (1798). *Child Psychology and Psychiatry Review*, *6*, 66–73.

Pastor, P., Reuben, C., Duran, C. & Hawkins, L. (2015). Association Between Diagnosed ADHD and Selected Characteristics Among Children Aged 4–17 Years: United States, 2011–2013. In National Survey of Children's Health Data Brief, #201. Hyattsville, MD: National Center for Health Statistics. See more at: http://www.chadd.org/understanding-adhd/about-adhd/data-and-statistics/general-prevalence.aspx#sthash.WBZ1StkQ.dpuf.

Patterson, G. R. (1982). *Coercive family process*. Eugene, OR: Castalia.

Pauls, D. L. (1991). Genetic factors in the expression of attention-deficit hyperactivity disorder. *Journal of Child and Adolescent Pharmacology*, *1*, 353–60.

Pavuluri, M. N., Yang, S., Kamineni, K., Passarotti, A. M., Srinivasan, G., Harral, E. M., et al. (2009). Diffusion tensor imaging study of white matter fiber tracts in pediatric bipolar disorder and attention deficit/hyperactivity disorder. *Biological Psychiatry*, *65*, 586–93.

Pelham, W. E., and Fabiano, G. A. (2001). Treatment of attention deficit hyperactivity disorder: The impact of comorbidity. *Clinical Psychology and Psychotherapy*, *8*, 315–29.

Pelham, W. E., and Hinshaw, S. P. (1992). Behavioral intervention for attention-deficit hyperactivity disorder. In S. M. Turner, K. S. Calhoun, and H. E. Adams (Eds.), *Handbook of clinical behavior therapy* (2nd ed., pp. 259–83). New York: Wiley.

Pelham, W. E., Wheeler, T., and Chronis, A. (1998). Empirically supported psychosocial treatments for ADHD. *Journal of Clinical Child Psychology*, *27*, 190–205.

Pennebaker, J. W. (2000). The effects of traumatic disclosure on physical and mental health; the values of writing and talking about upsetting events. In J. M. Volanti, D. Paton, and C. Dunning (Eds.), *Posttraumatic stress intervention: Challenges, issues and perspectives* (pp. 97–114). Springfield, IL: Charles C Thomas.

Piek, J. P., Pitcher, T. M., and Hay, D. A. (1999). Motor coordination and kinaesthesis in boys with attention deficit-hyperactivity disorder. *Developmental Medicine and Child Neurology*, *41*, 159–65.

Pizer R. (1998). *Building Bridges. The Negotiation of Paradox in Psychoanalysis*. Hillsdale, NJ: The Analytic Press .

Posner, M. I., and Petersen, S. E. (1990). The attention system of the human brain. *Annual Review of Neuroscience, 13*, 25–42.

Psychodynamic Diagnostic Manual Task Force. (2006). *Psychodynamic diagnostic manual.* Silver Spring, MD: Alliance of Psychoanalytic Organizations.

Quitkin, F., and Klein, F. (1969). Two behavioral syndromes in young adults related to possible minimal brain dysfunction. *Journal of Psychiatric Research, 7*(2), 131–42.

Rafalovich, S. (2001). The conceptual history of attention deficit hyperactivity disorder: Idiocy, imbecility, encephalitis and the child deviant, 1877–1929. *Deviant Behavior, an Interdisciplinary Journal, 22*, 93–115.

Rail, D., Scholtz, C., and Swash, M. (1981). Post-encephalitic parkinsonism: Current experience. *Journal of Neurology, Neurosurgery, and Psychiatry, 44*, 670–76.

Ramsay, J. R., and Rostain, A. L. (2008). *Cognitive–behavioral therapy for adult ADHD: An integrative psychosocial and medical approach.* New York: Taylor & Francis Group.

Rapin, I. (1964). Brain damage in children . In J. Brennemann (Ed.), *Practice of pediatrics, vol. 4* . Hagerstown, MD: MD Prior.

Reilley, S. P. (2005). Empirically informed attention-deficit/hyperactivity disorder evaluation of college students. *Journal of College Counseling, 8*, 153–64.

Resta, S. P., and Eliot, J. (1994). Written expression in boys with attention deficit disorder. *Perceptual and Motor Skills, 79*, 1131–38.

Robin, A. L., Kraus, D., Koepke, T., and Robin, R. A. (1987). *Growing up hyperactive in single versus two-parent families.* 95th Annual Convention of the American Psychological Association, New York.

Rodriguez-Srednicki, O., and Twaite, J. A. (2006). *Understanding, assessing, and treating adult victims of childhood abuse.* Lanham, MD: Jason Aronson.

Roessner, V., Becker, A., Rothenberger, A., Rhode, L. A., and Banaschewski, T. (2007). A cross-cultural comparison between samples of Brazilian and German children with ADHD/HD using the child behavior checklist. *European Archives of Psychiatry and Clinical Neuroscience, 257*, 351–59.

Rogers, A. (2007). *The unsayable: The hidden language of trauma.* New York: Ballantine Books .

Rogoff, B., Mistry, J. J., Goncu, A., and Mosier, C. (1993). Guided participation in cultural activity by toddlers and caregivers. *Monographs of the Society for Research in Child Development.*

Rorschach, H. (1942). Psychodiagnostics.

Rosenfeld, G. B., and Bradley, C. (1948). Childhood behavior sequelae of asphyxia in infancy. *Pediatrics, 2*, 74–84.

Rosenzweig, M. R., Bennett, E. L., and Diamond, M. C. (1972). Brain changes in response to experience. *Learning and Memory, 8*, 294–300.

Ross, D. M., and Ross, S. A. (1976). *Hyperactivity: Research, theory and action.* New York: Wiley & Sons.

Ross, D. M., and Ross, S. A. (1982). *Hyperactivity: Current issues, research and theory* (2nd ed.). New York: Wiley & Sons.

Roth, M. (1981). Foucault's "history of the present." *History and Theory, 20*(1), 32–46.

Rothenberg, M. A. (2004). Down to cases: The ethical value of "nonscientificity" in dyadic psychoanalysis. *Journal of the American Psychoanalytic Association, 52*, 126–50.

Rothenberger, A., and Neumärker, K. J. (2005). *Wissenschaftsgeschichte der ADHS.* Steinkopff, Darmstadt: Kramer-Pollnow im Spiegel der Zeit.

Rubia, K., Overmeyer, S., Taylor, E., Brammer, M., Williams, S. C. R., Simmons, A., et al. (1999). Hypofrontality in attention-deficit/hyperactivity disorder during higher-order motor control: A study with functional MRI. *American Journal of Psychiatry, 156*, 891–96.

Rustin, M. (2003). Research in the consulting room. *Journal of Child Psychotherapy, 29*(2), 137–45.

Salomonsson, B. (2004). Some psychoanalytic viewpoints on neuropsychiatric disorders in children. *International Journal of Psychoanalysis, 85*, 117–36.

Salomonsson, B. (2006). The impact of words on children with ADHD and DAMP: Consequences for psychoanalytic technique. *International Journal of Psychoanalysis, 87*(Pt 4), 1029–47.

Salomonsson, B. (2011). Psychoanalytic conceptualizations of the internal object in an ADHD child. *Journal of Infant, Child and Adolescent Psychotherapy, 10*, 87–102.

Salzinger, S., Feldman, R. S., Hammer, M., and Rosario, M. (1993). The effects of physical abuse on children's social relationships. *Child Development, 64*, 169–87.

Sameroff, A. J,. and Chandler, M. J. (1975). Reproductive risk and the continuum of caretaker causality. In F. B. Horowitz (Ed.), *Review of child development research, vol. 4.* Chicago: University of Chicago Press.

Scharff, J. S. (1992). *Projective and introjective identification and the use of the therapist's self.* Lanham, MD: Jason Aronson.

Schore, A. N. (2003). *Affect regulation and the repair of the self.* New York: W.W. Norton & Company.

Schulz, K. P., Fan, J., Tang, C. Y., Newcorn, J. H., Buchsbaum, M. S., Cheung, A. M., et al. (2004). Response inhibition in adolescents diagnosed with attention deficit hyperactivity disorder during childhood: An event-related FMRI study. *American Journal of Psychiatry, 161*, 1650–57.

Schulz, K. P., Newcorn, J. H., Fan, J., Tang, C. Y., and Halperin, J. M. (2005). Brain activation gradients in ventrolateral prefrontal cortex related to persistence of ADHD in adolescence. *Journal of the American Academy of Child and Adolescent Psychiatry, 44*, 47–54.

Schwartz, J. M., Stoessel, P. W., Baxter, L. R., Karron, M. et al. (1996). Systematic changes in cerebral glucose metabolic rate after successful behavior modification treatment of obsessive-compulsive disorder. *Archives of General Psychiatry, 53*(2), 109–13.

Selby, J. W., Calhoun, L. G., and Johnson, R. E. (2006). Perceived causes of psychological problems: An exploratory study. *Journal of Community Psychology, 5* (3), 290–94.

Seligman, M. E. P. (1972). Learned helplessness. *Annual Review of Medicine*, 23 (1), 407–12. doi:10.1146/annurev.me.23.020172.002203.

Semrud-Clikeman, M., Filipek, P. A., Biederman, J., Steingard, R., Kennedy, D., Renshaw, P., et al. (1994). Attention-deficit hyperactivity disorder: Magnetic resonance imaging morphometric analysis of the corpus callosum. *Journal of the American Academy of Child and Adolescent Psychiatry, 33*, 875–81.

Shaw, P., Eckstrand, K., Sharp, W., Blumenthal, J., Lerch, J. P., Greenstein, D., et al. (2007a). Attention-deficit/hyperactivity disorder is characterized by a delay in cortical maturation. *Proceedings of the National Academy of Sciences, U.S.A., 104*, 19649–54.

Shaw, P., Gornick, M., Lerch, J., Addington, A., Seal, J., Greenstein, D., et al. (2007b). Polymorphisms of the dopamine D4 receptor, clinical outcome, and cortical structure in attention-deficit/hyperactivity disorder. *Archives of General Psychiatry, 64*, 921–31.

Shaw, P., Lerch, J., Greenstein, D., Sharp, W., Clasen, L., Evans, A., et al. (2006). Longitudinal mapping of cortical thickness and clinical outcome in children and adolescents with attention-deficit/hyperactivity disorder. *Archives of General Psychiatry, 63*, 540–49.

Shaywitz, S. E., and Shaywitz, B. A. (1984). Diagnosis and management of attention deficit disorder: A pediatric perspective. *Pediatric Clinics of North America, 31*, 429–57.

Sherman, D. K., Iacono, W. G., and McGue, M. K. (1997). Attention-deficit hyperactivity disorder dimensions: A twin study of inattention and impulsivity-hyperactivity. *Journal of the American Academy of Child and Adolescent Psychiatry, 36*(6), 745–53.

Shields, A., and Cicchetti, D. (1998). Reactive aggression among maltreated children: The contributions of attention and emotion dysregulation. *Journal of Clinical Child Psychology, 27*, 381–95.

Shonk, S. M., and Cicchetti, D. (2001). Maltreatment, competency deficits, and risk for academic and behavioral maladjustment. *Developmental Psychology, 37*, 3–17.

Silk, T. J., Vance, A., Rinehart, N., Bradshaw, J. L., and Cunnington, R. (2009). White-matter abnormalities in attention deficit hyperactivity disorder: A diffusion tensor imaging study. *Human Brain Mapping, 30*, 2757–65.

Slomkowski, C., Klein, R., and Mannuzza, S. (1995). Is self-esteem an important outcome in hyperactive children? *Journal of Abnormal Child Psychology, 23* (3), 303–15.

Smith, H. F. (2003). Theory and practice: Intimate partnership or false connection? *Psychoanalysis Quarterly*, *72*, 1–12.

Sonuga-Barke E. J. S. (2005). Causal models of attention-deficit/hyperactivity disorder: From common simple deficits to multiple developmental pathways. *Biological Psychiatry*, *57*(11),1231–38. doi: 10.1016/j.biopsych.2004.09.008.

Sonuga-Barke, E. J., and Castellanos, F. X. (2007). Spontaneous attentional fluctuations in impaired states and pathological conditions: A neurobiological hypothesis. *Neuroscience and Biobehavioral Reviews*, *31*, 977–86.

Sowell, E. R., Thompson, P. M., Welcome, S. E., Henkenius, A. L., Toga, A. W., Peterson, B. S. (2003). Cortical abnormalities in children and adolescents with attention deficit hyperactivity disorder. *Lancet*, *362*, 1699–707.

Sprich-Buckminster, S., Biederman, J., Milberger, S., Faraone, S. V., and Lehman, B. K. (1993). Are perinatal complications relevant to the manifestation of ADD? Issues of comorbidity and familiarity. *Journal of the American Academy of Child and Adolescent Psychiatry*, *32*, 1032–37.

Sroubek, A., Kelly, M., and Li, X. (2013). Inattentiveness in attention-deficit/hyperactivity disorder. *Neuroscience Bulletin*, *29*(1), 103–10.

Stefanatos, G. A., and Wasserstein, J. (2001). Attention deficit/hyperactivity disorder as a right hemisphere syndrome. *Annals of the New York Academy of Sciences*, *931*, 172–95.

Still, G. F. (1902). Some abnormal psychical conditions in children: The Goulstonian lectures. *Lancet*, *1*, 1162–68.

Strauss, A. A., and Kephart, N .C. (1955). *Psychopathology and education of the brain-injured child. volume II. Progress in theory and clinic.* New York: Grune & Stratton.

Strauss, A. A., and Lehtinen, L. E. (1947). *Psychopathology and education of the brain-injured child.* New York: Grune & Stratton.

Sugarman, A. (2006). Attention deficit hyperactivity disorder and trauma. *International Journal of Psychoanalysis*, *87*, 237–41.

Sullivan, H. S. (1953). *The collected works (Vol. 1).* New York: W. W. Norton.

Surman, C. B., Biederman, J., Spencer, T., Miller, C. A., Petty, C. R., and Faraone, S. V. (2013). Neuropsychological deficits are not predictive of deficient emotional self-regulation in adults with ADHD. *Journal of Attention Disorders*, 1087054713476548.

Swanson, J. M. L., Elliott, G. R. , Greenhill, L. L. , Wigal, T. , Arnold, L. E. , Vitiello, B. , et al. (2007). Effects of stimulant medication on growth rates across 3 years in the MTA follow-up. *Journal of American Academy of Child and Adolescent Psychiatry*, *46*(8), 1015–27.

Szatmari, P., Oxford, D. R., and Boyle, M. H. (1989). Correlates, associated impairments and patterns of service utilization of children with ADHD: Finding from the Ontario child health study. *Journal of Child Psychology and Psychiatry*, *30*, 205–17.

Szymanski, K., Sapanski, L., and Conway, F. (2011). Trauma and ADHD—Association or diagnostic confusion? A clinical perspective. *Journal of Infant, Child and Adolescent Psychotherapy*, *10*(1), 51–59.

Tamm, L., Menon, V., Ringel, J., and Reiss, A. L. (2004). Event-related FMRI evidence of frontotemporal involvement in aberrant response inhibition and task switching in attention-deficit/hyperactivity disorder. *Journal of the American Academy of Child and Adolescent Psychiatry*, *43*, 1430–40.

Tangney, J. P. (1990). Assessing individual differences in proneness to shame and guilt: Development of the self-conscious affect and attribution inventory. *Journal of Personality and Social Psychology*, *59*, 102–11.

Target, M., and Fonagy, P. (1996). Playing with reality II: The development of psychic reality from a theoretical perspective. *International Journal of Psychoanalysis*, *77*, 459–79.

Taylor, S. E., and Brown, JD (1988). Illusion and well-being: A social psychological perspective on mental health. *Psychological Bulletin*, *103*, 193–210.

Thomas, A., and Chess, S. (1977). *Temperament and development.* New York: Brunner-Mazel.

Thome, J., and Jacobs, K. (2004). Attention deficit hyperactivity disorder (ADHD) in a 19th century children's book. *European Psychiatry*, *19*, 303–6.

Tomasello, M., and Akhtar, N. (1995). Two-year-olds use pragmatic cues to differentiate reference to objects and actions. *Cognitive Development*, *10*, 201–24.

Tong, L., Oates, K., and McDowell, M. (1987). Personality development following sexual abuse. *Child Abuse and Neglect, 11*, 371–83.

Treuting, J. J., and Hinshaw, S. P. (2001). Depression and self-esteem in boys with attention-deficit/hyperactivity disorder: Associations with comorbid aggression and explanatory attributional mechanisms. *Journal of Abnormal Child Psychology, 29*(1), 23–39.

Tsal, Y., Shalev, L., and Mevorach, C. (2005). The diversity of attention deficits in ADHD: The prevalence of four cognitive factors in ADHD versus controls. *Journal of Learning Disabilities, 38*, 142–57.

Uddin, L. Q., Kelly, A. M., Biswal, B. B., Margulies, D. S., Shehzad, Z., Shaw, D., et al. (2008). Network homogeneity reveals decreased integrity of default-mode network in ADHD. *Journal of Neuroscience Methods, 169*, 249–54.

U.S. Department of Health and Human Services. (2013). Summary health statistics for U.S. children. *National Health Survey*. Series 10. Number 258.

Vaidya, C. J., Austin, G., Kirkorian, G., Ridlehuber, H. W., Desmond, J. E., Glover, G. H., et al. (1998). Selective effects of methylphenidate in attention deficit hyperactivity disorder: A functional magnetic resonance study. *Proceedings of the National Academy of Sciences, U.S.A., 95*, 14494–99.

Valera, E. M., Faraone, S. V., Biederman, J., Poldrack, R. A., and Seidman, L. J. (2005). Functional neuroanatomy of working memory in adults with attention deficit/hyperactivity disorder. *Biological Psychiatry, 57*, 439–47.

van der Kolk, B. A., and McFarlane, A. (1996). The black hole of trauma. In B. A. van der Kolk, A. McFarlane, and L. Weisaeth (Eds.), *Traumatic stress: The effects of overwhelming experience on mind, body, and society* (pp. 3–23). New York: Guilford Press.

van der Oord, S., Prins, P. J., Oosterlaan, J., and Emmelkamp, P. M. (2012). The adolescent outcome of children with attention deficit hyperactivity disorder treated with methylphenidate or methylphenidate combined with multimodal behaviour therapy: Results of a naturalistic follow-up study. *Clinical Psychology & Psychotherapy, 19*(3), 270–78. doi: 10.1002/cpp.750.

Visser, S. N., Danielson, M. L., Bitsko, R. H., Holbrook, J. R., Kogan, M. D., Ghandour, R. M., . . . & Blumberg, S. J. (2014). Trends in the parent-report of health care provider-diagnosed and medicated attention-deficit/hyperactivity disorder: United States, 2003–2011. *Journal of the American Academy of Child & Adolescent Psychiatry, 53*(1), 34–46.

Von Economo, C. (1931). *Encephalitis lethargica. Its sequelae and treatment* (K. O. Newman Trans.). London: Oxford University Press.

Wachtel, P. (1977). *Psychoanalysis and behavior therapy: Toward an integration*. New York: Basic Books.

Weiss, G., and Hechtman, L. (1993). *Hyperactive children grown up: ADHD in children, adolescents, and adults* (2nd ed.). New York: Guilford.

Werry, J. S., and Wollersheim, J. M. (1989). Behavior therapy with children and adolescents: A twenty-year overview. *Journal of the American Academy of Child and Adolescent Psychiatry, 28*(1), 1–18. http://dx.doi.org/10.1097/00004583-198901000-00001.

Werry, J. S., Minde, K., Guzman, A., Weiss, G., Dogan, J., and Hoy, W. (1972). Studies on the hyperactive child-VII: Neurological status compared with neurotic and normal children. *American Journal of Orthopsychiatry, 42*, 441–51.

Whalen, C. K., and Henker, B. (1986). Cognitive behavior therapy for hyperactive children: What do we know? *Journal of Children in Contemporary Society, 19*, 123–41.

Whalen, C. K., and Henker, B. (1991). Therapies for hyperactive children: Comparisons, combinations, and compromises. *Journal of Consulting and Clinical Psychology, 59*(1), 126–37.

Whelan, D. A. (2004). On the intermingling of conflict and deficit: The case of a hospitalized boy with oppositional defiant disorder. *Journal of Infant and Child Psychotherapy, 311*, 119–37.

Whitmont, S., and Clark, C. (1996). Kinaesthetic acuity and fine motor skills in children with attention deficit hyperactivity disorder: A preliminary report. *Developmental Medicine and Child Neurology, 38*, 1091–98.

Widener, A. J. (1998). Beyond Ritalin: The importance of therapeutic work with parents and children diagnosed ADD/ADHD. *Journal of Child Psychotherapy, 24*, 267–81.

Winnicott, D. W. (1963). Regression as therapy illustrated by the case of a boy whose pathological dependence was adequately met by the parents. *British Journal of Medical Psychology, 36*(1), 1–12.

Winnicott, D. W. (1965). *The maturational processes and the facilitating environment: Studies
in the theory of emotional development* (p. 179). M. M. R. Khan (Ed.). London: Hogarth
Press.

Winnicott, D. W. (1967). Mirror-role of the mother and family in child development. In P.
Lomas (Ed.), *The predicament of the family: A psycho-analytical symposium* (pp. 26–33).
London: Hogarth.

Winnicott, D. W. (1986). *Home is where we start from: Essays by a psychoanalyst.* New York;
London: W.W. Norton & Company.

Wysong, J., and Rosenfeld, E. (Eds.). (1982). *An oral history of Gestalt therapy. Interviews
with Laura Perls, Isadore From, Erving Polster, Miriam Polster* (p. 6). Highland, NY: The
Gestalt Journal.

Yeh, M., McCabe, K., Hough, R. L., Lau, A., Fakhry, F., and Garland, A. (2005). Why bother
with beliefs? Examining relationships between race/ethnicity, parental beliefs about causes
of child problems, and mental health service use. *Journal of Consulting and Clinical
Psychology, 73*, 800–7.

Young, S. (2007). 6 Forensic Aspects of ADHD. *Handbook of attention deficit hyperactivity
disorder*, 91–108.

Young, S., Sedgwick, O., Fridman, M., Gudjonsson, G., Hodgkins, P., Lantigua, M., &
González, R. A. (2015). Co-morbid psychiatric disorders among incarcerated ADHD populations: a meta-analysis. *Psychological Medicine, 45*(12), 2499–2510.

Zelizer, V. A. R. (1985). *Pricing the priceless child: The changing social value of children.*
Princeton: Princeton University Press.

Zelizer, V. A. (2005). *Pricing the priceless child: The changing social value of children.*
Princeton, NJ: Princeton University Press.

Zelizer, V. A. (2010). *Economic lives: How culture shapes the economy.* Princeton, NJ: Princeton University Press.

Index

accommodation, 44, 100

ADD. *See* attention deficit disorder

ADHD. *See* attention deficit hyperactivity disorder

affect regulation, 16

aggression, 29–30

aggressor, identification with, 18

alpha function: to beta elements, 53; containing object and, 53; as ego, 54–55; of transformative experiences, 58

ambivalent attachment, 16

Andreasen, Nancy C., xxiii

anxiety, 63–64

APARTE: foundational principle of, 148–149; by Herrou, 148; parental environment of, 149; school environment of, 149

attachment, evolutionary theory of, 15–16

attachment style: ambivalent attachment from, 16; avoidant attachment from, 16; disorganized style from, 16; on psychological well-being, 16; secure attachment from, 16; self-regulation from, 17

"Attacks on Linking" (Bion), 54

attention, orienting of, 9

attention deficit disorder (ADD), xxiv

attention deficit hyperactivity disorder (ADHD): brain physiology and, xxi, xxv–xxvi; broad spectrum of, x;

Castellanos on, 4; conflict and, 1, 25; Crichton identifying of, xvii; by culture, 142–143; defined groups of, xxiv; developmental trajectory of, xxv; etiology of, 1; evolution of, xxx; as genetic disorder, xxvi, 6; history of, xvi; idiographic approach for, 14; interpersonal interactions with, ix–x, 3; medical model for, xvii; MTA of, 122; neurological factors influenced on, 3–4; as neuropsychiatric disorder, 30; pervasiveness of, 13; prevalence rates of, xv–xvi; psychoanalysis of, xvi–xvii; psychodynamic psychotherapy for, x, xii, 12, 13, 30–31, 33; psychological model for, xvii; psychological well-being of, xi; social construction of, 145; society and, 144–145; symptoms of, ix, xv, xviii

"atypical" type, 13

autism spectrum disorder, 102

avoidant attachment, 16

awareness, edge of, 24

Beck, Aaron T., 118

behavioral approach: for classroom management, 123, 124; efficacy of, 121; limitations of, 123–124; for neurological deficits, 121; parent training and, 121–122, 123; of psychodynamic psychotherapy, 118,

169

About the Author

Dr. **Francine Conway Jones** is dean and distinguished professor at the Graduate School of Applied and Professional Psychology, Rutgers, The State University of New Jersey and a licensed clinical psychologist in private practice. She has received degrees from Cornell University (Bachelor in Psychology), Columbia University (Master's in Clinical Social Work), and Adelphi University's Derner Institute for Advanced Psychological Studies (Doctor in Clinical Psychology). She serves as the research editor of the *Journal of Infant, Child and Adolescent Psychotherapy* and is a consulting editor for APA's Division 29 journal *Psychotherapy*. Dr. Conway has published numerous articles and book chapters on the emotional lives of children. Her recently published edited book, *Attention Deficit Hyperactivity Disorder: Integration of Cognitive, Neuropsychological and Psychodynamic Theoretical Perspectives in Psychotherapy*, based on the special issue of a journal attracted renowned national and international contributors. International scholars included Dr. Björn Salomonsson from the Swedish Psychoanalytic Society in Stockholm, Sweden; Dr. Marianne Leuzinger-Bohleber from the Sigmund Freud Institute; and Dr. Barry Jones from the Psychoanalysis Unit at the University College London. International recognition of her work has led to her research being featured on an ADHD international Web site and an invitation to present her research at the Sigmund Freud Institute in Frankfurt, Germany.

Dr. Conway has been treating children diagnosed with ADHD over the past fifteen years. In addition to her clinical experience, she has taught courses on ADHD and provided clinical supervision for students working with ADHD. She has a private practice in Scotch Plains, New Jersey, and New York.